Uncle John's presents

P9-CLR-660

Necessary Numbers

An Everyday Guide to Sizes, Measures, and More

MARY BLOCKSMA

PORTABLE PRESS
San Diego, California

Portable Press

An imprint of the Advantage Publishers Group

5880 Oberlin Drive, San Diego, CA 92121-4794

www.advantagebooksonline.com

Copyright © 2002 by Mary Blocksma

All notations of errors or omissions should be addressed to Portable Press, Editorial Department, at the above address.

Library of Congress Cataloging-in-Publication Data

Blocksma, Mary.
 Necessary numbers : an everyday guide to sizes, measures, and more / Mary Blocksma.
  p. cm.
 Rev. ed. of: Reading the numbers. 1989.
 Includes bibliographical references and index.
 ISBN 1-57145-866-2 (pbk.)
  1. Weights and measures. 2. Weights and measures—United States. I. Blocksma, Mary. Reading the numbers. II. Title.

QC88 .B535 2002
530.8—dc21   2002029078

Design and composition: Lois Stanfield, LightSource Images

Printed in Canada

1 2 3 4 5   06 05 04 03 02

To David Misner,
for loving this book

Contents

Acknowledgments

FOR HELP WITH THIS NEW EDITION, *Necessary Numbers*, I owe a debt of gratitude to a great number of people, beginning with the reference librarians at the Central Branch of the Bay County Library System, Bay City, Michigan, including Mary McManman, Tom Birch, Leslie Hammond, Mark Grotelueschen, and Ervin Bell, who tirelessly chased down elusive data when I could not find it myself.

Contributing ideas and patient lectures on subjects I could not get my mind around, or offering generous use of website material, were Bob Albrecht, Sebastopol, Calif.; Tom Starkweather, Bay City, Mich.; Rowland Bennett, director of the Maplewood Public Library, Maplewood, N.J.; Trevor Kimball of MyDesign-Primer.com; Her Majesty's Nautical Almanac Office, United Kingdom; the National Academy Press, Washington, D.C.; as well persons and websites too numerous to include here.

Then there are my experts, who, for no more payment than my thanks and a signed copy of this book, read the manuscript for errors: David Misner of Grand Haven, Michigan; Larry L. Smith of Seattle, Wash.; Bob Albrecht; my brother Dewey Blocksma of Beulah, Mich.; my sister Julia Blocksma of Middleton, Ver.; John Lejohn and Marion Sielinski of Bay City; Douglas Le Compte of the National Weather Service, Washington, D.C.; and Wim vanVugt of Holland, Mich. None of these volunteers is to blame for any of my oversights or errors, for which I take full responsibility.

Finally, to my cheering squad of family and friends in Bay City and nationwide, thanks for keeping me going, hearing me out, and plying me with libations when such were clearly called for. And for my son, Dylan Kuhn, who never ceases to believe as much in my possibilities as I believe in his, neither gigabytes nor yottagrams can contain my love.

Between all these lines find happy gratitude to the good people at Portable Press: JoAnn Padgett and Allen Orso for their enthusiastic support, and my tireless and cheerful editor, Jennifer Thornton, who kept her cool and sometimes mine as well, and managed to bring this book to a high shine. Thanks also to Lois Stanfield for her meticulous and inspired book design and art, and to Irving Kahn for having suggested this new edition.

TO THOSE WHO HELPED with *Reading the Numbers*, the first edition of this book, I reexpress my thanks to the many individuals, libraries, companies, and government agencies who responded generously and warmly to my many inquiries. I was especially astonished by the enthusiasm and support I received from persons at all levels of government—city, county, state, and federal—whose exceptionally patient and cheerful help have redefined the word "bureaucrat" for me. Special thanks belong to the following: AAA California; American Gas Association; American Heart Association; American Lung Association; American National Metric Council; American Paper Institute; Big O Tire Company; Building Division, City of Santa Rosa, Calif.; Bureau of Alcohol, Tobacco and Firearms; Bureau of Labor Statistics; California Department of Transportation; California Redwood Association; Chevron Research Company; Curtis and Turk, Healdsburg, Calif.; Federal Highway Administration; Federal Reserve System; Firestone Tire and Rubber Company; Hardin Mortgage Company, Santa Rosa, Calif.; Holland Public Library, Holland, Mich.; Hurty-Peck and Company; Industrial Fasteners Institute; National Association of Hosiery Manufacturers; University of California, Sonoma County Extension; National Academy of Sciences; National Bureau of Standards; National Fertilizer Development Center; National Highway Traffic Safety Administration; National Oceanic and Atmospheric Administration; National Office Products Association; National Weather Service; Office of Metric Programs, U.S. Department of Commerce; Pencil Makers Association; Petrini's Market, Santa Rosa, Calif.; San Francisco Fashion Institute; Social Security Administration; Sonoma County Mapping Division;

Sonoma County Public Library, Santa Rosa, Calif.; Tennessee Valley Authority; Tire Industry Safety Council; Uniform Code Council; U.S. Department of Energy; U.S. Geodetic Survey, Menlo Park, Calif.; U.S. Metric Association; U.S. Naval Observatory; U.S. Postal Service; U.S. Surgeon General's Office; and Wolverine Worldwide, Inc., Rockford, Mich.

Among the many individuals deserving special thanks are Valerie Antoine, executive director of the U.S. Metric Association; Carter Blocksma, Contour Designs, Grass Lake, Mich.; George Chrenka, Nu-Wool Company, Hudsonville, Mich.; Fred Dunnington, city planner of Middlebury, Vt.; John Gandy, Dorchester Industries, Shipyard Division, Dorchester, N.J.; Jack Herrod, General Pharmacy, Healdsburg, Calif.; Dr. William Klepczynski, Time Service Department, U.S. Naval Observatory; David McElroy, Oak Ridge National Laboratories, Tenn.; Chuck Northup; Donna Preckshot; Dr. Fenwick Riley; Bob Ulrich, *Modern Tire Dealer*; and Charles Wilson of Industrial Fasteners Institute.

Finally, I wish to acknowledge those persons whose influence on this book was truly major: librarians Helen Hinterader and Jane Erla of the Healdsburg Public Library, who cheerfully chased down the answers to questions, month after month, bringing many new sources to my attention; my agent, Gina Maccoby; my wonderful Viking Penguin editors, Tracy Brown and Mindy Werner; and above all, Bruce W. Schadel, who tirelessly discussed, read, and critiqued this book and without whom I wouldn't have written it. None of these persons, organizations, or agencies are responsible for any errors, for which the responsibility is entirely mine.

Foreword

I DISCOVERED THE FIRST EDITION of this book in a used-book store. I enjoyed it so much, I wanted to buy copies to share with my friends and business associates. Imagine my surprise when I found out this uniquely entertaining and informative book was no longer in print. I contacted a publishing friend, and he was as intrigued with the book as I was. He sought out the author, Mary Blocksma, and asked her to create a completely revised edition.

The first edition gave me so much pleasure, I am delighted to introduce this new, updated edition. The book's title says it all. Numbers are the key to the technological revolution. It was not all that long ago that *Time* named the computer as "Man of the Year," and shortly thereafter that the world made a quantum leap from analog to digital. No one knows for sure what the next big leap will be, but Mary Blocksma's book provides fast answers to questions about the numbers we encounter in our daily lives. Many of these numbers are old friends (or enemies) like calories. Others we take for granted, like highway, route, and interstate numbers. Some numbers we encounter out of necessity—when we need to buy windows or insulation and suddenly have to decipher R-values. Some are new friends, like financial indexes, as we become more involved in the stock market. You may think you know these numbers, but you don't. *Necessary Numbers* is the author's gift to you to help you take the "numb" out of numbers and learn the fascinating facts behind them.

I am sure you will enjoy this book as much as I do.

— Irving Kahn, CFA
  Chairman, Kahn Brothers & Company, Inc.

Introduction

HOW NUMBERS GOT OUT OF HAND

NUMBERS SEEM TO THRIVE in American life. It's impossible to avoid them. They come at us every day, from all directions, often at the most inconvenient of times. They find us on the highway and in the garden. They turn up at the gas station, bank, library, clothier's, jeweler's, doctor's office, supermarket, fabric store, office supply store, pharmacy, and even at the beach. They fly off the financial pages, our gas bills, our personal checks, and practically every piece of packaging we touch.

Most of us go glassy-eyed before a selection of tires (P195/60R15?), sunscreens (6? 15?), lightbulbs (hours? lumens?), or fertilizers (10-5-10 or 20-5-10?). And why not? No amount of American education—not a college degree, not even a Ph.D.—prepares us for these daily dilemmas. Numbers that we think we know, like the length of a yard and the time of day, are not always what they seem. Numbers on engine oil cans and those mileposts on the freeway have always been slightly ominous, at least to me. (Is there something here I should know?) The Consumer Price Index and the legal description on our property deeds have us on the run, not to mention those long, grim strings of numbers—checking account, bar code, ISBN, Social Security, and ZIP code (plus an additional four numbers).

How on earth did numbers proliferate like this?

The first units of measure used on the earth were calculated quite naturally by every human body. An inch was the width of a thumb, a foot was the length of a foot, a pace was two marching steps, a mile a thousand paces. Liquid volume began with a mouthful, and that measure was doubled again and again for larger measures. It was a handy and a friendly system, and kept the universe within a person's grasp.

Effective as the body system was, it became apparent that some sort of standard had to be found so that people with different-sized extremities could communicate. The problem landed in the leaders' laps, and soon most of the world was measured by the hands and feet—and even the girth—of kings and queens. Unfortunately (or fortunately, in some cases), kings and queens were frequently replaced, and each time it happened, a country's system of measurements had to be revised.

In Europe frustrated traders and scientists began demanding measurements they could count on for longer than the royal life span, as well as more accuracy. Eventually standard platinum measuring instruments were made—and were guarded like the royal jewels. Meanwhile, France devised the metric system, in which the meter was defined as one ten-millionth of the distance between the equator and the North Pole. Before the end of the nineteenth century, most of the world—except the United States and a few smaller countries—was metric.

It turned out, however, that the platinum meter became slightly distorted with time and temperature; worse, making copies of it was impossible. Scientists began searching for much larger, much smaller, and more accurate authorities. In 1960, the man-made meter was redefined in terms of the wavelength of light, then redefined again in 1983 using a laser. New units like parsecs, microns, attograms, and picoseconds began measuring an alarmingly expanding universe.

To cope with the numbers and information explosion, the computer was devised, and with it has come the binary number system, which uses only zero and one. Most of us are spared direct exposure to numbers like 0001101, but we haven't been spared their impact. What used to be spelled out in plain English is now often coded in a strange language of numbers, from food at the market (bar codes) to books (ISBN numbers), ID cards, Social Security numbers, and bank account numbers. Numbers are becoming longer, more numerous, foisting themselves upon us without so much as a brief explanation.

Tired of being intimidated, and probably knowing less about numbers than you do, I began asking those truly simple questions one is usually too embarrassed to ask. The answers were astonishingly elusive. You would think, for example, that "How much alcohol is in this can of beer?" could be settled at a local package store. Often, however, such innocent inquiries required an astonishing amount of research, with calls to federal offices at the highest levels.

The result of this and hundreds of other such questions is a collection, arranged alphabetically, of the subjects that bothered me most. This book is not intended to be comprehensive or definitive—there are too many numbers to try to explain them all, and some are changing even as I write. The real purpose here is to take the "numb" out of numbers, hoping that you'll find the explanations useful, the histories amusing, and the oddities of many of these number systems vastly reassuring.

M.B.

1989

NOTES ON *NECESSARY NUMBERS*

BEING A NUMERICALLY CHALLENGED PERSON, terrified by pixels, bar codes, exponents, and mysteriously lengthy identification numbers, I offer myself as an understanding and genuinely comforting companion to those who may still be resisting the recent avalanche of unfamiliar acronyms, numbers, and measures. Like many of you, I've grappled with those terrifying descriptive tags on scanners, digital cameras, and the like, often giving up before purchasing who knows what. Writing this book, I have faced down my fears, cajoling experts into explaining things again and again, asking "dumb" questions so you wouldn't have to, and then translating the answers into an alphabetical series of instructive amusements: short takes suitable for classrooms, libraries, the beach, and even the bathroom.

Several years ago, when Uncle John's Bathroom Readers Institute asked me for permission to use some of my essays from *Reading the Numbers*, I figured I'd really made it. The book had been a success—it was a Quality Paperback Book Club dual main selection and was included on *Scientific American*'s list of "1989 Best Science Books for Young People." Now I am pleased to have been asked to update the entire thing.

A professional librarian by training, I researched the first edition of this book, *Reading the Numbers* (Viking Penguin, 1989), by library and telephone. Much of the new information here, however, I tracked down on the World Wide Web. The Internet has changed the world; nearly thirty new subjects have been added to *Necessary Numbers*, and almost every entry has been updated or expanded. I even included hundreds of useful URLs.

LINKING

NECESSARY NUMBERS has been written as a reference and a good read for persons with or without access to the Internet. I intend the URLs—addresses to useful websites—to serve as enhancements, not completions, of the essays offered here. The URLs may also serve as doors to subjects that catch your fancy, or even as a short course in Internet research.

One of the problems here is that URLs can change. Also, even incredibly long URLs must be keyed in letter and punctuation perfect to work. I have therefore listed all the URLs, arranged alphabetically by subject, as links on my website. To find them, go to http://www.beaverislandarts.com. Under "Necessary Numbers," click on the first letter of the appropriate subject, and then on the desired URL.

That offered, welcome to the twenty-first century.

M.B.

2002

AGE, EXTRAORDINARY

THE AGE OF ANCIENT OBJECTS, such as prehistoric bones and arti-facts, and truly ancient objects, such as certain rocks and the earth itself, can often be calculated by analyzing the radioactive materials they contain. The calculations involve the radioactive elements' *half-life*, a term that may make your hair stand on end. Once you understand the idea, though, the dating process makes sense.

In 1900 Marie Curie discovered that certain rare elements (an element being a basic component of the universe, such as oxygen, hydrogen, carbon, sodium, etc.) become radioactive. At some point, a radioactive atom will begin to decay, giving off rays and particles, changing its basic structure, actually transforming into an entirely different element. This is truly startling behavior; we don't expect things to change their basic nature. Snakes do not change into birds, people don't become werewolves, and, despite centuries of experiments, lead (an element) cannot be turned into gold (another element). But a radioactive element continues transforming itself into other elements until it becomes a stable, nonradioactive element, and then it stops.

The timing of this transformation is also odd, because the indi-vidual atoms in a batch of radioactive materials are essentially ageless—they are no more apt to begin changing today than, in the case of uranium, for example, they were a million years ago.

Nevertheless, it can be predicted that in 4½ billion years, half the atoms in any given amount of uranium-238* will have changed to thorium-234. Thus 4½ billion years is called uranium-238's *half-life*. This does not mean, however, that it will take only 4½ billion years to transform the half that's left. In 4½ billion more years, only *half* the remaining uranium will change, leaving ¼ of the original amount. It will take 4½ billion more years to transform half of that, leaving ⅛ of the original amount. And so on. It is because of this awkward-to-calculate tailing-off process that scientists use the easier-to-calculate half-life—or the time it takes to make the first split.

A half-life need not be billions of years. Thorium-234, for example, has a half-life of twenty-four days. In twenty-four days half of the uranium-238 atoms that decayed into thorium-234 atoms will have changed into protactinium-234. The process continues until the uranium becomes lead, a stable, nonradioactive element. By measuring the amount of a radioactive material in a rock (or a very old artifact or bone), measuring the elements that this material turns into as it searches for stability, and then comparing these amounts, scientists can date ancient objects.

Different radioactive elements are useful for different ages. Uranium-238, with its extraordinarily long half-life, has been used to date rocks from 50 million to 4 billion years old—the earth itself has been dated at 5 billion years using this method. Potassium-40, with a half-life of 1.3 billion years, is often used to date younger rocks. Carbon-14, a radioactive element with a half-life of only 5,760 years (changing to carbon-12), is useful for dating prehistoric artifacts and bones—fossils of Neanderthal man have been dated at 50,000 years. Under 10,000 years, the carbon-14 method is accurate to within 100 years.

But even carbon-14 data changes with technology and new information. In 2001, thanks to a discovery in some limestone caves

---

* The number following an element's name is its atomic mass. This number distinguishes an element from its isotopes—i.e., atoms with the same chemical properties but with a different weight. For example, carbon-14 is an isotope of the element carbon.

in the Bahamas that suggested that climate changes could affect the amount of radioactive carbon in Earth's atmosphere, scientists had to readjust some of their carbon-14 dates by as much as 5,000 to 10,000 years!

AIR QUALITY INDEX (AQI)

AT THIS WRITING, the Central Los Angeles Air Monitoring Sub-region reports the Air Quality Index (AQI) for L.A. on its website as follows:

Currently: O_3—12 AQI, NO_2—54 AQI,
CO—19 AQI, PM 10—54 AQI

What on earth do those letters and numbers mean?

The Environmental Protection Agency (EPA) uses over a thousand monitors across the country to measure the levels in the air of five worrisome pollutants: ozone (O_3), nitrogen dioxide (NO_2), carbon monoxide (CO), sulfur dioxide (SO_2), and two grades of particulate matter—fine (PM 2.5) and coarse (PM 10). Particulate matter includes both solid particles and liquid droplets: a grade of PM 2.5 tends to result from fuel burning, such as that generated by traffic and power plants, while dust from unpaved roads would be measured as PM 10.

Although each pollutant is measured differently, the AQI uses a 1 to 500 scale to represent the level of public threat. Each level is assigned a color, making it simpler for newspapers and websites to report the AQI.

Using the above EPA chart and the symbols for the pollutants, it's easy to interpret that mysterious Los Angeles AQI report. For L.A., it looks like a pretty good day: only two figures nudge into the moderate, yellow category (particulate matter 10 and nitrogen dioxide, with high readings of 54). If the AQI is reported as one figure, L.A.'s AQI would be 54 NO_2 and PM 10. A single AQI figure represents *not an average* of all the AQI levels but the *highest* AQI reading for that day.

Air Quality Index (AQI) Values	Levels of Health Concern	Colors
When the AQI is in this range:	*...air quality conditions are:*	*...as symbolized by this color:*
0 to 50	Good	Green
51 to 100	Moderate	Yellow
101 to 150	Unhealthy for sensitive groups	Orange
151 to 200	Unhealthy	Red
201 to 300	Very Unhealthy	Purple
301 to 500	Hazardous	Maroon

Here's how each pollutant is measured:

Ozone (O_3)	100 AQI = 0.08 parts/million (an hour average)
Nitrogen dioxide (NO_2)	201 AQI = 0.65 parts/million (24-hour average)
Carbon monoxide (CO)	100 AQI = 9 parts/million (8-hour average)
Sulfur dioxide (SO_2)	100 AQI = 0.14 parts/million (24-hour average)
Particulate matter, fine (PM 2.5)	100 AQI = 40 micrograms/cubic meter (24-hour average)
Particulate matter, coarse (PM 10)	100 AQI = 150 micrograms/cubic meter (24-hour average)

Local and state agencies in cities with a population over 350,000 are required to inform the public daily of the Air Quality Index. Readings of over 100 must be accompanied by warnings to appropriate groups, such as children playing outdoors, persons with asthma, commuters, senior citizens, persons with heart problems, and so on. Even if you do not live in a large city, you still may be able to find a real time reading for your area on the Internet.

▶ To find a daily AQI for your city or area, or to read more about AQI reports, go to http://www.epa.gov/airnow. A search for your area— e.g., "AQI Michigan" or "AQI Los Angeles"—may lead you to even more detailed information. Remote or very clean areas, like the state of Wyoming, may not be reported.

ALCOHOL IN BEVERAGES

HOW DO YOU TELL how much alcohol is in what you're drinking? The percentage is clear enough on wine labels, but is 100 proof brandy 100 percent alcohol? And why is the alcohol content of malt beverages, at least in the United States, not on the label?

Wine and Wine Beverages

Wine and wine beverages are labeled with the percentage of alcohol content by volume, although the actual percentage can vary 1.5 percent either way—a wine labeled 12 percent alcohol by volume may contain from 10.5 percent to 13.5 percent alcohol.

Common Alcohol Contents

Wine coolers	3.5 to 7 percent
Table wines	7 to 14 percent
Dessert wines	14 to 21 percent
Distilled spirits	over 24 percent

Beer and Other Malt Alcoholic Beverages

Beer, by the federal government's decree, must contain at least .5 percent alcohol by volume to be considered beer. Most beers range between 4.4 percent and 5.5 percent alcohol by volume, but not always. Inquiries into the amount of alcohol in beer opens a real Pandora's box. It seems that the federal government has the most liberal requirements about beer, but that state, county, and even city or town governments can tighten these up. Even states with no regulations at all may contain towns or counties that are regulated, or even dry. This means that the same brand of beer might have a 3.2 percent alcohol content if bought in Colorado; 4 percent in California, where anything over 4 percent must be sold as malt liquor; or 4.8 percent, the average for most beers, in states with higher ceilings.

You'd think, with the furor over labeling these days, that the alcohol percentage would be found right next to the required-by-law health warning for pregnant women. Until recently, however, the labeling of the alcoholic content on malt beverages was actually prohibited except when required by state law. Apparently, Congress feared that alcohol content labeling would lead to a sort of high-octane race—beer companies would push beer by raising the alcohol content. Today, although it is now permissible, it is not required, and alcohol content labeling on beer is still rare.

How, then, do you know what strength beer you are getting? You don't, at least not until you can research it. Often even the vendor doesn't know.

Then there's light beer. Alcohol is highly caloric, accounting for about two-thirds of the calories in regular beer, so reducing the alcohol content cuts calories. In order for a company legally to call its beer "light," it must contain one-third fewer calories than the same company's regular beer.

If you can find your glasses and there's enough light in the bar, you can read the required fine-print calorie count on a can of light beer. The light beer labels we checked varied from 89 to 138. In fact, the number of calories in light beers varies so much that one company's "regular" may have only 5 or 10 more calories than another's "light." Since labels are not required on regular beer, which averages around 150 calories for a 12-ounce can, it's hard to know for sure.

Distilled Spirits

The alcohol content of liquors, such as whiskey, gin, and brandy, is expressed in proof degrees, a system used only by the U.S. government. Fortunately, the math required to find the percentage of alcohol is simple: divide the proof by 2; e.g., 100 proof whiskey contains 50 percent alcohol. The highest proof possible, of course, is 200, or 100 percent alcohol.

Extreme Measures

The American proof system is a cup of tea compared to Europe's muddle. For the past half-millennium, starting with the reign of Britain's Elizabeth I, European governments have sought to accurately measure the alcohol content of booze, all the better to tax it. The problem has been how to determine the strength of the batch in question. Quaffing the stuff (probably the first official measure) was unreliable, to say the least—one can only guess at the rates issued by the end of a taster's day. Governments were constantly looking for better ways.

For almost a century, various tests were applied to alcoholic beverages, ranging from whether a man in shorts could comfortably rise from an ale-coated bench (if he stuck, the tax rate went up) to mixing the stuff with gunpowder to see if it would burn brightly when lit (if it did, the tax rate doubled). What was needed was some sort of an instrument. Please.

Several instruments were eventually applied to the problem. One was the *saccharometer*, which, by measuring the amount of sugar in the solution to be fermented, could roughly predict the alcoholic outcome. In 1730 Clarke's *hydrometer*, which came with forty different weights, attempted to measure the density of liquor, alcohol being less dense than water.

In 1794 Bartholomew Sikes invented the first real *alcoholometer* along with a confusing scale, named for himself, that ranged from 0 degrees to 100 degrees Sikes. These were degrees, not percentages—a whiskey that was 50 percent alcohol by volume measured

87.6 degrees on the Sikes scale. Nevertheless, Sikes's scale, called U.K. proof, was used by Great Britain for over two hundred years. In Spain, the Cartier scale added to the confusion by introducing a scale ranging from 10 degrees Cartier (no alcohol) to 44 degrees Cartier (all alcohol). Germany's system measured the percentage of alcohol by weight, resembling none of the above.

Finally, in 1824, Gay Lussac, a highly respected French chemist, introduced a workable alcoholometer reporting measurements anyone could understand: actual percentages by volume. Zero degrees meant no alcohol and 100 degrees meant all alcohol, by volume. Lussac's system, the most rational system of all, has been the official measuring system in France and Belgium for over 175 years. With minor adjustments, it was recently adopted by the European Union, finally clearing up a measurement mess that persisted into the twenty-first century.

Today, all forms of alcoholic beverages in the United States—except, of course, for beer—are labeled with the EU's percent of alcohol by volume in addition to, where applicable, the U.S. proof.

▶ **To find the calorie count and alcohol content of your favorite malt beverage, go to http://www.alcoholreview.com.**

ALCOHOL, BLOOD LEVELS (BAC)

DRINKING AND DRIVING can be a fatal combination—a .10 percent blood alcohol concentration (BAC) increases the odds of an automobile accident eleven times over someone with a BAC of zero. Although driving anywhere in the United States with a .10 percent or higher BAC is illegal per se (meaning it is illegal in and of itself), the current trend is for states to set the legal limit at .08 for drivers over twenty-one and close to zero for drivers under twenty-one.

Many countries already have some form of .08 BAC laws, including Canada, Ireland, Italy, New Zealand, and Switzerland. At

.05, Australia, Austria, Denmark, Greece, the Netherlands, Norway, Portugal, and Spain are even stricter. Russia claims a .02 BAC.

In the United States, state governments determine BAC levels. To inspire their cooperation, the Congress waves money at them and may even threaten to withhold it. In 1982, the National Highway Traffic Safety Administration began offering highway grant funds to encourage .10 BAC per se laws, and even more for .08. In 1998, President Clinton proposed the Safe and Sober Streets Act, which would have withheld certain highway funds from states that did not enact a .08 BAC per se law by October 1, 2001. His effort failed, but later that year Congress did pass the Transportation Equity Act for the 21st Century, nicknamed TEA 21 (surely the result of someone's sense of humor). Although falling short of requiring a .08 BAC limit, TEA 21 offered tempting incentive grants to states that did. By 2002, nineteen states, Washington, D.C., and Puerto Rico had complied.

Blood Alcohol Concentration Chart

Weight	Drinks (Two-Hour Period) 1½ oz. 86 Proof Liquor or 12 oz. Beer											
100	1	2	3	4	5	6	7	8	9	10	11	12
120	1	2	3	4	5	6	7	8	9	10	11	12
140	1	2	3	4	5	6	7	8	9	10	11	12
160	1	2	3	4	5	6	7	8	9	10	11	12
180	1	2	3	4	5	6	7	8	9	10	11	12
200	1	2	3	4	5	6	7	8	9	10	11	12
220	1	2	3	4	5	6	7	8	9	10	11	12
240	1	2	3	4	5	6	7	8	9	10	11	12

Be Careful	Driving	Do Not Drive
BAC to .05	Impaired .05–.09	.10 and Up

Source: U.S. Department of Transportation, National Highway Safety Administration

Boating under the influence is equally unlawful in every state, but in addition to state BUI laws, there is also a federal law prohibiting operators from piloting a boat with a BAC of .10 or more. The U.S. Coast Guard may enforce this limit on all U.S. waters except those belonging solely to a state.

None of this information helps much, however, if you don't know what a .10 or .08 BAC means to your personal consumption. To help you figure out how much is too much, most state Departments of Motor Vehicles offer a chart similar to the one on page 13. Although criticized by organizations that discourage any drinking at all, BAC charts do offer some general guidelines to encourage drivers to respect the safety of others, use good judgment, hang on to their licenses and stay out of jail. Keeping in mind that many other factors can affect sobriety and that this kind of information may not be enough to get you home safely, you can use the chart to find out not only how many drinks will make you too drunk to drive, but how few may impair reflex time and depth perception.

▶ **You may find it useful to go to one of the many websites that estimate a possible BAC level. (Enter figures reflecting your usual drinking behavior before you drink away from home.) Find a BAC calculator at http://www.onlineconverters.com.**

ANALOG VS. DIGITAL

YOU MAY NOT have been aware of it, but until the last decade or so, you were living an analog life. The cameras you've been using all these years—that 35 mm job, not to mention the point-and-shoot number and even the handy occasional disposable—are analog cameras. The clock with hands that sweep around a full circle? That's an analog clock. Nearly every device on the planet is either analog or digital. Things analog are continuous, uninterrupted, while things digital measure values at intervals. A clock with hands is analog, because the hands physically touch not just the numbers but all the points between them; a digital clock displays changing numbers, the time at intervals. An analog photograph is a pattern of light that has actually touched film; a digital photo-graph is light "sensed" and remembered as soldierly rows of sepa-rate numerical formulas. (See *Cameras, Digital*, page 43.)

> ▶ For an interesting discussion on analog vs. digital, read "Is Life Analog or Digital?" by Freeman Dyson, professor of physics at the Institute for Advanced Study in Princeton, at http://www.edge.org/3rd_culture/dyson_ad/dyson_ad_print.html.

ANNUAL PERCENTAGE RATE (APR)

EVERY MORTGAGE COMES with two rates of interest—the nominal in-terest rate, or the one the loan is listed and advertised for, and the annual percentage rate, known as the APR, which can be ½ percent or more higher. This sounds sneaky. Are you being bamboozled?

Here's what's going on: You decide on a mortgage with an in-terest rate of 7.5 percent, but there are expenses that may leave you fairly shaken if you are a first-time borrower. Points (prepaid interest; see *Points, Mortgage*, page 189) and/or the appraisal, the credit report, processing, and other fees (inclusions vary) add to the total cost of the loan. The APR is the interest rate calculated on the total of these plus the loan amount, while the nominal in-terest rate is calculated only on the amount of the loan you applied for. Bamboozling has been outlawed in most states, which require lenders to inform you of the APR, particularly if it is appreciably higher than the nominal interest rate. If you aren't told, ask.

Your APR rate is usually listed on your credit card bills, where your unpaid balance is treated as a loan.

> ▶ To quickly calculate an APR, or even just a loan or mortgage payment, go to http://www.mortgage-calc.com. This site offers many kinds of calculators—just click on the one you want. For APR, enter the amount of the loan, the points, expenses, and the period of time of the loan: your monthly payment will be calculated for you.

ASPECT RATIO

IN THIS DIGITAL AGE, *aspect ratios* are showing up more and more on product descriptions for cameras, computer monitors, television screens, photographs, and tires, to name a few in this book. Explaining it once is, for this ordinary mortal, more than enough.

An aspect ratio is basically a set of two numbers, separated by a colon, describing the relationship of height to width. It's really just a fraction of the measurements—height over width—reduced to the lowest common denominator. So a square, which has the same height and width, has a 1:1 aspect ratio, no matter what the square measures. The popular 4" x 6" photographic print has a ratio of 2:3, since 4/6 can be reduced to 2/3. A 2:3 *aspect ratio*, however, is usually expressed as 1:5:1, which does not mean that the height is one and a half times longer than the width. It means that it takes one and a half (1.5) heights to make one (1) width.

To find any height/width aspect ratio, whether you are talking about pixels, millimeters, inches, or any other measure of length, *simply divide the height (the first number) into the width (the second number).* Here are a few common proportions if one number is reduced to 1 (good time for a calculator):

Common Aspect Ratios	
35 mm film	1.50:1
Photo paper 4" x 6"	1.50:1
Photo paper 8" x 10"	1.25:1
Some digital cameras	1.33:1
Computer monitor	1.33:1
8 1/2" x 11" paper	1.29:1
Television screen	1.33:1
Most movies before 1950	1.33:1
Most of today's movies:	
Academy Flat	1.85:1
Panavision/Cinemascope	2.35:1

Even aspect ratios have stories. A second look at that list will reveal that television screens, gaining popularity in the fifties, were first formatted to fit the movies. When theater audiences began to dwindle, the movie people changed the aspect ratios so that movies no longer could be seen free without special formatting. Today movies have to be either enlarged and cropped or accompanied by a strip of black on top and bottom to be seen on television.

BAR CODES

WHAT COULD BE MORE INHUMAN than the grim black symbol stamped on nearly everything these days, most often encountered as the aptly named Universal Product Code (UPC)? They even appear on oranges and bananas. Is it really necessary to make nearly everything for sale, and even the books in the library and our mail, look incarcerated? Well, ask no more. You are about to unlock those little bars. Bar codes can be fun!

Introduced at first for groceries in 1973, the UPC symbol has proliferated for thirty years, but except for holographic scanners and a sometimes compressed or extended appearance, they haven't changed much. Still, few of us know how they work.

The Code

The UPC bar code is exactly that—a twelve-digit computer code made up of bars that may be translated into Arabic numerals for humans. These twelve digits group into four numbers:

Source: Uniform Code Council, Inc. Used with permission.

0	The first digit, called the *number system character,* identifies the product. A 0 is assigned to all nationally branded products except the following: a 2 signals random weight items, such as cheese or meat; a 3 means drug and certain health-related products; a 4 means products marked for price reduction by the retailer; a 5 signals a coupon.
12345	The next five digits represent the manufacturer. This number is assigned by the Uniform Code Council (UCC) in Dayton, Ohio.
67890	The next five digits are assigned by the manufacturer to represent the product, and may include size, color, and other information.
5	The final digit is called the check digit. It signals the computer if one of the other digits is incorrect.

The price, by the way, is not part of most bar codes—that information is kept in the store's computer, which sends each price to the appropriate cash register as each bar code is scanned. Price changes, sales, and specials are introduced, and prices vary from store to store, making it impractical to include the price in the bar code. Coupon clippers should know that the coupon's bar code not only automatically deducts the amount of the coupon from your bill but also checks the grocery list to make sure you actually bought the product.

The Bars

The way the digits are turned into bars helps explain how the scanners "read" them. Each digit of the code is represented by two dark bars and two light "bars," or spaces, filling a space divided into seven equal parts.

Because the computer can read only yes or no, each number is coded into a seven-digit yes/no code using a one (bar) for yes and zero (space) for no. It's easy to see how a seven-digit code fills the spaces shown at the top of the next page.

SAMPLE "BAR" IN UPC SYMBOL.

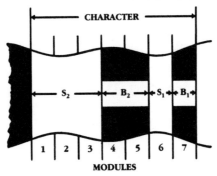

S_1 and S_2 are the two groups of light bars;
B_1 and B_2 are the two groups of dark bars.

Source: Uniform Code Council, Inc. Used with permission.

There are two ways to write each number: A code applied to a digit in a manufacturer's number always contains an odd number of ones (bars). This code is mirrored when applied to a product number digit—each one is turned into a zero, and each zero becomes a one, so that there is an even number of bars. (For example, a 5 is 0110001 in a manufacturer's number, but 1001110 in a product number.) This way, a manufacturer's number will not be confused with the product number. In the following chart, find the code for 1 through 9, with those used for the manufacturer's code on the left and the mirrored version for product code on the right. Remember, each 0 is a space and each 1 is a bar.

Digit	Manuf. No.	Product No.
0	0001101	1110010
1	0011001	1100110
2	0010011	1101100
3	0111101	1000010
4	0100011	1011100
5	0110001	1001110
6	0101111	1010000
7	0111011	1000100
8	0110111	1001000
9	0001011	1110100

In a bar code, three sets of double bars separate each of the four number groups, extending below the other bars. The number system character (left side) and the check digit (right side) are also represented by long bars just inside the outside double bars. The short bars encode the two five-digit numbers that represent the manufacturer and the product.

BREAKING THE BAR "CODE"

(NOT TO SCALE)

Source: Uniform Code Council, Inc. Used with permission.

The Scanner

In most supermarkets, the bar code is passed over a window through which an electronic scanner using a laser or a hologram translates the bars into time intervals, as it takes longer to pass over thick bars than thin ones. The scanner measures spaces the same way. The time intervals are then translated into digits. Because the product codes are not the same as manufacturer codes, the laser can read the bar code in any direction. Laser light, by the way, doesn't break down into a rainbow of colors like ordinary light—it is only one color. Scanners use red lasers, which is why red ink cannot be used to print bar codes—the laser can't "see" red. Holographic scanners can read a label at many different angles.

The Check Digit

Some people might like to know how the check digit works—how can a one-digit number catch any mistakes in the preceding eleven? Information from the Uniform Code Council says it works with the formula below. Try it on our sample bar code number, always starting from the left. In this case, the odd positions begin with 0 and the even positions with 1: 0 12345 67890

1. Add the numbers in odd positions: 2 + 4 + 6 + 8 + 0 = 20
2. Multiply total in Step 1 by 3: 3 × 20 = 60
3. Add the numbers in even positions: 1 + 3 + 5 + 7 + 9 = 25
4. Add the Step 3 total to the Step 2 total: 60 + 25 = 85
5. The number you need to add to reach a total that is divisible by 10 is your check number: 85 + 5 = 90, so the check digit is 5.

This really works—if numbers are transposed (a common mistake) or a wrong number is hit on a keyboard, the check digit will be wrong, and the keyboard operator will know to check the figures. But because the check digit is used mainly by computers, it's not always translated for the human eye into an Arabic numeral. You can still find the mistake, though, by using this formula.

▶ For more information on UPC bar codes, go to http://www.uc-council.org. Also check out Marshall Brain's book called *How Stuff Works,* or go to http://howstuffworks.com/upc.htm.

BAROMETRIC PRESSURE

WHEN THE BAROMETRIC PRESSURE reads 30.1, what does this number mean—30.1 what? And why is the range—29 to 31 on many home barometers—so small? You might assume that it means pounds of pressure or something metric for which an American equivalent was never found.

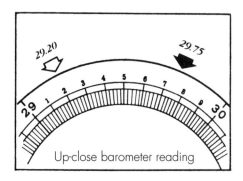

Up-close barometer reading

This barometer reads 29.75, up from the last reading of 29.20.
Source: Howard Miller Clock Company, Zeeland, Mich.

In 1643 a student of Galileo's named Torricelli took a tube about 34 inches long that was closed at one end, filled it with mercury, turned it upside down, and put the open end in a mercury pool. No matter when he did this experiment, the amount of mercury that stayed in the tube ranged from about 29 to 31 inches, depending on the air pressure.

Even though most of today's barometers are aneroid barometers, using a dry partial vacuum to determine the air pressure, the reading represents the inches of mercury that would have remained in a tube if mercury had been used instead.

How to Read the Barometer

The barometer uses decimal inches—each number, or inch, is divided into tenths. The tenths are divided into hundredths (although these are not marked on most home barometers). The barometric reading in the example is 29.75. Generally, a reading of over 30.2 is considered high and one below 29.7 low. Low air pressure brings inclement weather; high air pressure brings fair. To tell whether the air pressure is rising or falling (if the next reading is higher or lower than the last), line up the stationary needle with the barometer needle. Check later to see if the reading is higher or lower than the stationary needle.

If you know what direction the wind is coming from, you can take a stab at predicting the weather. As a rule, winds from the east quadrants and a falling barometer indicate foul weather. Winds shifting to the west quadrants indicate clearing and fair weather. How fast and how far the barometer falls can give you an idea how fast a storm is approaching and how intense it is. The following chart will hardly be enough on which to base accurate weather predictions—meteorologists still miss, even with the benefit of satellites and electronics. Still, it does give a feel for how those numbers, combined with a glance at your wind sock or weather vane, translate into reality.

Barometer Conversion Table

Hectopascals/millibars	Inches	Millimeters
992	29.29	744.1
996	29.41	747.1
1000	29.53	750.1
1004	29.65	753.1
1008	29.77	756.1
1012	29.88	759.1
1016	30.00	762.1
1020	30.12	765.1
1024	30.24	768.1
1028	30.36	771.1
1032	30.48	774.1

Wind-Barometer Table

Wind Direction	Barometer Reading (Inches), Normalized to Sea Level	Character of Weather This Indicates
SW to NW	30.10 to 30.20 and steady	Fair, with slight temp. changes for 1 to 2 days
	30.10 to 30.20 and rising rapidly	Fair, followed within 2 days by rain
	30.20 or above and stationary	Fair, with no decided temp. change
	30.20 or above and falling slowly	Slowly rising temp. and fair for 2 days
S to SE	30.10 to 30.20 and falling slowly	Rain within 24 hours
	30.10 to 30.20 and falling rapidly	Wind increasing in force, and rain within 12 to 24 hours
SE to NE	30.10 to 30.20 and falling slowly	Rain in 12 to 18 hours
	30.10 to 30.20 and falling rapidly	Increasing wind, and rain within 12 hours
E to NE	30.10 or above and falling slowly	In summer, with light winds, rain may not fall for several days. In winter, rain within 24 hours
	30.10 or above and falling rapidly	In summer, rain probably within 12 to 24 hours. In winter, rain or snow with increasing winds possible

Wind-Barometer Table (continued)

Wind Direction	Barometer Reading (Inches), Normalized to Sea Level	Character of Weather This Indicates
SE to NE	30.00 or below and falling slowly	Rain will continue 1 to 2 days
	30.00 or below and falling rapidly	Rain, with high wind, followed within 36 hours by clearing, and in winter by colder temps
S to SW	30.00 or below and rising slowly	Clearing within a few hours and fair for several days
S to E	29.80 or below and falling rapidly	Severe storm imminent, followed within 24 hours by clearing and in winter by colder temps
E to N	29.80 or below and falling rapidly	Severe NE gale and heavy precipitation; in winter, heavy snow, followed by cold wave
Going to W	29.80 or below and rising rapidly	Clearing and colder

Source: "The Aneroid Barometer," U.S. Department of Commerce, Weather Bureau

With barometers manufactured anywhere outside the United States, pressure might be measured in either millimeters, millibars, or hectopascals. Exactly what a millibar or hectopascal means falls, for this book, anyway, into the TMI—Too Much Information—category. However, these measures require a conversion table (see page 23) if you are to read the wind-barometer table.

The Drastic Effects of Altitude on Barometers

If you moved to Denver from an area close to sea level, you might well assume your barometer was broken when you unpacked it—the needle wouldn't register anything. The atmospheric pressure is quite different at higher altitudes, and the readings of your barometer will be roughly 1 inch lower for every 1,000 feet higher you take it—even a trip of 100 feet will change the reading one-tenth of an inch. At 5,000 feet, the mean barometric pressure is 24.89 inches of mercury, a number so low that it's not even on your barometer.

How to fix this? A barometric pressure reading given in weather reports is usually "normalized" to what it would be at *mean sea level*. To adjust your barometer, get a "normalized" report and reset your barometer needle to that reading. It won't be entirely accurate, since other factors affect barometric pressure readings, but it will be close.

Altitude

An *altimeter* is essentially a flying barometer, an aircraft instrument that measures its height above mean sea level. It makes sense: a barometer measures the pressure that the weight a column of air exerts on a particular place or object. The higher the altitude, the thinner the air and the lower the pressure, so an air pressure reading can be converted into an altitude reading. In reality, an altimeter measures the weight of the air *above* the aircraft, translating that into the number of feet *below* it (adjusted to sea level). American aircraft, at least the smaller ones, report this measure in feet. Internationally, altitude may be measured in millibars (see conversion table on page 23).

There are two readings on an altimeter: height above mean sea level plus a barometric pressure reading. So how does a pilot know where the ground is? For short hops over relatively flat areas—from an island to the mainland, for example—the pilot can set the altimeter at *field level*, so that when the plane is on the ground, the altimeter reads zero. More commonly, readings from air control towers are entered in the barometric window, which corrects the altitude reading if the plane has covered some distance. If no reading is available, a "normal" barometer reading of 29.92 (1013.3 millibars) is usually used.

To know one's clearance of, say, Colorado's Pikes Peak, however, one needs a radar altimeter, which measures the time it takes for radio waves to bounce from below and translates that into distance. This kind of altimeter is handy for night flying, blind landings, and making topographic maps from satellites. Small aneroid altimeters weighing around 3 ounces (or about 90 grams) can be carried by mountain climbers to chart their arduous progress.

BEADS

NOT ONLY ARE BEADS SIZED five ways to Sunday, but they are usually pictured greatly enlarged. If you've ever tried to buy beads from a catalog or on the Internet, you are probably totally flummoxed as to how big those beads in the photographs really are. Beads so small it takes thirty to make an inch can appear practically jumbo. Furthermore, bead size systems use both the metric system and the inch.

Metric Length

Most beads, especially medium and large beads, are sized by millimeters (mm). Since an inch measures 25.4 millimeters, you can do a quick bead-size approximation by rounding the millimeters to 24 and then calculating the number of beads per inch:

2 mm beads	12 per inch
4 mm beads	6 per inch
8 mm beads	3 per inch
12 mm beads	2 per inch

Remember: *the bigger the millimeter size, the bigger the bead.* The chart below, though neither exact nor complete, should help approximate some sample millimeter-sized beads.

2 mm 3 mm 4 mm 6 mm 8 mm 10 mm 12 mm 14 mm 16 mm 18 mm 20 mm

The Aught System

Seed beads—tiny beads used in jewelry, embroidery and bead-weaving— usually come in sizes that look like this: 6/0, 8/0, and so on. The zero, always present, signals the *aught system* (zeros are called aughts in some places). While this sounds metric, it's not: the number preceding the slash-zero apparently once represented the number of beads to an inch. It no longer does, but what *is* still true is this: *the bigger the aught size, the smaller the bead.*

Aught (Seed Bead) Size	Measure in Millimeters
6/0	3.3
7/0	2.9
8/0	2.5
9/0	2.2
10/0	2.0
11/0	1.8
12/0	1.7
13/0	1.5
14/0	1.4
15/0	1.3
16/0	1.2
18/0	1.1
20/0	1.0
22/0	.9

Metric Weight

Beads, and especially bead mixes, are often sold by metric weight, frequently in clumps of 100 grams (about 3½ ounces), 500 grams (half a kilo, or just over a pound), or a kilo (almost 2¼ pounds). Very expensive beads, usually sized by millimeter and weight, may be priced by the gram, say three dollars per gram, sometimes giving you the weight and letting you do the math.

The weight of a bead depends as much on what it's made of as its size. If a company does not say how many of a particular bead or bead assortment are found in, say, a 100-gram packet, it can be difficult to know how many you are getting. For a rough seed bead guide, estimate 120 size 11/0 seed beads per gram and 250 size 15/0 seed beads per gram.

Quantity

Beads sold by quantity—say, six beads for $3.95—are usually sized in millimeters, but not always. A wholesale quantity term is *mass*, which, in the bead world, represents neither weight nor area: *1 mass = 1,200 (usually identical) beads*, no matter what size the beads are.

Strand

Beads are sometimes sold by the *strand*—lengths of strung beads—and while the beads themselves are probably sized by millimeter, the strands are measured in inches. Strands often come in 16-inch, 20-inch, or 24-inch lengths. A *hank* is a dozen (12) 20-inch strands, or 240 inches of beads.

▶ For a complete bead-size education as well as more accurate and complete sizing charts, go to http://www.jewelry-tools.com/WJU/techniques/measures. Under "Bead Measures," click "Sizes." For another useful bead measure website, especially for seed beads, go to http://www.2bead.com/2bead2/Sizes.asp.

BINOCULARS

· ·

BINOCULARS COME in such a strange variety of sizes—6 × 15, 7 × 35, 8 × 42, or 10 × 50, to name just a few—that when you go to buy a pair, you can't imagine which one would be best. Is bigger better? Should you ask for the highest possible magnification? And what do those numbers mean, anyway?

Binoculars are sized by three basic numbers: the *power of magnification*, the *size of the "objective" lens*, and the *size of the field of view*. Magnification (the number before the "×") is the number of times the lens magnifies an object—anywhere from six to ten times. The size of the objective lens (the number after the "×") is the diameter of the large lens in millimeters—usually between 15 mm and 50 mm. The field of view is usually measured in feet as seen from 1,000 yards away—typically 315 to 640 feet.

What you want from binoculars is a sharp, bright image, the result of a combination of magnification and lens size, and bigger is not, for most purposes, better. There are trade-offs: Higher magnification makes the image dimmer, so bigger objective lenses are needed to compensate. (The larger the lens, the more light it collects.) But bigger objective lenses make the binoculars bulkier and heavier. This can be more inconvenient—higher magnification makes it harder to hold a steady image, a problem made worse by a heavy instrument. Thus 10X is about the practical limit.

Your intended binocular use will help you decide on a size. A reliably good size for bird-watching and all-purpose daytime use seems to be the middle-of-the-road 7 × 35 or 8 × 42, regular or wide-angle, while 7 × 50 works best for stargazing and other night use. Sizes larger than that—higher magnification and/or bigger lenses—work well for hunting. Smaller sizes are good for relatively close activities such as spectator sports, boating, and indoor use.

So what's the difference between passable ($100) binoculars, good ($400 or more) binoculars, and fabulous (over $1,000) binoculars? Aside from quality of image, waterproofing, ease of focus, and ease on the neck muscles, a good pair of binoculars will hold its alignment through the trials of normal field life. Better binoculars don't cause eye strain when viewing for more than thirty or forty seconds. If these prisms are not perfectly aligned, you will start seeing double and your eyes can suffer. Bargain binoculars can become easily misaligned or damaged.

Other features can influence a choice: a rocker focus is quick but not as sharp as the rotating wheel focus. And spectacled gazers who must keep their glasses on should consider special extensions. (If you have to take your glasses off, don't lay them in the weeds—a warning born of shattering personal experience.)

Experts recommend that you buy a pair that you've actually tried, as the fit and performance of binoculars seem to vary enormously, even within the same size and price ranges. When trying out a pair, look into dark areas such as a darkened room or a shaded spot outside; all binoculars perform well in bright light.

▶ Excellent recent articles on selecting binoculars for particular activities, such as bird-watching, boating, and stargazing, can be found at INFO-TRAC, a collection of online databases offered by many public libraries, some of whom make it available on their websites to library-card holders.

BLOOD PRESSURE
....

UNTIL THE LAST DECADE OR SO, many doctors felt that your blood pressure was theirs to know and yours to worry about. Today, however, people are encouraged to find out their blood pressure. Blood pressure is always given in two numbers: systolic pressure over diastolic pressure—120 over 80, for example. When people report high blood pressure, they often use the systolic number. Alarming as the number may sound, it's not usually the only one used to measure "high blood pressure."

Systolic pressure (the high number) is the pressure of blood against the artery walls when the heart contracts. The diastolic pressure (low number) is the pressure of blood against the artery walls when the heart is at rest. The systolic pressure is always higher than the diastolic because blood is pushed through the artery faster at the peak of the heart's pumping action. But it's the diastolic pressure that shows how much resistance has built up in the system, and it is this number that often concerns doctors most.

Find below the chart from "The Sixth Report of the Joint National Committee on Prevention, Detection, Evaluation, and Treatment of High Blood Pressure," published by the National Institutes of Health:

Classification of Blood Pressure for Adults Age 18 and Older

Category	Systolic (mm Hg)		Diastolic (mm Hg)
Optimal	less than 120	and	less than 80
Normal	less than 130	and	less than 85
High-normal	130–139	or	85–89
Hypertension			
Stage 1	140–159	or	90–99
Stage 2	160–179	or	100–109
Stage 3	180 or more	or	100 or more

Source: National Institutes of Health

What do those numbers mean? While the barometer measures air pressure in inches of mercury, the *sphygmomanometer*—that pumped-up cuff that puts pressure on your upper arm—measures blood pressure in millimeters (mm) of mercury (Hg). Although pressure is shown by a needle on a dial, the numbers still represent the millimeters the mercury would show if a mercury sphygmomanometer had been used. *Hypertension* is the word used to describe abnormally high levels of blood pressure.

▶ To find where you stand on the blood pressure classification chart, go to http://www.about-hypertension.com and click on "Risk Factors." Find up-to-date information on blood pressure and other health matters on http://www.healthfinder.gov.

BODY FAT

THERE ARE A NUMBER of depressing ways to measure body fat, including a measuring tape, but the worst of them is the fat caliper, or skin fold caliper, which some people actually purchase and allow in their homes. Applying one of these instruments to oneself, much less letting anyone else do it, has to be more disquieting than trying on swimsuits. Just the idea of it is enough to put some of us off our feed. Still, the issue of body fat, a national health hazard second only to smoking, really must be addressed. If you need another way to measure body fat, here it is.

Human bodies are made of water, muscle, and bone, among other essentials, but for many of us, a quarter of our body is fat. That's right: 25 percent body fat is (according to Linear Software) an average body fat percentage for a 26- to 45-year-old man and ideal for a man over 55, or average for a woman 16 to 25, ideal if she's between 26 and 55, and absolutely athletic if she's older than that.

It's a relief to know that there is no one optimum percentage of body fat for everybody. The percentage of body fat changes naturally with age, gender, and conditions such as pregnancy and lactation. In fact, if you consider yourself in fairly good shape, you might be pleasantly surprised at how well you score. An author of a certain age who exercises only moderately and who by one website's calculation must confess to 24 percent body fat has been declared (to her delight) "ideal." (Here's a caveat, however: although online fat calculators beat pinching oneself with calipers, the estimates among websites do tend to vary, especially when using different sets of factors.)

▶ For a "body fat estimator," click "Online Athletic Calculators" at http://www.stevenscreek.com. To see what this may say about your health status, go to http://www.linear-software.com/bodycomppic.html. To find out more about body fat percentages, or to calculate your body fat and health risk category based on height, weight, and age, go to the "Body Fat Lab" at http://www.shapeup.org.

BODY MASS INDEX
∙∙∙

FINDING OUT if you were officially overweight used to be easy—you checked yourself on a height-and-weight chart (often issued by an insurance company) and that was that. Today the U.S. Department of Health and Human Services has introduced a complication: body mass index (BMI). To find your BMI, you have to divide your weight in kilograms by your height in meters squared.

What? You don't *know* your weight in kilograms? You don't measure your height in meters (squared)? No matter. You can find your BMI on the height-and-weight chart provided on page 35, or use an online BMI calculator.

Although this chart may seem a little more forgiving than the old ones, it's just one factor to consider in evaluating your health risks. Another important body mass factor is your shape—the medical community appears to agree that excess abdominal fat, often called an "apple shape," may place you at greater risk of health problems than if you are "pear shaped," even if your BMI is fine. Your waist (just above your navel) should not measure over 35 inches for women or 40 inches for men.

▶ If you know your weight, let the Obesity Education Initiative calculate your body mass index for you. Go to http://www.nhlbisupport.com/bmi. To find a BMI chart for children, go to the Center for Chronic Disease Prevention and Health Promotion at http://www.cdc.gov/nccdphp/dnpa/bmi.

BMI (BODY MASS INDEX)

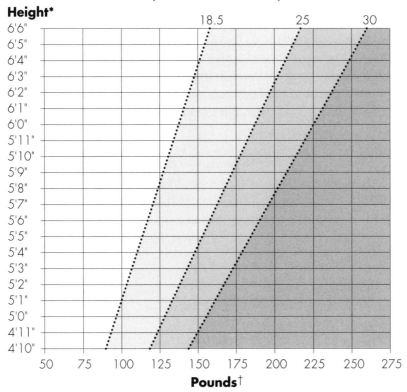

Pounds†

*Without shoes
†Without clothes

BMI measures weight in relation to height. The BMI ranges shown above are for adults. They are not exact ranges of healthy and unhealthy weights. However, they show that health risk increases at higher levels of overweight and obesity. Even within the healthy BMI range, weight gains can carry health risks for adults.

Directions: Find your weight on the bottom of the graph. Go straight up from that point until you come to the line that matches your height. Then look to find your weight group.

Healthy Weight BMI from 18.5 up to 25 refers to healthy weight.

Overweight BMI from 25 up to 30 refers to overweight.

Obese BMI 30 or higher refers to obesity. Obese persons are also overweight.

Source: Report of the Dietary Guidelines Advisory Committee on the Dietary Guidelines for Americans, 2000, page 3.

BRASSIERES

···

DON'T LAUGH—this is a challenging subject. Brassieres have two measurements: a band size and a cup size. Measuring the band is easy enough: you measure around the rib cage just under the breasts. The cup size, however, has been subject to a formula that falls short of higher math but does remind one of those add-this-subtract-that party tricks.

The traditional method for finding your cup size:
1. Measure your rib cage for band size.
2. Add 5 inches.
3. Round off to the nearest even number.
4. Now measure around the fullest part of your bust while wearing a bra.
5. Subtract your rib cage measurement from your bust measurement.
6. You now have the key to your cup size.

Answer	1"	2"	3"	4"	5"	6"	7"
Cup Size	A	B	C	D	DD	DDD	F

Plastic surgeon Edward A. Pechter recently began an article titled "Breast Measurement" with this statement: "It is often reported that 70 percent of women wear the wrong size bras." Dr. Pechter, who apparently does breast augmentations, suggests a saner way to find one's cup size: measuring across the top of one "unclothed" breast. His cup-size chart would look like this:

Breast Circumference	7"	8"	9"	10"
Cup Size		A	B	C	D

Your author, having endured the first formula under fitting room duress—it actually did work—has subjected Dr. Pechter's formula to primary research and happily reports that it works just as well.

CALENDAR

••

THERE'S AN OLD JOKE that says the camel is convoluted because it was built by committee. Well, the camel is a keen piece of work compared to the calendar. The calendar was built by a whole string of committees, beginning with an ancient Babylonian committee and followed in later centuries by more committees appointed by pharaohs, emperors, caesars, and a pope. That date book of yours is actually an abysmal mess that survives only because you—and the rest of us—are blindly devoted to it. Unless scientists can sneak through a change behind our backs, as they did when they redefined the second (see *Time Units*, page 244), we won't let them alter our sacred sense of time.

For starters, our months, which are based on but don't really follow the moon's cycles, are of lengths so unpredictable that no Ph.D. has topped this nursery rhyme evolved from a 1562 poem by Richard Grafton:

Thirty days hath September,
April, June, and November;
All the rest have thirty-one,
Except February alone,
Which has twenty-eight days clear
And twenty-nine in each leap year.

Now consider the weeks, which divide the months in a most erratic fashion, not even bothering to start each month with a fresh week. (See *Week*, page 268.) Only February divides evenly into weeks (except in leap years). Even the year doesn't divide evenly into fifty-two weeks—it's one day (two in leap years) too long. In addition, you need a new calendar every year, since the configuration is never the same two years running.

The reason for the confusion is that early on, committees began connecting time to the cycles of the earth, moon, and sun, which, though fairly predictable, are not really compatible.

A day	is based on the time it takes the earth to do a complete spin on its axis, although the time it takes can vary slightly.
A month	is based on the time it takes the moon to go around the earth, which is 29 days, 12 hours, 44 minutes, and 2.8 seconds.
A year	is based on the time it takes the earth to go around the sun, or about 365 days, 5 hours, 48 minutes, and 46 seconds.

Dividing solar time into dependable calendar units has long been a frustrating problem. An ancient Babylonian committee established a 354-day year, divided into 12 moon cycles, each 29½ days long. This was eleven days short of the solar year, however, and their seasons began to drift. They fixed this by adding extra days to the calendar when it seemed to need some.

The Egyptians, still B.C., divided their year into twelve 30-day months, totaling 360 days, adding 5 days at the end to make 365. However, the year is actually more like 365¼ days long, so after centuries of use, their calendar was seriously off.

The Romans also had a lunar calendar, but they began with ten months—six had 31 days and four had 30 days, adding up to 304 days. The extra 61¼ days fell in winter when the priests must have assumed everyone was too depressed to notice, since they simply waited that long to announce the new year. Eventually the Romans added a couple more months, changing the number of days in each, until Julius Caesar managed to make twelve months add up to an exact 365¼-day year in 46 B.C. by adding a day—thus our leap year—every four years.

This would have worked if the year weren't actually eleven minutes shorter than that. By 1582 the seasons were so out of kilter that Pope Gregory XIII (see *Roman Numerals*, page 208) modified the calendar by refining the leap year—leap years would still be every fourth year, but years beginning a new century would not be leap years unless evenly divisible by 400. (The year 2000, divisible by 400, was a leap year. The year 1900 was not.)

Pope Gregory's calendar was off by only 26 seconds a year, which means it gets out of sync one day every 3,323 years. This has

WORLD CALENDAR ASSOCIATION CALENDAR

January								February								March						
S	M	T	W	T	F	S		S	M	T	W	T	F	S		S	M	T	W	T	F	S
1	2	3	4	5	6	7				1	2	3	4							1	2
8	9	10	11	12	13	14		5	6	7	8	9	10	11		3	4	5	6	7	8	9
15	16	17	18	19	20	21		12	13	14	15	16	17	18		10	11	12	13	14	15	16
22	23	24	25	26	27	28		19	20	21	22	23	24	25		17	18	19	20	21	22	23
29	30	31						26	27	28	29	30				24	25	26	27	28	29	30

April								May								June							
S	M	T	W	T	F	S		S	M	T	W	T	F	S		S	M	T	W	T	F	S	
1	2	3	4	5	6	7				1	2	3	4							1	2	
8	9	10	11	12	13	14		5	6	7	8	9	10	11		3	4	5	6	7	8	9	
15	16	17	18	19	20	21		12	13	14	15	16	17	18		10	11	12	13	14	15	16	
22	23	24	25	26	27	28		19	20	21	22	23	24	25		17	18	19	20	21	22	23	
29	30	31						26	27	28	29	30				24	25	26	27	28	29	30	W

July								August								September						
S	M	T	W	T	F	S		S	M	T	W	T	F	S		S	M	T	W	T	F	S
1	2	3	4	5	6	7				1	2	3	4							1	2
8	9	10	11	12	13	14		5	6	7	8	9	10	11		3	4	5	6	7	8	9
15	16	17	18	19	20	21		12	13	14	15	16	17	18		10	11	12	13	14	15	16
22	23	24	25	26	27	28		19	20	21	22	23	24	25		17	18	19	20	21	22	23
29	30	31						26	27	28	29	30				24	25	26	27	28	29	30

October								November								December							
S	M	T	W	T	F	S		S	M	T	W	T	F	S		S	M	T	W	T	F	S	
1	2	3	4	5	6	7				1	2	3	4							1	2	
8	9	10	11	12	13	14		5	6	7	8	9	10	11		3	4	5	6	7	8	9	
15	16	17	18	19	20	21		12	13	14	15	16	17	18		10	11	12	13	14	15	16	
22	23	24	25	26	27	28		19	20	21	22	23	24	25		17	18	19	20	21	22	23	
29	30	31						26	27	28	29	30				24	25	26	27	28	29	30	W

been an acceptable margin of error to most countries, who slowly began adopting the Gregorian calendar: Great Britain—and the American colonies—adopted it in 1752; then Japan in 1873 and China in 1912, with Russia resisting until 1918. As you see, history's been hung up on it for more than four hundred years.

Committees are still picking at the calendar even now. A new calendar has been suggested by the World Calendar Association that divides the year into four equal quarters of 13 weeks each, with a "World's Day" added at the end—an 8-day week at the end of December—to make 365 days (see illustration). In leap years another World's Day would be added to the end of June as well. This calendar is so sensible that it probably will never catch on, but wouldn't it be wonderful to be able to use the same calendar every year?

▶ The World Calendar is only one of many alternative calendars. To check out some others, do a search for "alternative calendars."

CAMERAS, FILM

THERE ARE TWO KINDS of cameras: film-based, sometimes called analog (see *Analog vs. Digital*, page 14), and digital. This entry will deal primarily with the widely used 35 mm camera (if you favor a non–35 mm point-and-shoot camera, proceed directly to *Film* on page 99). If you are a professional using a camera of a different size, many of the numbers that follow here will not apply, but hey, you already know this stuff. If you use an ordinary adjustable 35 mm camera, however, there's your first number. And if you've been so intimidated by those numbers ringing the lens barrel that you've never taken it off A (automatic), perhaps it's time to pause and face the f-stops.

Lenses

The size of a lens is not its width, as you may have supposed, but its length, measured in millimeters from an optical point on the lens to the film. A camera is usually referred to by the size of its shortest lens—e.g., a 35 mm camera comes with a lens that measures 35 mm long. This is considered a short lens and it actually is, physically, short, making the camera quite portable.

The longer the lens—called *focal length*—the narrower the field of view and the greater the magnification. If you look through the viewfinder/lens of a 35 mm camera, things will appear more distant than they do with the naked eye. A 50 mm lens will bring things as close as you naturally see them. To magnify them more, you can go to a 100 mm, 200 mm, 500 mm, or 1,000 mm lens. This used to require separate, screw-on lenses, but most cameras today are equipped with a *zoom lens* that allows many focal lengths in one lens, with standard ranges from 35 mm to 70 mm or 105 mm. A short, 24 mm *wide-angle lens* takes wide, panoramic shots. A long *telephoto lens* magnifies distant objects to make them appear closer.

Exposure

A camera is essentially a dark box with a hole that allows a certain amount of light to hit a piece of chemically treated film for a certain length of time. How much light gets in is called the *exposure*, controlled by (1) the size of the hole; (2) how long the hole stays open; (3) how fast the film reacts to light; (4) the strength of the light that's available.

The settings, or numbers involved, are not hard to understand. The hard part is knowing how to combine them—but it helps to know how each aspect of exposure works.

F-Stops. Inside the camera is a diaphragm that can physically adjust to change the size of the hole, or *aperture*, that lets in the light. The aperture size is controlled by *f-stops*, represented by numbers found around the lens barrel. There are usually seven of them:

2   2.8   4   5.6   8   11   16

Each f-stop lets in half the light of the stop before it. So f-stop 2.8 lets in half as much light as f-stop 2, but twice as much light as f-stop 4.

The f-stop you use helps determine your *depth of field*, meaning the portion of your picture that will be in focus. (Other factors are *lens size* and the *distance* of the object you are focused on.) *The larger the f-stop number, the smaller the aperture* and the more of your picture will be in focus. In fact, so little light gets into a pinhole camera that the entire field is in perfect focus. Coordinating the seven f-stops with the seven shutter speeds is a matter of practice, know-how, and artistry.

Shutter Speed. When you take a picture, another mechanical device inside the camera called a *shutter* opens briefly to allow light to hit the film. How long it stays open is the *shutter speed*, and is measured in fractions of a second. A suggested shutter speed often appears inside the camera's viewfinder: 1 = 1 second, 2 = $1/2$ second, 4 = $1/4$ second, 50 = $1/50$ second, 100 = $1/100$ second, 250 = $1/250$ second, 500 = $1/500$ second, and so on. There are shutter speeds up to $1/500,000$ second!

A fast shutter speed of 500 will freeze action; a slow speed of 50 will blur it. Slow speeds require steady hands or a tripod for clarity.

Available Light. Photographers are keenly aware of light: type (daylight, interior light, flash), direction, and angle. The camera measures the level of light and, if the camera is set on automatic, adjusts the exposure settings appropriately.

ISO. Film speed is measured with ISO (International Standards Organization) numbers: 50 for slow film, 100 and 200 for film used in daylight. 400 is considered fast film, or film that reacts quickly to light, and is useful for indoor action shots. (For more on film, see *Film*, page 99.)

▶ For more extensive explanations on the workings of cameras, go to http://www.howstuffworks.com and http://www.photosecrets.com.

CAMERAS, DIGITAL
•••

AMONG THE MASSES of new measures and sizes brought to you by the digital age, pixels may be one of the least understood. Still, digital cameras are the name of the game. If you don't have one, you probably want one or think you might soon. Perhaps you are just put off by those pesky pixels.

Not to worry—it's pixel time.

A digital camera is a filmless device that uses an image sensor (usually a charge-coupled device [CCD], or, in less expensive cameras, a complementary metal oxide semiconductor called a CMOS) to convert photons (light) into electrical charges. This data is stored on a *memory card* and can be reformulated in thousands of rows of tiny square *pixels.*

Take a look at partial catalog descriptions of four digital cameras:

Olympus Brio D-100 $199.00
- 1.3 megapixels with 1280 x 960 resolution
- digital 2x zoom
- supplied with 8 MB SmartMedia card

Olympus C-700 Ultra Zoom $399.00
- 2.11 megapixels resolution
- 10x optical zoom
- 16 MB SmartMedia card

Olympus C-4040 $899.00
- 4.1 megapixel CCD for resolution up to
  3200 x 2400 pixels
- 3x zoom lens
- 16 MB SmartMedia card

Olympus E20N SLR Pro Digital $1,999.00
- 5.0 effective megapixel CCD
- 4x glass zoom lens
- 32 MB SmartMedia card

Source: Porter's Photo-Digital-Video A-69 Catalog, March 30, 2002

Pixels

The amount of detail that a camera can capture is measured in *pixels*, a term short for *picture element*. It prints as a little square. Generally speaking, the more pixels your camera can capture, the sharper the image, or *resolution*.

How many pixels are enough? At the low end, good for e-mailing or websites, is 640 × 480 pixels, or about 300,000 pixels. To print quality images, however, go for at least one *megapixel* (a million pixels), which gives a resolution of 1216 × 912. The more pixels, the higher the resolution and, of course, the higher the price of the camera and the fewer pictures you can cram on your memory card. (Note that the total pixel figure may be more than width times height; apparently some are applied to necessary camera functions.)

The highest end digital camera listed above offers 5 megapixels. While this sounds impressive, at this writing even the highest resolution digital image can't begin to compare with the resolution of an image captured on film. One of the priciest (about $15,000) digital cameras can capture 15 megapixels, but it would take over 70 megapixels to equal a print from 35 mm film. Which is why most digital photographs will not hugely enlarge with clarity. But this often doesn't matter. The human eye can't differentiate one from the other, so for most applications a good digital image works well.

Zoom Lenses

Zoom lenses, even optical ones, are described by their magnifying power: 2X is two times magnification, 4X is four times, 10X is ten times, and so on.

Memory

Digital images are stored on a memory card instead of on film. The images are transferred from the card to your computer and the card can be used again. Memory cards come in binary sizes and are measured in *megabytes*, just like computer memory (see *Computers, Personal*, page 63). Popular sizes to date are 32 MB, 64 MB, and 128 MB.

How many images, or "pictures," you can put on a card depends on the size of the card and the size of the file for each image. The image file size depends not only on the density of the resolution (the number of pixels), which is obvious, but also the kind of memory—TIFF, JPEG, or other types of memory—used to store the images. TIFF uses much more memory than JPEG but prints with better resolution. Which kind of memory you choose depends on how you want to use the images. Better resolution and smaller memory demands will likely improve with future models.

▶ **For a more extensive explanation of digital camera workings, go to "Digital Cameras," at Marshall Brain's How Stuff Works website, http://www.howstuffworks.com/digital-camera.htm, or take "A Short Course in Choosing a Digital Camera," http://www.shortcourses.com.**

CANS
....

YOU MIGHT OCCASIONALLY come across an old recipe that calls for a No. 2 can of beans, but you're not sure how large a No. 2 can is. You still can't be sure. For one thing, the can size number is no longer to be found on the label. Yesterday's No. 2 can is around 20 ounces by weight but 18 fluid ounces. Today's No. 2 can, as defined by the can industry, is 20.55 ounces by weight.

While there are exact measurement requirements for various can sizes, down to the last sixteenth of an inch, most cookbook users today need only be aware that in the United States, a metal can announces its capacity in one of two ways: *fluid ounces* or by weight in *avoirdupois ounces*. Fluid and weight measurements will not likely be the same. The metric equivalents, usually shown in parentheses, provide another clue: milliliters (ml) for fluid ounces and grams (g) when measured by weight.

> ▶ **If you can't sleep until you know the exact capacity and dimensions of today's cans, go to http://www.cancentral.com.**

CHECKS

AT THE BOTTOM of your business or personal check is a line of numbers in a large, bold, squarish font. Why do these numbers look so strange?

Banks have long used a system called *magnetic ink character recognition* (MICR), which allows scanners to read numbers printed with magnetic ink in a special font. Technology hurtles on, however, so today some scanners use *optical character recognition* (OCR), which does not require special inks or odd fonts. Banks still requiring magnetic ink can translate OCR fonts into MICR, which is why you occasionally may find a strip adhered to the bottom of a canceled check.

But when bank tellers ask for your checking account number, which of that long string of numbers do they want?

There is no straightforward answer. Often it's the last six digits. Sometimes it's more. Sometimes it's a group somewhere in the middle. To figure out your account number, write out the line of

Source: Federal Reserve Bank of New York, U.S. Department of the Treasury.

numbers from the bottom of a returned check in a large, friendly hand, substituting a pleasant space for the eye-bending squiggles.

All the numbers printed in the upper corners of the check are repeated on the bottom except for the first number on top of the fraction, in this case 50. This is the American Banking Association number for the state or area in which your bank is located. Now find the numbers in the upper corners of the check that are repeated in the bottom string. Cross them out. The group of numbers remaining is your account number.

~~0213~~/~~0226~~/~~8~~ / ~~1234~~ / <u>07889</u> / ~~0687~~ / 000000~~10295~~

0213	is the bank's Federal Reserve District, office and state or special collection arrangement. Cross it out.
0226	is your bank's identification number. Cross it out.
8	is the check digit (see *Bar Codes*, page 17). Cross it out.
1234	represents your particular bank branch. Cross it out.
0687	is your check number. Cross it out.
102.95	is the amount you wrote the check for, printed on the bottom of the check when it is returned with your statement.
07889	is your account number.

CHOLESTEROL

CHOLESTEROL HAS BECOME a bad word in the American diet these days, and it doesn't seem fair—it is indispensable for the manufacture of sex hormones, not to mention brain and nervous system growth. Furthermore, although it's true that one kind of cholesterol clogs the inside of your arteries like layers of grease down the kitchen drainpipes, there's another type of cholesterol that does just the opposite—it actually helps clean the harmful kind out.

Still, there's reason to be concerned: bad cholesterol can cause atherosclerosis (hardening of the arteries), a major cause of heart disease. Most blood cholesterol tests report the overall cholesterol present in your blood. The American Heart Association (AHA) and most doctors now feel any count over 200 is undesirable—that's 200 mg of cholesterol per deciliter of blood. If your level is between 200 and 239, you're considered to have "borderline-high" blood cholesterol. Anything over 240 is considered high.

Your risk of heart disease can be more accurately calculated, however, if another test is done that measures the clogging cholesterol, called LDL (low-density lipoproteins), which may cause heart disease, and the declogging cholesterol, called HDL (high-density lipoproteins), which tends to fight heart disease. The AHA recommends that everyone have this test done by the age of thirty (twenty, if there's a history of heart disease in your family), repeating it every three years. Add triglycerides, associated with cholesterol as they are yet another fatty substance in the blood to worry about, and here are some generally accepted limits:

	Good	Borderline	Undesirable
Total cholesterol	Below 200	200–240	Above 240
LDL cholesterol	Below 130	130–160	Above 160
HDL cholesterol	Above 45	35–45	Below 35
Triglycerides	Below 200	200–400	Above 400

Keep in mind that these are 2002 numbers. It's risky to report the latest in cholesterol research—so many studies are being done, and the news does seem to change from year to year, if not from month to month. But controlling your cholesterol is important. Most people can do it by avoiding animal fats in their diets. American Heart Association studies show that the average American man consumes about 500 mg of cholesterol every day, and the average woman 320 mg. The AHA recommends an intake of no more than 200 mg daily for people with coronary heart disease, diabetes, or high LDL cholesterol; 300 mg daily for those who don't.

By cutting down on red meats, dairy products, and fast foods, you may reduce your risk of heart disease. And if you've never understood the flap over eggs, consider this: just one medium egg at 274 mg of cholesterol is over the daily limit (200 mg) for some of us and just under (300 mg) for the rest. That's one egg! You can eat five cups of ice cream (1 cup = 51 mg), four burgers (1 plain quarter-pound burger = 77 mg) or a half a cup of butter (1 tbsp. = 31) before you get to that number.

▶ **If you know your cholesterol count, you can estimate your ten-year risk of having a heart attack at http:/hin.nhlbi.nih.gov/atpiii/calculator.asp. To find the fat content of popular fast food, go to http://fatcalories.com. You can also do an Internet search for "cholesterol calculator."**

CIRCLES

IT'S NOT A BAD IDEA to know your way around the circle, since so many essentials in life are based on it—clocks, angles, maps, and compasses, to name just a few. Fortunately, the circle is elegantly simple—a gentle line without beginning or end that is equidistant from the center at all points. The fact that the circle is divided into 360 degrees is common knowledge, but who did the dividing? And why 360?

The same people who invented the wheel five or six thousand years ago—the Mesopotamians—also fancied the number 60, basing their entire number system on it. No one seems to know exactly why—it might even have been related to trade. For commercial purposes, it's helpful to use a number that has many factors (see *Commercial Items*, page 59), and 60 has twelve of them, more than any other manageable number—it can be evenly divided by 1, 2, 3, 4, 5, 6, 10, 12, 15, 20, 30, and 60: very useful for marketing. Whatever the reason, the Egyptians used it to divide the circle into 360 degrees (60 × 6), and gave us the symbol for degrees (°). The Egyptians divided spheres into 360 degrees as well, assigning the first latitude and longitude lines to the earth (see *Latitude and Longitude*, page 147).

This ancient system for dividing the circle has persisted to the present. Each degree of the circle is divided into 60 minutes (60') and each minute into 60 seconds (60"), divisions that also apply to coordinates for places, compass directions, angles, and, of course, the minutes and seconds of time.

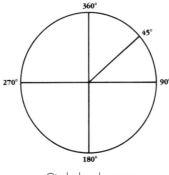

Circle by degrees

Easy as Pi

At first glance, measuring the circumference (distance around the edge) and the area inside the circle appears to defy familiar, un-bending measuring tools, like rulers. And it would, actually, ex-cept for a magical number, discovered about 4,000 years ago, that makes it a piece of cake—or, more to the point, pi. Pi, symbolized by the Greek letter π, is simply the number of times the diameter of a circle will go around the edge—always 3.1416 times (pi has been calculated to something like a billion decimal places, but most people stop at four). This means that you *can* use your ruler to measure the circle—all you need to measure is the diameter or the radius (half the diameter).

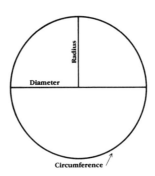

If the diameter (d) is 6", the radius (r) is 3" and the circumference (C) 18.85".

The formulas are simple, but remember that if you measure in feet or inches, the answers will be in decimal feet or decimal inches. The examples that follow apply to a circle with a diameter of 6 inches.

$$d\pi = \text{circumference (C)}$$
(6 inches x 3.1416 = 18.85 inches)
OR
$$2\pi r = C$$
(2 x 3.1416 x 3 inches = 18.85 inches)

You can also use pi to find the area in square inches (or square centimeters or whatever measure you're using) by squaring the radius (multiplying it by itself) and multiplying that by pi (the example applies to the above circle, which has a radius of 3 inches):

$$\pi r^2 = \text{area}$$
(3.1416 x 9 [3 inches squared] = 28.27 square inches)

So how do you remember a number like pi? Close approximations are 3.14 and 22/7. Or look at your calculator—most calculators have the symbol for pi on one of the buttons. Push it and pi will appear.

CLOTHING (SIZES)

THE SIZES FOR MOST AMERICAN CLOTHING—men's, women's, and children's—are based on anthropometric studies, which measured the size of the varying human, in this case American, form. The first anthropometric studies used by the clothing industry for women's as well as men's apparel were conducted during World War II by the U.S. Armed Forces, which had to measure their burgeoning ranks for uniforms. Another study, measuring 150,000 children in sixteen states, was done by the Department of Agriculture at about the same time. American clothing sizes, even women's sizes, are still frequently based on these studies. The clothing industry has also introduced the Small-Medium-Large sizes (S-M-L), sometimes adding an Extra-Small (XS) and an Extra-Large (XL), which can apply to almost any article of clothing on the market. To figure out how the system works, you can safely assume that each letter represents two, sometimes three, numbered sizes, spreading over the size range. There is much license taken here, however; one company's Large might be another's Medium, especially if the first was made in the Far East, where the anthropometric measurements tend to be smaller.

Clothing, Babies'

What could be more frustrating than trying to buy clothing for somebody else's baby? If you've never purchased baby clothes before, you could easily blunder, for the sizes are misleading. The confusion begins with three sizing systems:

The age system may include the following sizes: newborn, 3 months, 6 months, 12 months, 18 months, 24 months, and 36 months. Motherly wisdom has it that you multiply the child's age by two—assuming the infant is not a preemie or especially large for its age—in order to get the right fit (for example, a 6-month-old baby would wear a 12-months size). When the child is around 12 months, however, you buy the Toddler sizes, which begin with the year-old baby and end with the 4-year-old: 1T to 4T. Sizes followed by a T are supposed to have extra room for diapers (although T may sometimes mean Tall).

The weight system is supposed to apply to the following ages: up to 14 pounds for newborn to 3 months, 15 to 20 pounds for up to 6 months, 21 to 26 pounds for up to 18 months, 27 to 32 pounds for up to 24 months, and so on—but brands vary.

The newborn to extra-large system is anybody's guess, for there are no government rules—only suggested guidelines—in the industry to encourage consistency. There is usually a weight or age on the label for guidance.

Choosing a size wouldn't be half so difficult if these systems were accurate—if a size 18-months sleeper actually fit an 18-month-old baby, or overalls for a 15- to 20-pounder fit your 19-pound nephew. Often, however, they turn out to be too small.

Perhaps babies are bigger than they used to be, or the clothes shrink with all the washings. Whatever the reason, what are you to do? Buy gifts one or two sizes bigger than what seems perfectly sensible. Babies grow fast, so if the cuties don't fit into them tomorrow, they probably will next week.

Clothing, Children's

A baby is considered by the clothing industry to have become a child when she or he can tear around independently and diaperless. Children's clothing sizes apply to both girls and boys, and, unfortunately, are no more dependable than infant and toddler sizes. Children's sizes continue to estimate age—2 through 6X (X meaning extra large). After size 6X, children experience one of the American rites of passage: girls and boys split up to find their finery in different departments.

Girls' sizes continue the children's sizes, using only even numbers after 7—8, 10, 12, 14, and 16. This is confusing because the most popular women's size numbers are exactly the same! Unlike women's sizes, girls' clothing may also be labeled for width. A teenage girl graduates to the Junior Department (see *Clothing, Women's*, page 54).

Boys' sizes, like girls' sizes, are based on age, even though it rarely applies. The size range is from 6 to 24, using only the even numbers (6, 8, 10, etc). Boys' clothes are usually labeled for width as well—slim, regular, and husky. The larger boys' clothes are often in a separate department for "young men," but the sizes sensibly continue the same system (unlike the odd-numbered Junior clothes for teenage girls). A teenage boy who can wear the larger boys' sizes can probably fit into men's sizes as well—the overlap is considerable. Young men's clothes are often cut slimmer, however, and the styles are more likely to reflect the current fads.

Clothing, Men's

No size system is so sensible as that applied to men's clothing. It is an island of reason in a sea of size insanity (see other *Clothing* entries). For one thing, the numbers that represent men's clothing sizes usually mean inches. For another, because sizes are actual measurements, they are consistent—a size 15 shirt's collar band measures 15 inches for any brand. Men are lucky for a third rea-son—better shirts and pants are often measured in two direc-tions, so alterations are frequently unnecessary.

Men's shirts and sweaters are often sized to fit a man's neck and arms, the measurements applying to the collar band and sleeve length (measuring from the base of the collar, over the shoulder to the edge of the cuff). Most collar band sizes increase every half inch from 14 to 16^1/2. The sleeve length usually measures from 32 to 36 inches.

Men's pants have two measurements: waist and inseam (crotch to hem measurement), so a short, thin man will not have to have a tall, thin man's pants shortened. (Women are not so lucky.) Waist sizes run from 28 to 42, inseams from about 28 to 36 inches. Men's coats and jackets (and sometimes sweaters) are sized by chest measurements in inches, going from 32 to 44 and higher.

The only monkey wrench in this system is the use of Extra Small (XS), Small (S), Medium (M), Large (L), and Extra Large (XL). These sizes most often apply to men's sportswear and un-derwear, but sometimes to shirts and sweaters as well, and they do vary some from brand to brand. The fit may not be as precise as measured sizes—in a Small, all measurements will be small, while a Large will have all large measurements, with Medium some-where in between.

Clothing, Women's

One of the more outrageous systems foisted upon American women is the sizing of their clothes. Women's clothing is not sized to the last half-inch as many men's clothes are, not only be-cause the huge variety of designs sometimes makes exact mea-surements difficult, but because the women's clothing industry seems reluctant to confront a woman with her own measure-ments. But if measurements can't be used, then how to label clothes for the vast variety of heights, girths, and shapes represented by American women?

The clothing industry has dealt with this problem with this solution: instead of dividing women's clothing into two groups—teenagers' clothing and adult clothing—it has divided women's apparel into no less than five main groups. Many women who flounder between one or another department don't realize that the real dividing factor is height and figure type. Here are some general, if unavoidably unreliable, guidelines:

	Sizes	Height	Figure Type
Junior	3-5-7-9-11-13-15	5'2" to 5'7"	slender
Misses	4-6-8-10-12-14-16-18	5'5" to 5'7"	developed and well proportioned
Petite	2P-4P-6P-8P-10P-12P-14P-16P	4'8" to 5'4"	developed and well proportioned
Half	even numbers from 10½ to 26½	5'2" to 5'4"	fuller and rounder than Misses sizes
Women's	even numbers from 34 to 52	5'5" to 5'8"	fuller and rounder than Misses

Based on data from *Figure Types and Size Ranges,* by Debbie Ann Gioello, courtesy of Fairchild Books, a division of Fairchild Publications, New York, NY.

Not one of the size types deals with a woman tall enough to be a model, whose lithe length every American woman is supposed to be striving to resemble. And it does sound as if the sizes assigned to women (34 to 52) were bust measurements, but do not be taken in by this: a size 34 fits a woman with a 38-inch bust and hips and a 29-inch waist.

Size-foolery is also used by the makers of "better" clothes—although there is general agreement in the clothing industry about size ranges, a woman who wears a size 14 in clothes she can afford frequently may fit nicely into a more expensive 12 or 10, a practice that many fashion experts seem to feel persuades the woman to buy pricier clothes. Styles vary greatly between size types as well.

Usually the bigger a woman is, the less trendy and exciting have been her style choices. This dreadful practice has incensed full-bodied women, so today special stores and departments are offering a more tempting variety.

▶ **To find roughly equivalent British, Continental, or Japanese sizes, go to http://www.fromto.as/clothing.htm.**

COMFORT INDEX (WEATHER)

WEATHER REPORTS often include figures that are not actually the weather but the weather's effects on the human body. In winter the wind can make lower temperatures feel colder. In summer the humidity can make high temperatures feel hotter. In either case the effects on the human body can be acutely, even dangerously, uncomfortable.

Windchill Index

Most people are familiar with the windchill index—a day with a temperature of 15 degrees Fahrenheit and a wind speed of 20 mph will be reported as having a windchill temperature of –2 degrees. This does not mean that the wind makes the air colder. It does mean that it makes people colder—that an appropriately bundled-up person's body will react to that wind and temperature as if it were –2 degrees. Although you lose one-fifth of your body heat by breathing, you can control some of the heat loss with extra layers of well-insulated clothing. The effects also vary some with the size of the person—small persons lose heat faster than large ones.

It's important to know the windchill on particularly cold and windy days to avoid *hypothermia*, or dangerously low body temperatures. On a dry winter day the cold can sneak up on you. Use the windchill chart on page 57 for guidance.

NEW WINDCHILL CHART

Wind Speed (mph)

	Calm	5	10	15	20	25	30	35	40	45	50	55	60
	40	36	34	32	30	29	28	28	27	26	26	25	25
	35	31	27	25	24	23	22	21	20	19	19	18	17
	30	25	21	19	17	16	15	14	13	12	12	11	10
	25	19	15	13	11	9	8	7	6	5	4	4	3
	20	13	9	6	4	3	1	0	−1	−2	−3	−3	−4
	15	7	3	0	−2	−4	−5	−7	−8	−9	−10	−11	−11
	10	1	−4	−7	−9	−11	−12	−14	−15	−16	−17	−18	−19
	5	−5	−10	−13	−15	−17	−19	−21	−22	−23	−24	−25	−26
	0	−11	−16	−19	−22	−24	−26	−27	−29	−30	−31	−32	−33
	−5	−16	−22	−26	−29	−31	−33	−34	−36	−37	−38	−39	−40
	−10	−22	−28	−32	−35	−37	−39	−41	−43	−44	−45	−46	−48
	−15	−28	−35	−39	−42	−44	−46	−48	−50	−51	−52	−54	−55
	−20	−34	−41	−45	−48	−51	−53	−55	−57	−58	−60	−61	−62
	−25	−40	−47	−51	−55	−58	−60	−62	−64	−65	−67	−68	−69
	−30	−46	−53	−58	−61	−64	−67	−69	−71	−72	−74	−75	−76
	−35	−52	−59	−64	−68	−71	−73	−76	−78	−79	−81	−82	−84
	−40	−57	−66	−71	−74	−78	−80	−82	−84	−86	−88	−89	−91
	−45	−63	−72	−77	−81	−84	−87	−89	−91	−93	−95	−97	−98

Temperature (°F) (vertical axis label on left)

▒ Frostbite occurs in 15 minutes or less

Windchill (°F) = 35.74 + 0.6215T − 35.75($V^{0.16}$) + 0.4275T($V^{0.16}$)
Where T = air temperature (°F); V = wind speed (mph)

Source: National Weather Service, U.S. Department of Commerce

Note that this chart is not the same chart used in the 1989 edition of this book. In August 2001, the American National Weather Service, together with the Meteorological Services of Canada, announced a new windchill temperature index for the 2001/2002 winter season. The new system attempts to internationally standardize the windchill index, upgrading the old 1945 index using new technologies. The new windchill index is quite different, one reason being that the wind speed is now calculated at 5 feet, the average height of the human body's face, instead of 33 feet, the standard *anemometer*—wind speed calculator—height.

Heat Index

Perspiring is the human body's cooling system, and it works quite well in summer as long as the air is dry. Damp air doesn't allow good evaporation, however, so the humidity can really bother you—pleasant temperatures in the low 80s can feel oppressive if the relative humidity is over 70 percent. In fact, the average person

HEAT INDEX TABLE

Heat Index	Effects on the Human Body
130 or above	Heatstroke likely with continued exposure
105 to 130	Heatstroke likely with prolonged exposure
90 to 105	Heatstroke possible with prolonged exposure

Air Temperature (°F)

Relative Humidity	70	75	80	85	90	95	100	105	110	115	120
30	67	73	78	84	90	96	104	113	123	135	148
35	67	73	79	85	91	98	107	118	130	143	
40	68	74	79	86	93	101	110	123	137	151	
45	68	74	80	87	95	104	115	129	143		
50	69	75	81	88	96	107	120	135	150		
55	69	75	81	89	98	110	126	142			
60	70	76	82	90	100	114	132	149			
65	70	76	83	91	102	119	138				
70	70	77	85	93	106	124	144				
75	70	77	86	95	109	130					
80	71	78	86	97	113	136					
85	71	78	87	99	117						
90	71	79	88	102	122						
95	71	79	89	105							
100	72	80	91	108							

Source: National Weather Service, U.S. Department of Commerce

can be safely outside in a 100-degree temperature with 90 percent relative humidity for only ten minutes. The effects of humidity and temperature on the human body is reported as the *humiture*, or sometimes as the *heat stress index*. When the heat stress index is high, outdoor activities can be dangerous to your health.

Unlike the windchill index, the heat index table has remained unchanged except in format.

▶ To see the difference between the old and new windchill indexes, go to http://weather.gov/om/windchill/index/shtml. Find the windchill calculator, enter wind speed and temperature, and voilà!

COMMERCIAL ITEMS

WHY IS IT THAT OUR DOLLAR is based on the number ten (10 × 10 = 100), but the things we buy with it are sold by the dozen? When the contemporary trend is toward the ten-based metric system, why do manufacturers and commercial establishments still frequently base their trade on the number twelve?

Actually, when it comes to selling and pricing things, twelve is a much more useful number than ten, because it has more *factors*, or divisors. The number ten has only four divisors—1, 2, 5, and 10—while twelve can be divided by 1, 2, 3, 4, 6, and 12, making it much more flexible. This convenience may partially explain why the number twelve has been popular for hundreds of years, with twelve inches making up a foot, and twelve ounces the troy pound (see *Weight*, page 269).

Science writer Isaac Asimov, noting these advantages in his book *Realm of Numbers*, suggests that if humans had been born with six fingers on each hand instead of five, our number system would likely be based on twelve instead of ten!

Commercial items are counted in multiples of twelve: 1 dozen = 12 items; 12 dozen = 1 gross; 12 gross = 1 great gross (1,728 items).

COMPASS

ON THE FACE OF IT, the compass seems unbelievably simple and handy—it's affordable, portable, and, unless corrected, its little magnetic needle always points to magnetic north. It's even easier to read than it used to be. Before 1920 there were 32 bewildering direction points—north, north by east, north-northeast, northeast, northeast by east, east-northeast, east by north, and east, to name only eight.

Today you simply read clockwise from zero to 360—north is 0 degrees, east is 90 degrees, south is 180 degrees, and west is 270 degrees. (Like the circle, the compass is divided into 360 degrees.)

COMPASS

Source: Thermometer Corporation of America

If you're lost in the woods and you've remembered your compass, you probably assume that all you have to do is line up north on the compass with the needle, and you'll get an accurate read of all the other directions. Unfortunately, you may also need to consider the whereabouts of magnetic north.

Magnetic north is not the same as true north, but you might assume that it's pretty close. Even if you know that magnetic north moves around a bit, you probably envision it moving around the North Pole. But magnetic north is located about a thousand miles from the North Pole, about halfway between the U.S. border and

Alaska. In fact, it is changing so fast that it is predicted to soon leave Canada, heading for Russia through Alaska. Such an eccentric location can seriously throw off a compass reading—if you're lost in Alaska or the Yukon, for example, your compass won't point anywhere near north; it might, in fact, point south. Even in the "Lower Forty-nine," the only way to get an accurate reading from your compass is to know the number of degrees you need to correct for—a correction known as the *declination*.

You'd think that this sort of essential information would be easy to find, but it isn't. For one thing, the declination—how many degrees to add or subtract to find true north—changes about a quarter of a degree every year. This is not serious, but means that older maps can be off a degree or more.

How essential this information is to you depends on where you plan to do your adventuring—as you can see on the following rough estimate of declinations, it's those of you in western and northeastern states whose compasses will be farthest off. If you're

UNITED STATES MAGNETIC FIELD CHART, 1995: DECLINATION

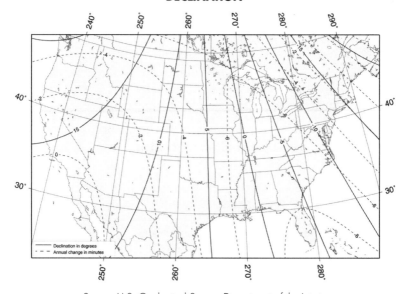

Source: U.S. Geological Survey, Department of the Interior

lucky, you'll be outdooring in more centrally located states where there's only a 5 degree or less correction, probably okay in a pinch: Wisconsin, Illinois, Michigan, Ohio, West Virginia, Indiana, Kentucky, Tennessee, western North Carolina, South Carolina, Georgia, Alabama, most of Mississippi, and Florida.

The intent of all this information is not to instruct you in compass finesse, but simply to warn you about making dangerous assumptions about the compass's accuracy. The degrees of correction are usually included on good topographical maps, along with the expected annual change for that area. Authorities at the National Cartographic Information Center recommend finding true north the old-fashioned way—by locating the North Star (the very bright star in a direct line with the top star on the front edge of the Big Dipper), because it never deviates from true north more than one degree. If you line up "north" on your compass with the North Star, you will see how many degrees' difference there is between true north and magnetic north, to which the needle is pointing.

Or you can go the new-fashioned way—the *Global Positioning System (GPS)*, headquartered at Schriever Air Force Base, owned and operated by the U.S. Department of Defense for the U.S. military, but available to private firms and individuals. GPS typically uses four satellites to show the position of anyone carrying a compatible instrument. There are close to twenty-four active GPS satellites in orbit.

If you're simply using the compass to orient yourself so you don't start going in circles, you don't need to worry about declination. Declination is most important when you are trying to follow a map.

> ▶ To find the declination for your area, go to the National Geophysical Data Center at http://ngdc.noaa.gov and click on "Geomagnetism," or go to http://resurgentsoftware.com/geomag.html. A footnote: the needles on the earliest compasses, used by the Chinese about 1000 A.D., were marked to point south!

COMPUTERS, PERSONAL (PCs)

THE COMPUTER WORLD is so full of numbers, you hardly need sound effects to make you feel trapped in *Scream 3*, but there are some that you really must deal with if you are going to consider buying a personal computer. Whether you are in a computer store, looking at a catalog, or browsing the web, and even if your son, daughter, or grandchild is at your elbow providing reassurance, you will still have to make your choice based at least in part on this kind of information:

Model	RAM	HD	Modem	MHz
Power Mac G4	256MB	40GB	56K	800
iMac G4 Super-Drive	512MB	60GB	6K	800

Yikes! you cry, if you're still with us. (If you're not, you gave up already or this is kindergarten stuff to you.) What *are* these numbers? What is the normal range? Are these high or low? good or bad? And those abbreviations! Doesn't anyone ever *spell* anything anymore?

If you are not of a generation that has known these acronyms since second grade, you have a right to confusion. Computer people have redefined or shortened so many familiar words, even metric prefixes that are practically sacred, that at times you may *think* you know what they're talking about, but trust me, you don't. To understand anything at all, it helps to spell out computer memory in bits and bytes.

Bits and Bytes

A unit of memory in a computer is contained in a *byte*. A byte can store one character of text, such as a "b," a comma, or a space (for image bytes, called *pixels*, see page 44). Each of these bytes is made up of an eight-digit yes-no (1-0) code, much like a bar code (see page 17). Each of those digits is a *bit*, short for binary digit.

The yes-no nature of computer intelligence has led to a 2-based number system, rather than a 10-based number system, even though some of the prefixes sound 10-based (metric). In computer memory, *kilo-* only sort of means thousand and *mega-* only sort of means million: a *kilobyte*, or 1K, consists of 1,024 bytes and a *megabyte* is 1,024 kilobytes (or 1,048,576 bytes). When you push each system—the 2-based and the 10-based—to a billion, you get the following, which demonstrates why memory chunks almost always come in strange-sounding numbers like 128, 256, or 512.

Powers of 2	*Powers of 10*
2 bytes	10
4 bytes	100
8 bytes	1,000 = 1 K
16 bytes	10,000
32 bytes	100,000
64 bytes	1,000,000 = 1 M
128 bytes	10,000,000
256 bytes	100,000,000
512 bytes	1,000,000,000 = 1 billion or 1 G
1,024 bytes = 1 K (kilobyte)	
2,048 bytes = 2 K	
4,096 bytes = 4 K	
8,192 bytes = 8 K	
16,384 bytes = 16 K	
32,768 bytes= 32 K	
65,536 bytes = 64 K	
131,072 bytes = 128 K	
262,144 bytes = 256 K	
524,288 bytes = 512 K	
1,048,576 bytes = 1,024 K = 1 M (megabyte)	
1,024 M = 1 G (gigabyte)	

To summarize:

Computer Memory Units
8 bits = 1 character = 1 byte
1,024 bytes = 1 kilobyte (K or KB)
1,024 kilobytes (K) = 1 megabyte (M or MB)
1,024 megabytes = 1 gigabyte (G or GB) = 1,073,741,824 bytes

What do these figures mean to you and your purchase? Since computers store text using 1 byte per character, including spaces, a typical typed, double-spaced page of about 350 words is about 2,000 characters, requiring 2K of computer memory. Drawings, charts, music, images, photos, art, and software add not just kilobytes but a megabyte load. How many megabytes and gigabytes a PC can deal with or store is represented by bytes of *memory*.

ROM and RAM

Two major kinds of computer memory have such similar acronyms that the uninitiated often confuse them. It helps to remember what the acronyms stand for. *ROM (read-only memory)* directs the computer's functions. You normally do not alter the contents of ROM, which remain the same whether the power is on or off.

The contents of *RAM (random-access memory)* are lost when the power goes off. RAM is like a tabletop where you can spread out your tools and projects and produce results. The bigger the table, the more work you can do at once. But there the metaphor stops: if you don't put your work away when you are finished—in literal computer terms, *save* it—you will probably lose it.

The size of a computer's RAM is important: the larger the RAM, the more programs you can run simultaneously and the larger the project you can work on. You need enough RAM to run your favorite programs with room left for other functions. RAM size keeps growing. Programs you want to run are getting bigger and adding more and more bells and whistles as technology allows for graphics, animation, movies, photography, and other memory gobblers. To demonstrate: the first edition of this book was written in 1988 on one of the first Macintosh computers with a RAM of *512 kilobytes*. In 2002, this new edition is being produced on a low-end two-year-old iMac with a RAM of *131,072 kilobytes*, or 128 megabytes.

Hard Disk (HD)

Programs, operating systems, and your work are stored on a rapidly spinning platter inside your computer called a *hard disk*, or

HD. These days, hard disk capacity is measured in *gigabytes* (G or GB), meaning *billions of bytes*. Your author's computer has a hard disk capacity of 20 gigabytes, which has proved more than enough for hundreds of scanned paintings, large layout and photo programs, a website, and several copies each of several full-length books with accompanying art files and notes. If you worry that you'll need more storage space than the gigabytes generally available, you need a professional's advice.

Megahertz (mHz)

Computers are getting faster all the time; how fast is measured in *megahertz* (mHz, or millions of cycles per second). The number of megahertz represents the speed of a computer's central processing unit (CPU), but this figure can be misleading. Computer performance is influenced by more than the speed of the processor. If, for example, the "highways" (called *buses* in computertown) between the processor and the various storage and memory facilities are slow, it doesn't matter how fast the processor is, the computer will be slow, too. Performance also depends on how much the processor can process at once.

Ethernet

Sometimes figures are supplied for Ethernet, a program developed by Xerox that facilitates the connection of a local area network (LAN). The version numbers tell how much data can be transferred between computers *per second*. The 100 Base-T, for example, can transfer 100 mbps (megabits per second). A gigabit Ethernet can transfer 1 gbps (gigabit per second). If you are working alone, you don't need to worry about Ethernet.

▶ For a more detailed computer education, go to Marshall Brain's fabulous website at http://www.howstuffworks.com/computer-memory. To find good definitions of computer terms, go to http://pcwebopaedia.com.

CONSUMER PRICE INDEX (CPI)
••

THE CONSUMER PRICE INDEX (CPI) has been described as an "economic speedometer"; it measures the *percent* increase or decrease in the prices of 211 goods and services bought by an average urban family over various amounts of time. A general summary in a daily newspaper might look something like this:

Consumer Price Index for All Urban Consumers (CPI-U)
These are the price indexes for January 2002. The percent change from December 2001 has been seasonally adjusted. 1982–84 = 100 unless otherwise noted.

	Index	Percent change from Jan. 2001	Percent change from Dec. 2001
All items	177.1	1.1	0.2
Food and Beverage	188.2	2.8	0.3
Housing	177.6	2.0	0.2
Apparel	120.4	–4.0	–.7
Transportation	148.6	–3.8	0.3
Medical Care	279.6	4.7	0.5
Recreation*	105.7	1.5	0.2
Education and Communication*	107.2	3.2	0.3

*Indexed on a December 1997 = 100 base.

Three easy keys unlock the mysteries of the CPI: (1) The figures are percentages—price *indexes*, not prices. (2) The index numbers *begin* with 100, unlike the percentages you are used to, which begin with zero, e.g., the first index figure—177.1—means 77.1 percent. More than what? you ask. (3) The percentages are based how much more or less a particular or group of items or services cost compared to a *base year or period*, which is always specified. If more than one base period is used, it's usually in a footnote.

Thus, in this CPI report, all items were 77.1 percent more expensive in January 2002 than the same items were in 1982–84, while education and communication cost 7.2 percent more than they did in December 1997 (see the footnote). The different base year explains why education appears to have suffered so little inflation: it's compared to a period five years ago, while most of the other figures are compared to a period twenty years ago.

The percent change is usually supplied for the previous month (in this case, December 2001) and the same month from the previous year (January 2001). Sometimes a *seasonally adjusted* figure is given to account for holidays.

The formats for all the CPI reports are similar: if you can read this index, you can read the rest of them. There are two main CPIs, both published monthly: (1) *All Urban Consumers (CPI-U)*, based on the expenditures of almost all residents of urban and metropolitan areas, and (2) *Urban Wage Earners and Clerical Workers (CPI-W)*, which tends to differ slightly from the first. The CPI-U and the CPI-W are published for twenty-six cities: monthly for the New York City, Chicago, and Los Angeles metropolitan areas; every other month for eleven other large cities; and twice a year for twelve more.

Then there are the detailed CPI reports, a statistical paradise. For example, you can really get a feel for American eating habits: this January 2002 CPI-U says we spend .08 percent of our budget on bananas, .20 percent on candy and chewing gum, and 6.2 percent on food away from home.

Recent Changes in the CPI

The Consumer Price Index affects just about everybody. It influences cost of living allowances, alimony checks, Social Security checks, veterans' benefits, IRS tax brackets, and Federal Reserve interest rates. It's no wonder that the Bureau of Labor Statistics (BLS) has come under scrutiny and criticism, in particular for tardiness of data and other problems that resulted in an inflated inflation figure. In 1996 the BLS was mandated by Congress to, among other things, update, use more accurate methods to decide the "weight" (importance) of items and services, take account of the way price changes influence consumers to switch and substitute, and work toward making the CPI more of a cost-of-living index.

Things are slowly improving. In August 2002, the BLS will begin supplementing the regular CPI reports with a new *chain* CPI, which will deal with the substitution problem.

> ▶ CPI reports can be found by telephone, at libraries, in newspapers, and online. For any statistics, including the most recent, go to http://www.bls.gov/cpi/home.htm. To calculate what a dollar will buy now compared to any date of your choosing, go to http://minneapolisfed.org/economy/calc/cpihome.html. For a terrific explanation of CPI, go to http://www.bls.gov/cpi/cpifaq.htm.

COPYRIGHT PAGE
••

IF YOU NEED TO KNOW when a book was published, you look on the flip side of the page announcing the title, author, and publisher. There you will find the copyright date, usually preceded by a circled "c." That's clear enough. But what are all those other numbers for?

Library of Congress Cataloging-in-Publication Data
Blocksma, Mary.
Reading the numbers : a survival guide to the measurements, numbers, and sizes encountered in everyday life / Mary Blocksma.
p. cm.
ISBN 0 14 01.0654 5
1. Weights and measures. 2. Weights and measures—United States.
I. Title.
QC88.B54 1989
530.8—dc19 88-23219

Most of the remaining numbers are included under the Library of Congress heading for librarians ordering and cataloging books.

QC88.B54	is the Library of Congress classification number. Every book published by a United States publisher is classified by the Library of Congress.
1989	is the year the book was published.
530.8	is the suggested Dewey Decimal classification for smaller libraries.
88-23219	is the number used by librarians to order catalog cards.
ISBN	0 14 01.0654 5 (See *ISBNs,* page 144.)

A short printing history is often found at the bottom of the page—a strange string of numbers that looks something like this:

1 3 5 7 9 10 8 6 4 2

Publishers use these numbers to keep track of the book's printing history without having to reset the page with each new printing—they simply remove the numbers that no longer apply. Read the lowest number for the number of the printing.

CREDIT CARDS

CREDIT CARDS actually came into use in the 1920s, when individual companies would issue them to their customers. We called them "charge cards," and often had a wad of them, a separate card held for each department store or other preferred business or shopping destination. In 1958 American Express issued a universal card that could be used at many businesses, but it too was, and still is, essentially a charge card, the balance required to be paid off monthly. Credit cards as most Americans use them (the majority of Americans carry at least one) did not arrive until 1959, when Bank of America began issuing cards—eventually, in 1976, called Visa cards—which could not only be used universally but could carry a balance upon which the holder was charged interest.

It's important to understand what is *not* a credit card: cards like American Express (except for their Optima and Blue cards) and Diners Club are not credit cards but *charge cards*. Charge card accounts are expected to be paid in full, monthly. Then there are *debit cards*, sometimes called *check cards*, which function the same way as writing a check would, except that your checking account is docked immediately, not later when a paper check would have arrived at your bank. A check card can also double as an ATM (automated teller machine) card, allowing you to make transactions at ATMs.

A credit card, such as Visa or MasterCard, carries a balance with an annual percentage rate (APR, see page 15) of interest that, along with a 20- to 25-day grace period, varies depending on the companies and the particular card. According to Federal Reserve regulations, banks must send you a statement at least 14 days before your payment is due, and most companies give you at least 20 days to pay up. Interest rates vary wildly: at this writing, they can be found from 4.6% APR to over 20% APR. It pays to shop around before falling for one of the many offers you may be receiving almost daily.

Most of us are more familiar with credit card numbers than we wish we were, but what do the numbers mean? Here is part of the mystery: most credit and debit cards consist of thirteen to sixteen digits. You can tell by the prefix (the first numbers on the left) what type of card it is:

Diners Club or Carte Blanche (300–305, 36 or 38)
American Express (34 or 37)
Visa (4)
MasterCard (51–55)
Discover (6011)

The last number, or the number at the far right, is the check digit (see *Bar Codes*, page 17), which can be used only to make sure the numbers are legitimate card numbers, not to determine whether it has been stolen or is over its limit or any other problems. The numbers in between represent the bank and individual account numbers.

Very basic information about the cardholder is contained in the magnetic strip on the back of most credit cards, allowing cards to be swiped through a card-reader and read electronically. A fairly new kind of card called the Smart Card, currently used more extensively in Europe than in the United States, contains a microprocessor capable of storing much more data. One Smart Card may soon replace all one's money and other cards and serve many other functions as well.

▶ To find current interest rates and other factors that make for the best deal for you on a credit card, go to http://www.kiplinger.com/managing/cash/credit. For more than you ever wanted to know about how credit cards work, go to http://www.howstuffworks.com/credit-card.

CROCHET HOOKS

•••

BEGINNING CROCHETERS who think they'll just pop in to the craft store and pick up a crochet hook will soon find themselves in a measurement morass. Not only are crochet hooks made of different materials—steel, aluminum/plastic, brass, bone, and wood—but each of these uses its own unique, inexplicable size system. We're talking five size systems here.

This is further confused by the fact that Canadian/U.S. size systems are completely different from U.K. systems, which differ from the metric, or Continental, systems. And if you want to be really picky, the crochet hook companies are not in complete agreement: for example, the Boye equivalent to the U.S. size $10^{1/2}$, or K, aluminum hook is size 6.0, while Bates's is 6.5 and Britanny's is size 5.75. Go figure.

It may help to narrow the field to the two most-used types of crochet hooks: steel hooks, used for thin cotton threads, and aluminum or plastic hooks, used mainly for yarns and thicker threads. But just to put an extra spin on the game, notice that *in American sizes, steel hooks get bigger as the sizes get smaller, while aluminum hooks do the opposite, increasing in size along with the size number.*

Aluminum Crochet Hook Conversion Chart

Canadian and U.K. sizes

000	00	0	2	3	4	5	6	7	8	–	9	10	11	–	12	13	14

Metric sizes

10.0	9.00	8.00	7.00	6.50	6.00	5.50	5.00	4.50	4.00	3.75	3.50	3.25	3.00	2.75	2.50	2.25	2.00

U.S. sizes

N	M	L	–	K	J	I	H		G	F	E	D		C		B	
15	13	11		10.5	10	9	8		7	6	5	4	3		2		1

Steel Crochet Hook Conversion Chart

Canadian and U.S. sizes

00	0	1	2	3	4	5	6	7	8	9	10	11	12	13	14

Metric sizes

3.00	2.50	2.00	1.95	1.85	1.75	1.70	1.60	1.50	1.25	1.15	1.00	0.80	0.75	0.70	0.60

U.K. sizes

–	00	1	–	–	2	–	–	2.5	3	–	4	–	5	–	6

Source: Crochet hook conversion charts courtesy of Crochet Treasures, http://www.crochettreasures/conversion.htm.

Although most crochet patterns suggest a hook size, a *gauge* is usually supplied to make sure that the hook fits your crochet style—how loosely or tightly you do your stitches. Usually, a gauge is a patch of a few inches or a pattern motif. Unless you're a veteran, it's best to take time to do the gauge.

▶ **For size conversions by crochet hook company, go to http:// geocities.com/Heartland/Ridge/4564/conversion.html. For brass and wood sizes, go to http://home.fuse.net/SouthwestOhioCrochetGuild/ hooks.htm.**

CURRENCY

NEARLY ALL the U.S. "greenbacks" used today are Federal Reserve notes, produced by the Bureau of Printing and Engraving in Washington, D.C., and now available only in denominations of $1, $2, $5, $10, $20, $50, and $100. There was a time, however, when you could get $500, $1,000, $5,000, and $10,000 notes. Although the Federal Reserve stopped printing those huge denominations in 1945, they weren't withdrawn from circulation until 1969. The actual size of currency today is also smaller—until 1929, bills measured 7.42 × 3.13 inches. This was fairly large compared to today's bills at 6.14 × 2.61 inches.

Our currency remained unchanged for thirty years. Then a new series of bills, called the Series 1996, was introduced, with enlarged portraits of the presidents and new and modified security features designed to deter counterfeiting.

The new $100 note was issued in 1996, the $50 note in 1997, the $20 note in 1998, and the $10 and $5 notes in 1999. At this writing, the Federal Reserve has not decided to revamp the $1 note, the only "old" bill left.

What do the numbers mean on the face of today's currency?

Source: U.S. Federal Reserve Bank of Atlanta

Federal Reserve Districts

There are twelve Federal Reserve Banks in the United States, so the country is divided into twelve Federal Reserve Districts, each issuing its own notes according to its region's needs. You can tell which

MAP OF FEDERAL RESERVE DISTRICTS

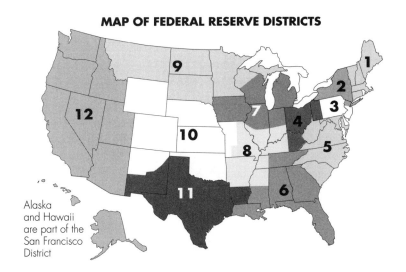

Alaska and Hawaii are part of the San Francisco District

bank issued the notes in your pocket by checking the letter and number under the serial number in the upper-left-hand corner:

1 and/or A	=	Boston
2 and/or B	=	New York
3 and/or C	=	Philadelphia
4 and/or D	=	Cleveland
5 and/or E	=	Richmond
6 and/or F	=	Atlanta
7 and/or G	=	Chicago
8 and/or H	=	St. Louis
9 and/or I	=	Minneapolis
10 and/or J	=	Kansas City
11 and/or K	=	Dallas
12 and/or L	=	San Francisco

Locate your Federal Reserve District on the map; then check your currency. Most of the bills in your pocket probably carry the same Federal Reserve Bank letter.

Serial Numbers

Federal Reserve notes are numbered in lots of one hundred million, with a "star" note substituted for the one-hundred-millionth note. The first run will carry the suffix letter A, progressing through Z for succeeding runs (but omitting the letter O so it won't get mixed up with zero). When you consider that there are several billion $1 notes alone in circulation, it is amazing to realize that no two notes of the same kind, denomination, and series have the same serial number!

Star Notes. If a note is damaged during printing, interrupting the number series, it is replaced with a star note, which is exactly like it except that a star takes the place of the suffix letter—e.g., F00000004*.

Series Number. The year the design of the note was first used is shown as the series number, to the lower left of the president's portrait. If only a minor change is made, one not requiring a new engraving plate, a letter will appear after the year, starting with A for the first change in that series; e.g., 1996B would indicate that two minor changes had been made.

Note Check Letter and Plate Serial Number. In the lower-left-hand corner is a small capital letter followed by a number. This is the note position, or check letter, indicating the position of the note on the printing plate. The newer presses print thirty-two notes to a sheet. The same letter appears at the lower right of the president, followed by another number, which is the plate serial number, or the number of the plate from which the note was printed. "A 46," for example, would be the forty-sixth plate made for that type, denomination, and series of note.

▶ To learn more about U.S. currency, check out the "Dollars and Cents" brochure at http://www.frbatlanta.org. To convert U.S. dollars into foreign currency, or vice versa, go to XE.com's Universal Currency Converter, http://www.xe.com/ucc.

DOW JONES INDUSTRIAL AVERAGE
∙∙

A DECADE AGO, millions of people still wondered what those nightly Dow Jones numbers meant, and now, well, there's maybe only hundreds of thousands of us. So for this rapidly dwindling but nevertheless intelligent group, we ask: What are points anyway, and what is the Dow Jones the average of?

Dow Jones reports three averages: the Transportation Average, the Utilities Average, and the Industrial Average. However, when you hear a "Dow" or "Dow Jones" or "Dow Jones Average" figure, you can safely assume that what is being referred to is the Dow Jones Industrial Average—the average cost per share of stock from thirty companies chosen by the Board of the New York Stock Exchange as the most outstanding companies reflecting the variety of American business to represent the stock market. And the "points" can be directly translated into dollars and cents.

In January 1987 the Dow Jones Industrial Average went over 2,000 points for the first time in its ninety-one-year history. At the time, its highest-priced stock sold for about $122.85 a share, and its lowest-priced stock was $5.37. In fact, if you added up all thirty stocks, they totaled only $1,780. How could the average have been higher than the sum total? The answer has to do with stock "splits" and "substitutions."

The first Dow Jones Averages report, which appeared in *The Wall Street Journal* in 1896, really was a simple average—Mr. Charles Dow, who devised the system and founded a financial publishing company with Edward Jones, simply added up the prices of twelve stocks and divided by twelve. However, the companies' stocks began rising. To make stock shares affordable to small investors, companies began to split their shares when the prices got too high. (Most stocks are split before they reach $100.)

Finding the average was no longer simple. When a company split its stock, it halved the share size, so it could offer twice the shares at half the price. The market hadn't fallen, but if a simple average was calculated, the Dow Jones would go down. So Dow

Jones no longer divided the total stock prices by the number of companies, but by a *divisor,* a number that would make the final "average" the same as it would have been before the split. The first divisor used was 16.67. Over the years, as companies were added to the list and stocks split, over and over again, the divisor got lower and lower, until it reached 1. When the average went over 2,000 points, the divisor was 0.877, even less than 1, which made it a multiplier. The 2,000 figure represents the price per share of stock if there had never been any splits or substitutions.

Despite ups and downs, the Dow Jones Industrial Average has been on the rise. In 1906 the stock market closed at over 100; in November 1972 it first closed over 1,000; and in January 1987, with much hoopla, it passed the 2,000 mark. On March 30, 1999, the average broke 10,000, and by 2002, still over 10,000, the divisor was down to 0.20. The Dow Jones shows how the average price per share of stock has risen—shares worth $100 in 1906 might well have sold for $2,000 in 1987 and $10,000 in the twenty-first century.

The New York Stock Exchange, indexing only thirty companies, is just one of many stock exchanges; the others represent thousands of other companies and are open to what is called the small investor. Among the most often reported indexes are the Nasdaq (National Association of Securities Dealers Automated Quotations system) and the S&P (Standard & Poor's) 500.

▶ **For the latest report of the Dow Jones, Nasdaq, and the S&P 500, go to http://www.kiplinger.com.**

DWELLINGS (SIZE)
. . . .

THE SIZE OF A HOUSE is always described in square feet. But how do you know from the real estate ad that caught your eye whether the 1,200-square-foot home with the backyard peach orchard is big enough to warrant a visit? Faced with hundreds of ads, you need some way to sort out the best bets. What does 1,200 square feet mean?

The square-foot description is a measure of the inside finished living space. This includes all the finished floor space in the house, so if there are two floors, the second floor is counted as well. Not included are the garage, outside porches, decks, or an unfinished basement.

A house is usually measured by an appraiser hired by a bank or mortgage company to help establish the home's market value. The appraiser works from the outside, measuring off a rectangle, then adding the living spaces that lie outside it and subtracting the empty areas inside. The final figure, therefore, includes the space occupied by inside and outside walls. (In some areas—your real estate agent should know if this applies to you—it is customary to measure the house from the inside, a tedious procedure that re-quires measuring every room. This final figure does not include the walls, so it would be somewhat smaller.)

So how big is 1,200 square feet? Real estate agents report that you never know for sure until you see the place, but as a rule of thumb, a 1,000-square-foot house is considered small, a 1,500-square-foot house average, while one with more than 2,000 feet is pleasantly large.

Once you know the square feet, look for the number of bed-rooms. If the 1,200-square-foot house with the orchard has three bedrooms, the living spaces left might make for a snug fit. If it has only one bedroom, however, the place might well feel palatial!

EARTHQUAKES

•••

THE FIRST NUMBER that a news service usually picks up when reporting an earthquake is its magnitude on the Richter scale, a 1 to 8 scale that is extremely difficult to translate into actual effects. How great is a 3.5 earthquake, and is a 7.0 earthquake twice as great, or more? Most of us would like to know at what point life and/or property are threatened.

The first scale used to measure earthquakes gauged just that. It was devised by Italian seismologist Giuseppe Mercalli in 1902 and revised by American scientists in 1936. Mercalli interviewed earthquake survivors, and then used a 1 to 12 scale (designated by Roman numerals) to describe the effects. It was much like Beaufort's scale describing the effects of wind speeds (see *Wind*, page 272). Here it is, with approximate Richter figures included:

The Mercalli Scale

Mercalli	Mercalli Characteristics	Approx. Richter
I	Detectable only by seismographs	Less than 3.5
II	Feeble: noticed only by some people at rest	3.5
III	Slight: similar to vibrations of a passing truck	4.2
IV	Moderate: felt indoors; parked cars rock	4.5
V	Rather strong: felt generally; sleepers wake	4.8
VI	Strong: trees sway; furniture moves; some damage	5.4
VII	Very strong: general alarm; walls crack	6.1
VIII	Destructive: weak structures damaged; walls fall	6.5
IX	Ruinous: some houses collapse as ground cracks	6.9
X	Disastrous: many buildings destroyed; rails bend	7.3
XI	Very disastrous: few buildings survive; landslides	8.1
XII	Catastrophic: total destruction; ground forms waves	Greater than 8.1

Although Mercalli's scale is still useful for getting a general idea of earthquake effects, it lacks accuracy—damage done by earthquakes is influenced by many factors, including population density, type of ground involved, building structures, etc. Furthermore, it does not measure the earthquake itself. Seismologist Charles F. Richter was bothered by all this and in the 1930s devised a system, which he never intended to become so universally used, to measure the actual "magnitude" of the quake, a term he used to take the emphasis off the effects (intensity) and place it on the physical activity—the earth's action—during the quake.

The result was the Richter scale, sometimes misleading because it is not actually a 1 to 8 but a *1 to 10 million* scale. Each level indicates a tenfold increase in magnitude from the level before, making a 6.0 quake not twice as great as a 3.0 quake, but a thousand times greater, and an 8.0 ten million times greater than a 1.0. Here is a translation of the Richter scale:

The Richter Scale

Richter Number	Increase in Magnitude
1	1
2	10
3	100
4	1,000
5	10,000
6	100,000
7	1,000,000
8	10,000,000

Richter measured earthquakes using a seismograph to record the size and time of tremors. He measured an earthquake by relating the *amplitude* (the distance the ground moves between waves, measured in millimeters on seismograph records) to the time between the primary (first) and secondary (second) tremors, much like an obstetrician judging the stage of labor by timing contractions and analyzing their intensity.

Today earthquakes are measured on a 1 to 10 *moment magnitude scale*, using more sophisticated instruments than Richter had at his disposal. The numbers are similar for earthquakes up to 7 on the Richter scale, but change for the really big ones: the highest measure on record is 9.5, an earthquake in the Pacific Ocean off the coast of Chile in 1960 which went off Richter's scale at 8.5.

Earthquakes are scary, and no country takes them more seriously than the United States. The world's foremost collection of earthquake data lies in Golden, Colorado, at the U.S. Geological Survey's National Earthquake Information Center. Here 60,000 seismic readings are collected every month from twelve seismograph installations across the United States, 650 stations around the world, and many more that give information when called upon. Most rescue operations to any earthquake-hit area of the world begin with a signal from Golden.

Unfortunately, although scientists can make long-term predictions about where an earthquake may occur, even sophisticated electronic ears listening for ground activity still can't reliably predict exactly when.

▶ For an extensive glossary of earthquake terminology, go to http://vulcan.wr.usgs.gov/Glossary/Seismicity. To review recent earthquake activity, go to http://earthquake.usgs.gov.

ELECTRICITY
• •

IT'S TIME TO SORT OUT those one-syllable words that have been confounding you all these years—words like "amps," "volts," "watts," and "ohms" that are often preceded by a number probably meaningless to you unless it's translated into dollars on your power bill. If you are like many people, the best you've done so far is figure out that a 100-watt lightbulb is brighter than a 40-watt lightbulb (even if it often costs the same).

To begin with, *amps*, short for amperes, are the measure of actual electrical current (electrons per second) that flows along the wires in your house.

Volts are the measure of the pressure pumping the amps into, say, your house. (If amps were water, volts would be the water pressure forcing the water through the pipes.) High voltage pumps move amps along a wire more rapidly than low voltage. Normal voltage for most homes is 120 volts.

Ohms are a measure of the resistance that slows the flow of amps. The higher the ohms—the more resistance created—the fewer amps can get past. Ohms (or resistance) can be increased by using, among other objects, thinner wires or resistors, devices that control the amount of current that can enter an electrical appliance. These are very important, as few appliances require the full force of 120 volts.

Watts are a measure of work—the amount of work an appliance is capable of. If you continue with the water analogy, watts are the power that amps (water) have when propelled at certain volts (pressure) past a resistance of a certain number of ohms (through a hose of a certain size and coming out of a nozzle with a particular opening). So the resistance in a 40-watt lightbulb lets in less current than the resistance in a 100-watt lightbulb, producing fewer watts.

This can all be summed up in a few little equations:

$$\text{watts (power)} = \text{volts (pressure)} \times \text{amps (current)}$$

OR

$$\text{amps (current)} = \frac{\text{volts (pressure)}}{\text{ohms (resistance)}}$$

OR

1 watt = 1 amp flowing at 1 volt pressure

OR

1 volt will drive 1 amp through the resistance of 1 ohm

You pay for electricity by the *kilowatt hour* (kWh), which is the amount of energy required to produce 1,000 watts of power (*kilo* meaning thousand) for 1 hour. Check your electric meter: some meters simply show a number, while others show four or five little "clocks," which are read from left to right. If your meter read-ings are not remotely transmitted, a meter reader may come around once a month or so to record this number. Last month's reading is subtracted from the current reading so the electric company will know how much you've used.

HOW TO READ YOUR ELECTRIC METER

Because the dials are geared to each other, the pointers on some dials turn clockwise; on others, counterclockwise. Read the dials from left to right. When a pointer is between two numbers, always read the smaller number. This reading is 7-3-1-5-6 kilowatt-hours.

Source: Pacific Gas and Electric Company. Used with permission.

To calculate the cost of your appliances, first check your latest electric bill for your local per-kilowatt-hour charges. To find out how long one of your appliances takes to use up a kilowatt hour (1,000 watts/hour), divide 1,000 by the wattage of the appliance. For example, a 200-watt television will give you 5 hours of enter-tainment for 1 kilowatt hour of electrical power (1,000 divided by 200). Divide your cost per kilowatt hour by the number of hours the TV runs for that amount (5 hours), and you can determine your cost per hour. It's surprising how much—or how little— electricity appliances really use.

How much does it actually cost you to run those indispensable appliances in your house? In 2001, a national average was 8.4 cents/kWh. In 2002, California's Pacific Gas & Electric Company was charging 14 cents/kWh. Even if your cost is different, the following information from that company does make for some very interesting comparisons:

Estimated Kilowatt Appetites of Some Common Electric Appliances at 14¢ per Kilowatt Hour

Appliance	Cost per hour	Cost per use	Cost per month
Central air conditioner, 1,500 sq. feet (used 24 hr/day)	.67		387.00
Evaporative cooler (used 24 hr/day)		.07	50.40
1,500-watt portable heater		.21	
Water heater, per person			22.54
Washing machine (with electrically heated water) cold/cold warm/cold hot/warm		.05 .30 .82	
Dryer		.40	
Dishwasher (with electrically heated water)		.52	
Dishwasher set to "energy saver"		.46	
18 cubic foot refrigerator			15.60
Oven	.32		
Range, per burner	.18		
Microwave oven	.04/10 minutes		
Toaster oven	.17		
Coffeemaker		.02	

(continued)

**Estimated Kilowatt Appetites of Some Common
Electric Appliances at 14¢ per Kilowatt Hour (continued)**

Appliance	Cost per hour	Cost per use	Cost per month
2-slice toaster		.01	
Personal computer	.01		
Color monitor	.08		
LCD monitor	.02/10 hours		
Laser printer (on but idle)	.01		
Laser printer printing	.03		
Ink-jet printer	.03		
Telephone answering machine			.43
Digital clock			.40
27-inch color TV	.01		
VCR	.03/10 hours		
Satellite dish			.95
22-watt fluorescent lightbulb (12 hr/day, 30 days)	.00308		1.11
100-watt incandescent bulb (12 hr/day, 30 days)	.014		5.04
Electric blanket, twin		.07	2.10
Electric blanket, queen		.10	3.00
Water bed heater, queen			22.75
20-gallon aquarium heater			7.56
55-gallon aquarium heater			20.38

Source: Pacific Gas & Electric Company. Used with permission.

▶ For clear answers to frequently asked questions about electricity, go to William J. Beaty's Science Hobbyist website at http://www.amasci.com/elect/elefaq.html. Find the American Council for an Energy-Efficient Economy's up-to-date energy consumption ratings for home appliances, furnaces, and air conditioners at http://www.aceee.org/consumerguide. For an average cost-per-month calculator for home appliances, go to the Pacific Gas & Electric Company, http://www.pge.com and search for "energy calculator."

ENGINES (HORSEPOWER)

HORSEPOWER is one of those charming measures that drive scientists crazy, for it is based on an arbitrary, though lively, standard: the strength of a particular horse. One day Scottish inventor James Watt rigged up the horse of his choice with a rope and some pulleys so he could demonstrate the power (work capability) of his recently invented steam engine (patented in 1783). When Watt fastened a weight to one end of the rope and the horse to the other, he found that the horse, by moving forward, could raise a 3,300-pound weight ten feet into the air in one minute.

If Watt had increased the weight ten times, to 33,000 pounds, the horse would have raised it only one foot in one minute. Watt called the amount of work 1 *horsepower:* 1 horsepower was equal to 33,000 foot-pounds per minute, a measure that is still used today, although more commonly referred to as 550 foot-pounds per second (33,000 divided by 60 seconds). As horses were one of the main energy sources of that day, these were terms the general public could understand.

Watt labeled his steam engines in equivalent horsepower—a 10 horsepower engine could do the work of ten horses—i.e., could lift 5,500 pounds per second. Today the work capability of many engines is still labeled in horsepower. The horsepower of an engine results from a variety of factors, including the size of the engine, measured in cubic centimeters (cc's—see *Motorcycles,* page

171), engine design, etc. Note that if the horse can't lift the weight, no work is done and no power is developed. The horse provides the force: work = force × distance; power = force × distance ÷ time. So you might say that a 100 hp engine can work 100 times faster than a horse.

It is interesting to think in terms of actual horses doing the work of the following common gasoline engines:

Garbage disposal	$1/2$ horsepower (hp)
Power lawn mower	3 hp
Riding lawn mower	8 hp
Motorcycles	10 to 100 hp
Small one-engine airplane	30 hp
Small car	75 to 80 hp
Passenger car	80 to 300 hp
Small trucks	100 hp and up
Sports cars	up to 450 hp
Small six-passenger, two-engine airplane	400 hp/engine
B36 four-engine bomber	3,650 hp/engine

Horsepower can, by the way, be translated into "watts," another way to measure power, not invented by Watt but named in his honor anyway (see *Electricity*, page 82): 1 horsepower = 746 watts.

▶ **For higher hp information on horsepower, go to Marshall Brain's website at http://www.howstuffworks.com/horsepower.htm.**

ENVELOPES

WE MAY TAKE ENVELOPES and snail mail privacy for granted, but as simple a protection as an envelope might be, it wasn't always so. Around four thousand years ago, the Babylonians came up with possibly the first envelopes: clay, baked around important documents. Paper letters became popular in Europe by the fifteenth century but were sent folded and sealed with wax. Even in this country envelopes were not used until 1839, when they were manufactured by hand. Ten years later, a machine was invented to turn them out faster. An improved model patented in 1898 guaranteed their use into the twenty-first century.

Envelope Sizes

Today letter envelopes are manufactured in sizes (unless custom ordered) that range from 5 to $15^{1}/2$. The four most popular sizes are: the *A-2 invitation* size ($4^{3}/8$" × $5^{3}/4$"), into which you can slip business stationery folded into quarters; the A-7 *invitation* size ($5^{1}/4$" × $7^{1}/4$"), a popular greeting card envelope; the *6 $^{3}/4$ commercial* size ($3^{5}/8$" × $6^{1}/2$"), often used for paying bills; and the larger, standard business envelope, *commercial size 10* ($4^{1}/8$" × $9^{1}/2$") accommodating an $8^{1}/2$ × 11-inch letter folded into thirds.

Sizes for large "manila" envelopes, often closed with a little metal clasp and made of heavy kraft or manila paper, range from #5 to #110. Popular sizes are #90 (9" × 12"), accommodating $8^{1}/2$ × 11-inch unfolded paper, and # 97 (10" × 13"), for a thicker stack of the same.

Many more envelope styles are available, with many sizes for each, including invitation (stubby rectangle), baronial (square), commercial (long rectangle), catalog, remittance, ticket, drug, policy, coin, and window envelopes. Envelopes can be purchased from office supply and general merchandise stores; specialty envelopes or large quantities can be obtained from websites, catalogs, paper specialty shops, and commercial printers.

Postal Regulations

Domestic Mail. Thanks to advanced mechanization of domestic mail handling, size limits have been imposed on the dimensions of mailable envelopes. At this writing, the minimum size accepted by the United States Postal Service is 5 inches long, $3^1/2$ inches tall, and 0.007 inches thick (have fun with that last one). An envelope taller than $6^1/8$ inches or longer than $11^1/2$ inches or thicker than $1/4$ inch is considered a "large envelope," for which one may be charged extra.

Maximum size for postcard postage is 6 inches long by $4^1/4$ inches high by 0.016 inch thick. Larger postcards must use the letter or large envelope rate (see also *Postal Rates,* page 192).

International Mail. The Universal Postal Union, an agency of the United Nations, regulates sizes of international mail: minimum letter size is $5^1/2$ inches (14 cm) long by $3^1/2$ inches (9 cm) high, and the maximum size is $9^1/4$ inches (23.5 cm) long by $4^2/3$ inches (12 cm) high.

▶ For the latest U.S. regulations on mailable envelopes, and for postage rates, go to the U.S. Postal Service website: http://postcalc.usps.gov. Find a more complete list of envelope sizes at My Design Primer: http://www.mydesignprimer.com/printing/50024.html.

EXPONENTS

••

IF YOUR MIND SHUTS DOWN when you see a number like 5.88×10^{12} (the number of miles light travels in one year), fearing some form of higher mathematics, you're in for a surprise. Exponents, as those small, elevated numbers are called, simply tell you how many times to multiply the number it modifies by that number (e.g., $4^3 = 4 \times 4 \times 4 = 64$). Exponents of ten work the same way and make it easier to count the zeros in tediously large or small numbers. The above number written out is awkward: 5,880,000,000,000 miles. Even worse, a beta ray particle has a mass of 0.00000000000000000000000000091 gram, more neatly written as 9.1×10^{-28} gram.

Here's how to read exponents of ten. For positive exponents, simply use as many zeros as the exponent reads:

$10 = 10^1$	ten
$100 = 10^2$	one hundred
$1,000 = 10^3$	one thousand
$10,000 = 10^4$	ten thousand
$100,000 = 10^5$	one hundred thousand
$1,000,000 = 10^6$	one million
$1,000,000,000 = 10^9$	one billion
$1,000,000,000,000 = 10^{12}$	one trillion
and so on . . .	

For negative exponents, add the zeros numbered in the exponent on the left, *less one*, or, more simply, move the decimal as many places to the left as numbered in the exponent. So the negatives look like this:

$0.01 = 10^{-2}$	one hundredth
$0.0001 = 10^{-4}$	one ten-thousandth
$0.00001 = 10^{-5}$	one one-hundred-thousandth
$0.000001 = 10^{-6}$	one millionth
$0.000000001 = 10^{-9}$	one billionth
$0.000000000001 = 10^{-12}$	one trillionth
and so on . . .	

Most numbers involving exponents are written as a multiplication function—the second number simply tells you how many places to move the decimal in the first number. When the exponent is positive, move the decimal point in the first number that many places to the right; e.g., in 5.6×10^6, move the decimal six times to the right, making 5,600,000. When the exponent is negative, move the decimal point that many places to the left, e.g., in 5.6×10^{-6}, move the decimal in 5.6 six places to the left, making 0.0000056.

Now try these:

A jumbo jet weighs about 3.75×10^5 kilograms.
A house spider weighs 10^{-4} kilogram.
Neptune is 2.677×10^{12} miles from Earth.
The mass of a hydrogen atom is 1.66×10^{-24} gram.

FERTILIZER

· ·

LOOKING AT THE FERTILIZER SHELVES at the local plant store can make you want to jam your green thumb in your pocket, find your car keys, and leave. The array of offerings is staggering. How can you possibly decide which one to buy?

It helps a little to understand the numbers. There are three numbers on every bag, box, and bottle of plant food (fertilizer), usually found on the label in large print, and separated by hyphens; e.g., 10-10-5. These nationally standard numbers represent the percentage, by weight, of the three chemical elements essential to plant growth contained in the fertilizer: nitrogen, phosphorus, and potassium, always in that order. This means that the above 10-10-5 fertilizer contains 10 percent nitrogen (N), 10 percent phosphorus (P), and 5 percent potassium (K). What's left—the other 75 percent, in this case—is inert (nonactive) matter.

What's important here is not how high the numbers are but the ratio, or balance, of the three numbers. For example, a 5-5-5 fertilizer is essentially the same as a 10-10-10 or a 30-30-30 fertilizer: they all have a 1-1-1 balance, and they will all have essentially the same effect. The difference between a 10-10-10 fertilizer and a 30-30-30 fertilizer is (1) the amount and/or frequency of applications, and (2) the price. The ratio you choose in a fertilizer depends on what you're feeding, your soil, and what kind of growth you may be trying to encourage: the first number (nitrogen) affects stem and leaf growth, the second number (phosphorus) encourages root growth, and the third number (potassium) is needed for flowers, fruits, and general all-around sturdiness.

In truth, there's so much disagreement on which combination of nutrients is best for which plant that even a fairly knowledgeable gardener may be tempted to toss in the trowel trying to decide what to use. For example, a recently sampled shelf of fertilizers offered three different plant foods for tomatoes. See the breakdown below.

Three Tomato Plant Foods

Fertilizer	Amount	Cost	N-P-K	Amount	Frequency
Brand 1	12 spikes	$1.89	8-24-8	2 per plant	every 2 months
Brand 2	1 1/2 lb.	$4.69	18-18-21	1 tbsp./gallon water	every 7–14 days
Brand 3	4 lb.	$2.15	8-12-6	7/8 cup/plant 1/8 cup/plant	at planting every 6 wks after

The disparity of price, pounds, and nutrients here is mind-boggling! The slow-release spikes will cost you 63 cents per plant (4 per plant per season), which seems quite high. But try to compare that cost with the others—you need to know how many tablespoons are in a pound (Brand 2), and how many cups are in a pound (Brand 3), a figure that will differ from plant food to plant food. Then how do you decide on the nutrient balance? You might be tempted to go with the highest numbers until you notice that you use only a tablespoon of it, but you use nearly a cup (at planting) of the one with the lowest numbers. Which ends up feeding the plant the most?

It's important to remember that it's the balance that's important, not high numbers. For tomatoes, you may decide that a fertilizer high in potassium (good for fruiting and flowering) may be the best choice, but then you may wonder why the others, also made specifically for tomatoes, offer a different balance—potassium is actually the lowest number in Brand 3!

If you can't figure out what you want, pick a general-purpose fertilizer that you can dump on everything without thinking about it. The recommendations for this differ widely, of course—some experts recommend a 1-2-2 ratio (such as 5-10-10), others a 1-1-1 ratio (such as 10-10-10), and an expert from the National Fertilizer Development Center suggests that a 4-1-2 ratio (such as 20-4-10) would suit most lawns and garden plants. Your soil may determine which to use, so you might want to have it tested if you're really serious about all this. It may be comforting to know, though, that an overdose of phosphorus (P) or potassium (K) is not harmful to most plants. (An exception is zoysia grass, which doesn't like too much phosphorus.) Other suggestions include asking the person who has the best garden in the neighborhood (your soils may be similar) what he or she uses; calling up your county coopera-tive/extension agent (see *Soil, Garden*, page 228), who may offer comforting advice; and/or starting a compost heap.

You should know that there are three kinds of fertilizer: organic, inorganic, and slow-release fertilizers. Organic fertilizers are slow-acting but long-lasting; most chemical fertilizers are fast-acting but require more frequent applications, with the exception of slow-release fertilizers. Slow-release fertilizers are useful for shrubs, trees, and lawns. Urea formaldehyde (sometimes called ureaform or nitraform) is a synthetic organic fertilizer (which sounds like a contradiction in terms). It dissolves more slowly than other fertilizers, sometimes taking two years to become available to plants. A sulfur-coated urea developed by the Tennessee Valley Authority is one of the cheapest slow-release fertilizers and an effective once-a-year nitrogen feeding for lawns.

Here are the ratios of some of those odd-sounding offerings at the plant store:

Some N-P-K Fertilizer Ratios

Ammonium nitrate	33-0-0
Ammonium sulfate	21-0-0
Blood meal	13-0-0
Bonemeal	1-23-0
Fish emulsion	5-1-1
Horse manure	1-1-1
Muriate of potash	0-0-60
Sulfate of potash	0-0-52
Super phosphate	0-20-0
Urea	46-0-0

Now, if you're still looking at the shelf, here are a few of the many recommendations from a wide variety of master gardeners and plant food companies. This list will give you an idea of what sort of balance different plants may require, although your soil will influence what you need in a fertilizer. To use a plant food (when and how much), follow the directions on the package or that of your chosen expert.

Other Nitrogen-Phosphorus-Potassium Recommendations

The most important consideration here is the balance of nutrients, not how high the numbers are, so only the lowest commonly used numbers of that balance will be mentioned. In other words, 15-30-15 fertilizer will be listed as 5-10-5, since that is the essential balance; higher numbers that provide that balance will work as well.

African violets	10-10-5 or 12-36-14
Azaleas, camellias, rhododendrons	10-8-7
Bulbs	4-12-8
Cacti and other succulents	5-10-5
Citrus	10-12-4 or 6-9-6

Other Nitrogen-Phosphorus-Potassium Recommendations (continued)

Evergreens	14-7-7 or 10-10-10 or 16-4-4
Ferns	fish emulsion (5-1-1)
Flower gardens	5-10-5 or 5-10-10 or 12-55-6
Houseplants (flowering)	5-10-5
Houseplants (foliage)	5-10-5 or 12-6-6
Lawns	5-10-5 or 10-6-4 or 36-6-6 or 22-3-3 or 8-12-24, etc.
Perennials	0-20-20
Roses	5-10-5 or 8-12-4
Trees and shrubs	10-6-4 or 12-4-8 or 20-10-5
Vegetables (good general): Beans, beets, broccoli, chard, cucumbers, eggplant, melon, onions, peppers, potatoes, spinach, tomatoes, turnips	5-10-5 or 10-10-10
Brussels sprouts, carrots, peas, sweet potatoes	5-10-5
Leafy vegetables, cauliflower, celery, corn, radishes	5-10-10
Vines	10-10-10 or 5-10-5 or 0-10-10 (for less foliage)

▶ **For everything you ever wanted to know about fertilizer, go to the website for the Fertilizer Institute at http://www.tfi.org. For an answer to a particular question you might pose to such an agency, go to http://www.e-answersonline.org and http://www.greensmiths.com/ information.htm.**

FIBONACCI SEQUENCE
· ·

WHILE YOU MAY RECOGNIZE most of the numbers in this book, predictable series of numbers swirl before you every day that may nevertheless take some pointing out. The most famous of these was announced in 1202 by Italian mathematician Leonardo Fibonacci (pronounced "Fee-bo-nah-chi") in his book called *Liber Abaci* (meaning "Book of the Abacus"), in which he not only helped introduce Arabic numerals (1, 2, 3, 4, 5, 6, 7, 8, 9) to Europe, but also suggested that a particular sequence of numbers recurs with unusual frequency in nature.

Fibonacci's sequence is a series of numbers in which, after starting with 0 and 1, each number is the sum of the preceding two. The resulting series is an infinite series of numbers called *the Fibonacci sequence* (0+1 = 1, 1+1 = 2, 1+2 = 3, 2+3 = 5, 3+5 = 8, and so on):

0, 1, 1, 2, 3, 5, 8, 13, 21, 34, 55, 89, 144, 233, 377, 610, 987, and so on

Apparently, the Fibonacci sequence is a *tendency* (although not actually a *law*) of nature, found, for example, in spiral arrangements such as a nautilus shell, the seeds on a sunflower, the florets on a cauliflower, and the "petals" of a pinecone. The way this series of numbers works into a spiral is demonstrated by the Fibonacci Rectangle, which begins with two size-1 squares, followed by a size-2 square (two size-1 squares), followed by a size-3 square, and so on. A spiral can be made by drawing a quarter-circle in each square.

Even your math-impaired author's rendition of Fibonacci's rectangle demonstrates clearly the way a sequence of squares built on Fibonacci numbers constructs a spiral. Fibonacci's sequence also occurs in the way many plants branch, flowers petal, and honeybee drones reproduce. According to Ron Knotts of the University of Surrey, you can even find Fibonacci numbers in a banana or an apple split "around the equator."

FIBONACCI'S RECTANGLES

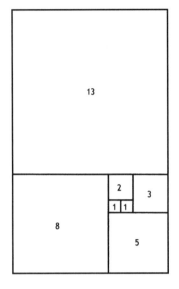 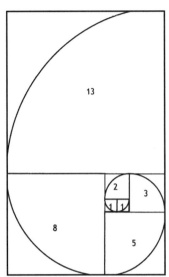

▶ For a more extensive exploration of the Fibonacci sequence and its implications, go to a long essay by Ron Knott of the University of Surrey, U.K., at http://www.mcs.surrey.ac.uk/Personal/R.Knott/Fibonacci/fib.html. For a more advanced approach to many aspects of number theory, including other number sequences, go to Eric Weisstein's "World of Mathematics" at http://mathworld.wolfram.com, and click on "Number Theory" and then "Sequences."

FILM

· ·

THE MANY BINS OF FILM BOXES at the discount store or the cubbies at the camera shop can be pretty intimidating. To narrow the choices, here are a few film factors to consider; keep in mind, of course, that this is a very basic on-the-fly guide.

Film Size and Type

Only one film size will fit your camera, probably 110 for a simple point-and-shoot camera or 135 for a 35 mm camera. You do, however, have a choice as to type of film:

- *Color print film* accounts for more than 98 percent of all film bought. Print film is *negative* (the developed film shows opposite colors to the print).

- *Color slide film* contains the word "chrome" in the name—e.g., Kodachrome, Fujichrome, Ektachrome, Elite Chrome, etc. It's used mostly for art, publication, slide shows, and other professional projects. Slide film is called *positive*, as the developed film is the same as the print.

- *Black-and-white film* is often used by photographers who can develop it themselves. However, "black-and-white" film declaring "Process C-41" is actually a color film without the color base and requires a color processing lab.

- *Specialty film* is made for cameras such as Polaroids.

- *Film-loaded panoramic one-use cameras* make panoramic-looking prints by enlarging the print and cutting off the top and bottom. These prints can sometimes be grainy.

- *Tungsten-balanced film* is specially treated to work well with indoor, incandescent light. Some film containers are labeled "daylight," used for outdoor or flash photography, or "tungsten," used indoors. (Fluorescent lighting fits neither category very well.)

Number of Exposures

Every film package announces the number of exposures, meaning prints or slides, per roll: most commonly 12, 24, or 36. Longer rolls often used by professional photographers or skilled amateurs can be purchased from photo specialty shops, catalogs, and websites.

Film Speed

The number indicating how "fast" or "sensitive to light" a film is, once called the *ASA number*, is now the *ISO number*, set by the International Standards Organization. Usual film speeds available for print and slide film include 50, 100, 200, 400, and 800. The "degree" figure printed after the ISO number is the European equivalent. *DX*, by the way, signals that the ISO can be read automatically by your camera using the silver shapes on the side of the film canister. If your camera is an old one, don't forget to reset the ISO each time you load it.

Remember: *low is slow. The higher the ISO number, the faster—more sensitive to light—the film.* Slow film requires more light and a steadier hand than fast film. Fast film can capture faster action and work in dimmer light.

ISO 50	Very slow. Needs long exposure, lots of light, and a tripod.
ISO 100	Fairly slow. Good daylight film. Fine grain, so good for enlargements 11" x 14" and larger.
ISO 200	Good compromise between 100 and 400.
ISO 400	Fast. Good for indoor and action shots. Traditionally, 400 film was much grainier than ISO 100 film, but film companies have worked hard to reduce the graininess of faster film. You probably won't notice it unless you're going larger than 8" x 10".
ISO 800	Many disposable cameras use 800 film. It's fast, good for indoor and action shots, and doesn't require a rock-steady hand.

ISO 1600   This is the fastest professional film found in the author's photo catalog, but of course, there's probably something even faster out there by now!

▶ **For an extensive Kodak film education, go to http://www.kodak.com/ global/en/consumer/pictureTaking and click on "Choosing Film."**

FINANCIAL INDEXES

NEWSPAPERS, MAGAZINES, and websites frequently report statistics collected by agencies and departments of the federal government, using an index system that looks odd if you don't know how to read it. Such statistics are not hard to read, though, and are worth the few minutes it takes to figure out—many of these numbers are of great interest to the nation's financiers as well as to those of us interested in the economy.

The *Consumer Price Index* and the *gross national product* are explained in separate entries, but there are many others, such as the *Leading Economic Indicators*, an index from the U.S. Department of Commerce that combines ten factors to represent a percent increase or decrease over 1996. To read the percentage, subtract 100 from the number given. For example, in February 2002, the baseline was 1996 (1996 = 100) for Leading Indicators, which stood at 112.4, a 12.4 percent performance increase over 1996. Index figures usually include percent changes from previous months and years as well. Some describe them in print, others display them in a chart or graph.

Many other indexes work the same way. Just remember that when an index names a base year to equal 100, it is comparing the latest figures to those of an earlier time, or a series of earlier times, in order to show growth or lack of it. The year the figures are being compared to is usually shown at the top of each index: Leading Indicators currently uses 1996 as its base, while Industrial

Industrial Production and Capacity Utilization: Summary
Seasonally Adjusted

Industrial Production	1992 = 100				Percent Change				
	2001 Nov.	Dec.	2002 Jan.	Feb.	2001 Nov.	Dec.	2002 Jan.	Feb.	Feb. '01 to Feb. '02
Total Index	137.2	136.8	137.1	137.6	-.3	-.3	.2	.4	-4.1
Previous Estimates	137.1	136.7	136.5		-.4	-.3	-.1		
Major Market Groups									
Products, Total	126.7	126.6	126.4	126.7	-.1	-.1	-.1	.2	-4.1
Consumer Goods	120.0	120.8	120.4	120.8	.3	.7	-.3	.3	-.4
Business Equipment	167.2	164.2	164.5	163.9	.2	-1.8	.1	-.4	-12.0
Construction Supplies	134.0	135.3	135.2	136.4	-.4	.9	0	.9	-1.6
Materials	154.8	153.8	155.0	156.0	-.7	-.7	.8	.6	-4.0
Major Industry Groups									
Manufacturing	142.0	141.5	141.9	142.3	-.1	-.3	.3	.3	-4.1
Durable	174.3	173.9	174.6	175.3	.2	-.2	.4	.4	-5.1
Nondurable	110.2	109.7	110.0	110.1	-.5	-.5	.2	.1	-3.0
Mining	99.0	97.3	97.0	96.4	-.4	-1.8	-.3	-.7	-5.7
Utilities	116.2	117.3	116.9	120.1	-2.7	.9	-.3	2.7	-2.7

Production compares its figures to 1992. Any number over 100 shows percentage of growth; numbers under 100 show percentage of decline.

For an example of a *summary chart* (more detailed information is available at the Federal Reserve website given at the end of this entry), look at the example (opposite) of an *industrial production* index, released on the 15th of every month. Comparative statistics are provided for the previous four months, with the percent change, for a variety of market and industry groups.

▶ For the Federal Reserve's latest industrial production figures, go to http://www.federalreserve.gov/releases/G17. For a succinct rundown on the latest government statistics, go to the White House Economic Statistics Briefing Room at http://www.whitehouse.gov/fsbr/esbr.html.

FIREARMS
••

PEOPLE WHO SHY AWAY from guns may be puzzled by the way they are sized: the size number goes up with the increased size of some firearms, while for others, the bigger the size, the smaller the weapon. Why is this?

It mostly depends on whether a gun shoots one projectile at a time or sprays a whole lot of them. Handguns, rifles, and even cannons are sized by the diameter of the ammunition (bullet/cannonball) that fits the *bore* (the inside of the barrel), measured either in decimal inches or millimeters. So a .22 caliber gun has a .22-inch bore and takes .22-inch bullets. A .38 caliber gun has a .38-inch bore and takes .38-inch bullets. In reality, the caliber is not an exact measure of the bullet or the bore, both of which are slightly smaller.

A shotgun, usually used for hunting small game, sprays prey with a shower of *shot*, or small solid round lead pellets. Shotgun size is expressed as *gauge*, a number once determined by how many balls of lead the diameter of the bore would take to weigh a pound (avoirdupois; see page 271). The smaller the shotgun, the smaller the lead balls, therefore the larger the number in a pound. Thus the higher the gauge, the smaller the bore. A 12-gauge shotgun bore measures .729 inches (18.52 mm), while a 20-gauge measures .615 inches (15.90 mm). An exception is the shotgun with the smallest bore—0.410 inches—which is described by the actual measure of the bore.

FIREWOOD

Firewood may not be one of your life's necessities, but many of us still like to keep the home fires burning. Ordering firewood invites an escape from computers, pixels, and metric everything. Even the anxieties seem earthy and olden: Should you get whole logs or split? Big or small? Exactly how much is a "cord" or a "truckload" or a "face cord"? Will you be cheated? How will you know? Is cheap softwood a better deal than expensive hardwood? How do you know if a full cord of pine at $150 is more economical than a face cord of 18-inch oak for the same price?

Firewood is usually sold by the *cord*, an inexact measure but useful for something as awkward as firewood. A cord is a stack of firewood that measures 8 × 4 × 4 feet, or 8 × 8 × 2 feet, which amounts to the same thing. How much firewood is actually in a cord varies with how tightly the vendor packs the wood—although a cord contains 128 cubic feet, the actual wood in it may measure anywhere from 65 to 100 cubic feet, depending on the air spaces. Some people are convinced that small logs make a tighter cord, others argue that large logs make a heavier cord, but most people agree that big logs with small logs filling in the spaces between them is best. (Old-time wisdom has it that the holes can be big enough to let a squirrel through, but not a cat.)

Many reputable firewood dealers have their firewood stacked on their lots in measurable fashion where you can examine it; others have figured out what fraction of a cord fits in their delivery truck. How do you know how much you are getting? You can take the dealer's word for it or you can restack the firewood and measure it.

Another confusing but popular measure of firewood is the *face cord*, also known as the *short cord*. The face cord is a stack of logs measuring 8 feet × 4 feet × whatever the length of the logs. So if you have 2-foot logs, you'll have half a cord (8 × 4 × 2 feet), but 16 inches or 25 inches or any other length log still makes a face cord if the "face," or outside, measures 8 × 4 feet. How do you compare the price of a face cord to that of a full cord? Look up the cubic feet for varying face cords below—or figure it yourself by finding the cubic inches (96 inches × 48 inches × the length of the logs in inches) and dividing by 1,728 (the number of cubic inches in a cubic foot)—and divide this figure into the price. For example: A face cord of 14-inch logs is 37.3 cubic feet. Divide the cubic feet into the price, say, $40, and you find you are paying $1.07 per cubic foot. Compare this to a full cord for, say, $105; $105 divided by 128 cubic feet (one cord = 128 cubic feet) gets you $0.82 per cubic foot, a much better deal.

Cubic Feet for Some Firewood Measures

Full cord	128.0 cu. ft.
Face cord of 12" logs (1/4 cord)	32.0 cu. ft.
Face cord of 14" logs	37.3 cu. ft.
Face cord of 15" logs	40.0 cu. ft.
Face cord of 16" logs	42.6 cu. ft.
Face cord of 18" logs	48.0 cu. ft.
Face cord of 20" logs	53.3 cu. ft.
Face cord of 22" logs	58.6 cu. ft.
Face cord of 24" logs (1/2 cord)	64.0 cu. ft.
Face cord of 25" logs	66.6 cu. ft.
Face cord of 30" logs	80.0 cu. ft.

Although in some states it's illegal to sell firewood by anything but the cord or fraction thereof, one still sees it for sale by the "truckload," sometimes called a "run," which is as much as that size truck can carry. Although the rule of thumb is that a 1/2-ton pickup can carry 1/2 cord and a 1-ton pickup a full cord, it really depends on the weight of the wood, the height of the truck bed's sides, and whether special frames have been mounted. If you are truly unlucky, you may also be faced with "stove cords," "fitted cords," or "fireplace cords." With any of these "measures," one clue to what you're getting is the weight: A typical cord of hardwood weighs $1^{1}/2$ to 2 tons. Anyone who claims to dump a cord of hardwood on your property with one $1/2$-ton truckload is fudging. (See pages 107-108 for weights of some other woods.)

In the end, the best measure of firewood may be the one most rarely used—*weight*. The amount of heat you get from your firewood is the same *per pound* for *all* firewood—one source says you will have about 7,000 Btu's (see page 120) from a pound of wood, while another source puts the figure at 6,400 Btu's. The important thing is this: no matter what kind of wood you use, you usually get the same heat value per pound. The denser, or harder, the wood, the heavier it is and the more pounds—and heat—you'll have per cord. The only true way to evaluate your wood is by price per pound, which you can figure out if you know the average weight per cubic foot of your firewood. Divide the price per cubic foot of firewood by the pounds per cubic foot that it weighs, and then you will know what you are paying for every 6,400 Btu's of heat. For example, a $100 cord of white fir costs 78 cents per cubic foot ($100 divided by 128 cubic feet). White fir weighs 28 pounds per cubic foot, so one pound costs about 3 cents, producing 6,400 Btu's of heat. This is just an educated guess—the cubic feet you figured above is not solid wood but stacked wood with air holes; the firewood must be dry (figures in the chart that follows are based on a 20 percent moisture content); and the cords must be honest—but it is an interesting way to compare firewood deals or the value of one kind of wood with another.

Approximate Weight per Cubic Foot of Some Common Woods

Types of Hardwood	Lb./cu. ft.	Types of Softwood	Lb./cu. ft.
Alder, red	38	Bald cypress	32.5
Apple	48.7	Cedar:	
Ash:		Alaska	32.5
Black	46	Atlantic-white	24
Green	41.5	Eastern red	34
White	43	Northern white	23
Aspen, quaking	27	Port-Orford	30.5
Basswood	25	Western red	24
Beech	44	Douglas fir	33–35
Birch:		Fir:	
Paper	37.5	Balsalm	26
Sweet	46	California red	27.5
Yellow	43	Grand	27
Butternut	27.5	Pacific Silver	31
Cherry	36.5	Subalpine	24
Chestnut	31	White	28
Cottonwood	24	Hemlock:	
Elm:		Eastern	29
American	36	Western	32.5
Rock	45	Mountain	32.6
Slippery	37.5	Larch	37.5
Hackberry	38	Pine:	
Hickory, pecan	47	Eastern white	26
Hickory, true:		Jack	31
Mockernut	51	Loblolly	36.5
Pignut	53	Lodgepole	36.5
Shagbark	51	Longleaf	42
Shellbark	50	Pitch	36.5
Honey locust	47	Pond	40
Locust, black	53	Ponderosa	29
Magnolia, southern	36	Red	32
Maple:		Sand	36
Bigleaf	34	Shortleaf	36.5
Black	41	Slash	42
Red	38	Spruce	32
Silver	34	Sugar	26
Sugar	44	Virginia	35
Oak, red:		Western white	27
Black	44	Redwood:	
Cherrybark	48	Old-growth	29
Laurel	44	Young-growth	26
Northern red	44		

(continued)

Approximate Weight per Cubic Foot of Some Common Woods (cont)

Types of Hardwood	Lb./cu. ft.	Types of Softwood	Lb./cu. ft.
Oak, red:		Spruce:	
Pin	43	Black	29
Scarlet	47	Engelmann	25.5
Southern red	41	Red	29
Water or Willow	44	Sitka	28
Oak, white:		White	28
Bur	45.5	Tamarack	38
Chestnut	45		
Live	67		
Post	47		
Swamp chestnut	47		
Swampy white	51		
White	47		
Sassafras	32.5		
Sweet gum	36		
Sycamore	36		
Tan oak	45.5		
Tupelo	36		
Walnut, black	40		
Willow, black	27.5		

Adapted from specific gravity figures for hardwoods and softwoods offered in *Agriculture Handbook No. 72, Wood Handbook: Wood as an Engineering Material,* by Forest Products Laboratory, Forest Service, U.S. Department of Agriculture, 1974.

FOOD (ENERGY VALUES)

YOU MAY THINK that your food contains calories, or perhaps is even made of calories, but this is not true. The calorie count isn't a measure of the content of food, but of the energy value of food. It's confusing, because not only are calories metric, but there are calories and there are Calories, and they are not equal.

A calorie is a measure of energy, and it comes in two sizes, small and large. The small calorie, used by scientists and by metric system countries to measure heat/energy, is defined as the amount of energy needed to raise the temperature of 1 gram of water 1 degree Celsius, or from 14.5 degrees C to 15.5 degrees C. It takes 1,000 of these small calories to make a kilocalorie, also known as the large

Calorie—or the amount of energy it takes to raise 1 kilogram of water 1 degree Celsius. It is this large Calorie that is used to measure the fuel value of food; i.e., the amount of energy it takes to raise 1 kilogram of water 1 degree C. Since the small calorie isn't commonly used in this country, we don't bother to capitalize the "c."

Food is potent. A pound of TNT, for example, has the same energy value as your average fast-food quarter-pound cheeseburger (500 calories). It's quite possible, however, that you think of calories not in terms of energy, but in terms of fat, and you're not far off. Generally speaking each pound of you represents about 3,500 calories. To lose a pound, you need to take in 3,500 fewer calories than you burn. But before you start a diet, try to determine where the calories are that you're eating—a little rearrangement can cut out quite a few without radically reducing your meal size. Naturally, you should check with your health practitioner before going on a diet.

How many calories should a health-conscious person consume, on average, per day? The chart on page 110 presents the recommendations of the U.S. Food and Drug Administration. (It's interesting to note that food labeling is now based on a 2,000-calorie intake, although many other numbers appear on the Recommended Energy Intake chart.)

You consume the recommended calories from the three basic types of foods you eat: fats, proteins, and carbohydrates. A gram of protein has an energy value of 4 calories, and a gram of carbohydrate has an energy value of 4 calories, but a gram of fat has 9 calories, more than twice that of the first two. This is worse news than you think—it has been estimated that 40 percent of the calories in the typical American diet is fat. If you are typical, another 20 percent of your daily calories are simple carbohydrates (sugars), leaving only 40 percent of your diet for protein and complex carbohydrates (grains, fruits, and vegetables). Here's the recommended balance from the U.S. Food and Drug Administration:

- 10% protein
- 30% fat (including 10% saturated fat)
- 60% carbohydrates (grains, fruits, vegetables, sugars)
- fiber based on 11.5 grams of fiber per 1,000 calories

Recommended Energy Intake

Category	Age	Calories per Day		
		Light Activity	Moderate Activity	Heavy Activity
Children	4–6		1,800	
	7–10		2,000	
Males	11–14		2,500	
	15–18		3,000	
	19–24	2,700	3,000	3,600
	25–50	3,000	3,200	4,000
	51+		2,300*	
Females	11–18		2,200	
	19–24	2,000	2,100	2,600
	25–50	2,200	2,300	2,800
	51+		1,900*	

Pregnant women in their second and third trimesters should add 300 calories to the figure the table indicates for their age. Nursing mothers should add 500.

*Based on light to moderate activity

Activity Levels

Very light: Driving, typing, painting, laboratory work, ironing, sewing, cooking, playing cards, playing a musical instrument, other seated or standing activities

Light: Housecleaning, child care, garage work, electrical trade work, restaurant work, golf, sailing, table tennis, walking on a level surface at 2.5 to 3 miles per hour

Moderate: Weeding, hoeing, carrying a load, cycling, skiing, tennis, dancing, walking 3.5 to 4 miles per hour

Heavy: Heavy manual digging or chopping, basketball, climbing, football, soccer, carrying a load uphill

Source: U.S. Food and Drug Administration

One of the simplest ways to cut calories is to eat less sugar and fat, remembering that fat, including butter and margarine, adds up quickly—about 100 calories per tablespoon—and that sugar contains 48 calories per tablespoon. You can probably cut more than 300 calories from your daily intake by eliminating most of your sugar and fat, without affecting the size of your meals.

Exercise, however, not only burns calories but can jump-start your metabolism, which also burns calories. In fact, studies have shown that if you don't exercise when you diet, your body may adjust its metabolism to fewer calories. This means that if you normally eat 2,200 calories but cut that to 1,200, your body may adjust so completely that, although you lose weight at first, after a while 1,200 calories may become your weight maintenance amount and any you take in over that could put weight on you. You may end up heavier than you were before you began the diet.

The effective way to lose weight, many experts say, is to combine a smaller calorie cutback from the right places with daily or frequent exercise. And that's good news, because exercise has great side effects, like keeping your bones and heart strong, your cholesterol down, and your spirits up.

This is not a diet book, but try a little math: if you burn off an extra 200 calories per day with exercise, and cut out 300 calories, that's 500 per day, enough to let you lose a pound a week! This is 10 pounds in 10 weeks, without cutting your meal size by much or by going on a crash diet that may make you bigger than when you began.

Calories to Burn

Activity	Calories burned per half hour
Sleeping Watching TV	30 to 36
Doing sedentary work/play Driving the car Playing a musical instrument Sewing Ironing	up to 75
Level walking, 2.5–3 m.p.h. Fixing the car Doing carpentry work Shopping with light load Playing golf Sailing	75 to 147

(continued)

Calories to Burn (continued)

Activity	Calories burned per half hour
Playing Ping-Pong Playing volleyball	75 to 147
Walking 3.5–4 m.p.h. Weeding Scrubbing floors Bicycling Skiing Playing tennis Dancing	150 to 222
Backpacking uphill Playing basketball Playing football Swimming Climbing	223 to 360

Source: Recommended Dietary Allowances. Used with permission from the National Academy Press, Washington, D.C.

▶ **For a good exercise/calorie calculator, go to http://www.msnbc.com/ modules/quizzes/caloriecalc.asp. To find a longer list of activities with calorie counts, go to the NutriStrategy website at http:// nutristrategy.com/activitylist.htm. To find out how many minutes you must exercise to burn off calories from various foods, or for a good calorie counter, go to Anne Collins's website at http:// www.annecollins.com/exercise-calories.**

FOOD GRADING
•••

A TV QUIZ SHOW host once asked whether "Choice" or "Prime" was the better beef, and the contestant didn't know. Not surprising, since the U.S. Department of Agriculture (USDA), responsible for most food grading, uses one system for beef and lamb, another for pork, and yet another for poultry. In addition, fresh fruits and vegetables are graded differently from canned ones, and eggs have yet a different grading—buy Grade A poultry and you get the best, but grade A eggs are only second best.

Typical Federal Grades for Foods

Food	Best	2nd Best	3rd Best
Beef, lamb, and veal	Prime	Choice	Good
Pork	Acceptable	Unacceptable	
Poultry	A	B	C
Fish*	A	B	C
Eggs and butter, Cheddar cheese	AA	A	B
Fresh fruits and vegetables†	U.S. Fancy	U.S. No. 1	U.S. No. 2
Canned fruits and vegetables, frozen juices, jams, and jellies†	A	B	C

*A voluntary inspection program by U.S. Department of Commerce.

†These designations may vary for some products.

Source: Agriculture Marketing Service, U.S. Department of Agriculture.

Inspection stamps seem to be a waste of time unless consumers have a clear idea of what they mean. Your only recourse may be to check the chart above. How do you know the grade on food products, especially fresh produce? Most of the time, you don't; however, many quality stores will tell you if you ask—the grade is usually printed on the cartons produce is shipped in.

COMMON GRADE MARKS

Meat
Beef, Lamb, Veal

Poultry
Chickens, Turkeys, Ducks, Geese

Fruits and Vegetables and Related Products
Fresh fruits and vegetables

U.S. Fancy (This grade name is more likely to be found without the shield.)

Canned and frozen fruits and vegetables. Dried or dehydrated fruits. Fruit and vegetable juices, canned and frozen. Jams, jellies, preserves. Peanut butter. Honey. Catsup, tomato paste.

Eggs

Source: Agricultural Marketing Service, U.S. Department of Agriculture.

Food inspection for safety, or wholesomeness, is mandatory, enacted at taxpayers' expense by the USDA's Food Safety and Inspection Service (FSIS). Grades for quality, as illustrated above, are voluntary, paid for by the food producers, processors, or companies that use them.

Eggs

Eggs are of special interest: in addition to voluntary quality grading, such as AA, A, or B, there is a regulation "weight class" for eggs. Eggs are sized not by the size of the eggs themselves, but by the net weight of a dozen: for example, 12 eggs must weigh in at 30 ounces to be called "Jumbo." Here are the sizes:

U.S. Weight Class for Eggs

Size or Weight Class	Minimum Net Weight per Dozen
Jumbo	30 ounces
Extra Large	27 ounces
Large	24 ounces
Medium	21 ounces
Small	18 ounces
Peewee	15 ounces

Poultry

Poultry also deserves a note: Grade A poultry is the only grade sold in markets; Grades B and C are usually used in processed products where the poultry meat is chopped, cut up, or ground. In other words, although that tablespoon of cubed chicken in your 99-cent frozen pasta meal was probably Grade B or C poultry, it nevertheless had to pass USDA safety inspection.

Fish and Seafood

Oddly, fish inspection is not only voluntary, but is provided by an entirely different department of government. NOAA—the National Oceanic and Atmospheric Administration—of the U.S. Department of Commerce offers voluntary inspection service, providing a grading mark that says "PUFI," meaning "processed under federal inspection," as well as a "lot inspection mark," sometimes found on retail packaging, that reads "USDC," or U.S. Department of Commerce, signifying that the product was sampled and inspected to conform with approved specifications or criteria.

▶ For more detailed information on food grading in the United States, go to http://www.ams.usda.gov. To find out more about U.S. food inspection, go to http://www.fsis.usda.gov/OA/pubs/ingrade.htm. For more about U.S. fish and seafood inspection, go to http://seafood.nmfs.gov.

FOOD LABELING
•••

FOOD LABELING has to be one of the most useful ways our government has found to spend our tax dollars. Valiant attempts (considering the bureaucracies involved) have been made to keep it
simple, readable, applicable, and useful, and it's getting better all
the time. You may need a rundown on the numbers, though, to
read them as swiftly as you must during a rush-hour shopping
run, or with a toddler in tow.

Since the government oversees and regulates food labeling, the
subject comes with a surfeit of acronyms. To keep you on board,
here are a few for you to refer back to when you begin to lose track:

FDA	Federal Food and Drug Administration; an agency of the USDHHS
USDHHS	U.S. Department of Health and Human Services
FSIS	Food Safety and Inspection Service; an agency of the USDA
USDA	U.S. Department of Agriculture
NLEA	Nutrition Labeling and Education Act of 1990
RDA	Recommended Daily Allowances; no longer used, and replaced by DV
DV	Daily Value (Percentage of recommended daily intake); comprised of DRVs and RDIs
DRVs	Daily Reference Values and
RDIs	Reference Daily Intakes

Here's the story: The Nutrition Labeling and Education Act of
1990, implemented in 1992 and 1993, requires nutrition labeling
for most foods and authorizes the use of nutrient content claims
and appropriate FDA-approved health claims. Even restaurant
foods must provide "reasonable basis" for any menu health claims
made for their offerings. Small timers, such as businesses with
fewer than one hundred full-time employees, may be excused
from labeling everything they produce, so you won't be arrested
for not analyzing your PTA bake sale goods.

The "Nutrition Facts" Label

Here is a typical required label, this one from a cereal box:

A food label is presented in seven parts:

Part 1 *Serving size and numbers of servings* are described in terms of kitchen measures, when possible, or pieces, or as a last resort, ounces (with the metric equivalent in parentheses).

Part 2 *Calories* are counted per serving, as well as calories from fat.

Part 3 *Analysis of food pyramid foods* requires two figures: The amount in grams or milligrams as well as the "% Daily Value" (meaning the percentage of this nutrient provided to a person consuming an average of 2,000 calories per day) are provided for fat (including saturated fat and cholesterol), sodium, carbohydrates (including fiber and sugar), and protein. *Note that to get the amount of complex carbohydrates, which is what you want and need for health, you have to subtract the simple carbohydrates (sugars) from the total carbohydrates.*

Part 4 *Vitamins and minerals* are listed as a Daily Value percentage, again, of a 2,000-calorie-per-day diet. (See also Vitamins and Minerals, page 262.)

Part 5 These are *explanatory notes,* including the information that the above figures are based on a 2,000-calorie-per-day diet. (Some labels also display percent figures for a 2,500-calorie-per-day diet.)

Part 6 This section recaps the *Dietary Reference Intakes,* meaning the recommended daily amount in grams per person (see page 262).

Part 7 *Ingredients* (not shown here), listed in order of amount by weight contained in the product, the largest amounts first.

Nutrition Facts

Serving Size 1 cup (58g)
Servings Per Container about 8

Amount Per Serving	Multi-Bran Chex	with ½ cup skim milk
Calories	200	240
Calories from Fat	15	15

	% Daily Value**	
Total Fat 1.5g*	**2%**	**3%**
Saturated Fat 0g	**0%**	**0%**
Polyunsaturated Fat 0.5g		
Monounsaturated Fat 0g		
Cholesterol 0mg	**0%**	**1%**
Sodium 380mg	**16%**	**19%**
Potassium 220mg	**6%**	**12%**
Total Carbohydrate 49g	**16%**	**18%**
Dietary Fiber 8g	**30%**	**30%**
Sugars 12g		
Other Carbohydrate 29g		
Protein 4g		

Vitamin A	10%	15%
Vitamin C	10%	10%
Calcium	10%	25%
Iron	90%	90%
Vitamin D	10%	25%
Thiamin	25%	30%
Riboflavin	25%	35%
Niacin	25%	25%
Vitamin B$_6$	25%	25%
Folic Acid	100%	100%
Vitamin B$_{12}$	25%	35%
Phosphorus	20%	35%
Magnesium	15%	20%
Zinc	25%	30%
Copper	4%	4%

*Amount in Cereal. A serving of cereal plus skim milk provides 1.5g total fat, less than 5mg cholesterol, 450mg sodium, 420mg potassium, 55g total carbohydrate (18g sugars) and 8g protein.
**Percent Daily Values are based on a 2,000 calorie diet. Your daily values may be higher or lower depending on your calorie needs:

		Calories:	2,000	2,500
Total Fat	Less than		65g	80g
Sat Fat	Less than		20g	25g
Cholesterol	Less than		300mg	300mg
Sodium	Less than		2,400mg	2,400mg
Potassium			3,500mg	3,500mg
Total Carbohydrate			300g	375g
Dietary Fiber			25g	30g

Source: General Mills, Inc. Used with permission.

Claims and Advertising

Did you know that simple words like *Lite, Low, Free,* and many more are regulated? The one your author has always hated is *More,* as well as comparative adjectives such as "Juicier!" "Brighter!" and "Shinier!" More than what? she wants to know. Brighter than what? Shinier than what?

At least the word "more" has now been regulated by the FDA: "More" means that a serving of food, whether altered or not, contains a nutrient that is at least 10 percent of the Daily Value more than the "reference" food, or "regular" version of that food. Similar restrictions have been issued for many words, including *Healthy, Reduced, High,* and *Fresh.*

Read those labels. They have all sorts of great information. Cereal boxes are a great place to start.

▶ **For a detailed explanation of food labeling, go to the FDA's article titled "The Food Label" at http://www.cfsan.fda.gov/~dms/fdnewlab.html. For more information on FDA, USDA, and FTC regulations as they affect nutrition, go to the very clear and informative website sponsored by the Council for Responsible Nutrition at http://www.crnusa.org/ Shellscireg000003.html. For ways food labeling can assist special diets, go to http://www.cfsan.fda.gov/~dms/fdspdiet.html. For U.S. dietary guidelines, go to http://www.nal.usda.gov/fnic/dga.**

GAS, NATURAL
· ·

EVERY HOME using natural gas has a gas meter, called a diaphragm type displacement meter, which measures in cubic feet how much gas you use. It does this by moving the gas through several chambers of a known size, so as one chamber is emptied, the one before it fills up, ensuring an even flow of gas at all times, while the meter registers how many times the chambers have been filled and emptied. This system is so effective that it seems to have escaped technology—unless you have one of the new, remotely read meters, the meter you use today may not have changed much in the 160 years since the first one was installed in 1843. Every month or so, some-one comes around to read the dials on your meter:

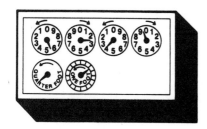

GAS METER

Reading left to right, this meter shows 5239 cubic feet of natural gas. When a needle is between numbers, always read the lower number.

Source: Pacific Gas and Electric Company. Used with permission.

The meter shows four dials in the top row: from left to right, they register cubic feet in the (1) hundred thousands (up to 1,000,000), (2) ten thousands (up to 100,000), (3) thousands (up to 10,000), and (4) hundreds (up to 1,000). To read the meter, read the dials from left to right, always using the smaller number when a pointer is between two numbers and ignoring the bottom dials, which are primarily for testing. The amount of gas you've used since the last reading is reached by subtracting that reading (the one on your last gas bill) from the current one. When your bill arrives, it will show the meter readings as a four-digit number, e.g., 5374 (prior) to 5457 (present), with a difference of 83, which means you have used 8,300 cubic feet of gas since your last bill. You may be charged for this amount, but it has probably been trans-lated into *therms*.

Therms are that latest twist in natural gas billing. *A therm is a unit of heat equal to 100,000 Btu's* (see page 120), and it takes 100 cubic feet of most natural gas to deliver this. But not all gas delivers the same amount of energy—some burns hotter than others—nor is all gas delivered at the same pressure, so your bill is adjusted to re-flect the actual energy value you've received by using a multiplier shown on your gas bill. The multiplier is a number that translates cubic feet of gas into therms.

How many therms does it take to run appliances in your home? Home heating is usually the highest, and it's hard to estimate, since home size, type of furnace, and insulation have so much effect on your bill. However, more and more effort is being put into making appliances energy-wise. Estimates vary, but here are a few general estimates made by several large energy companies:

Therm Estimates for Some Gas Appliances

Appliance	Therms
Water heater	5 per month per person
Clothes dryer	0.15 to 0.17 per load
Clothes washer (therms to heat water):	
warm wash, cold rinse	0.11 per load
hot wash, warm rinse	0.33 per load
Dishwasher (therms for hot water)	0.16 to 0.20 per load
Gas range:	
oven	0.20 per day
surface	0.10 per day
self-cleaning	0.50 per clean
pilot (older models)	0.20 per day
Gas log fireplace	0.20/hour
Pool heater (250,000 Btu's)	2.5 per hour
Space heat (forced air, 80,000 Btu's for a 1,750 sq. ft. house)	0.80 per working hour
Barbeque grill	0.25 per hour

Now, what about those Btu's?

If you've ever had to buy a furnace or a water heater, you've probably noticed that their heating capacities are given in Btu's, otherwise known as British thermal units. The Btu does not measure temperature, but energy—by International Code agreement 1 Btu = the amount of energy needed to raise the temperature of 1 pound (lb.) of water 1 degree Fahrenheit. Or put another way, 1 Btu is $1/180$ of the energy needed to raise the temperature of 1 lb. of water from freezing (32 degrees F) to boiling (212 degrees F). The amount of energy used by appliances is usually measured in Btu's: 1 therm will provide 100,000 Btu's.

In countries using the metric system, heat is not measured by the Btu, but by the *small calorie*. One small calorie = the amount of energy needed to raise the temperature of 1 gram of water by 1 degree Celsius, from 14.5 degrees C to 15.5 degrees C. It takes 1,000 small calories to make the *big Calorie* (kilocalorie) used to measure the energy values of food (see page 108). Since there are 252 small calories in 1 Btu, it takes about 4 Btu's to make one big Calorie.

These days, fuel efficiency is more important than ever. The Department of Energy (DOE) at the Environmental Protection Agency (EPA) has issued Annual Fuel Utilization Efficiency (AFUE) standards for nearly every possible appliance in your home and office. Those models that comply may display the Energy Star:

Source: Environmental Protection Agency, U.S. Department of Energy

▶ To check on the fuel efficiency rating for products using gas or electricity, go to the website for the Federal Energy Management Program (FEMP) at http://www.eren.doe.gov/femp/procurement/begin.html. For more energy-saving tips for gas appliances, go to the Sierra Pacific website at http://www.sierrapacific.com/services/energy and click on "Gas Energy Tips," then "Gas Wise Brochure." Get even more information and helpful links from the Department of Energy at http://www.eren.doe.gov/buildings/consumer_information/contact.html.

GASOLINE

....

IF YOU'VE EVER WONDERED about that octane number on the gas pump, you might have assumed that octane is much like the fat content of milk—regular is 2 percent, premium 4 percent, and super premium is close to half-and-half—without dealing with the actual number (87 what?). But although a high-octane gas is considered "rich," gasolines are not the same. At this very moment each oil company may be pumping several different blends of the same octane number—meaning the same grade, such as regular unleaded—in different parts of the country. In fact, the gas you pumped today is probably quite different from the gas you got from the same pump six months ago: climate affects gasoline performance—mainly volatility and anti-knock ability—so greatly that each oil company produces variations of each grade, much as beer manufacturers vary the alcohol content of a single brand of beer to meet the different legal requirements around the country (see *Alcohol in Beverages*, page 9).

Volatility

The first main performance feature of gasoline is its volatility, or tendency to vaporize. Volatility is necessary if the gasoline's to burn, but too much volatility can cause an engine to stall, while too little can leave an engine exposed to frictional heat and wear. Because volatility is greatly affected by temperature and humidity, maintaining the correct balance for different climates and seasons is tricky. The American Society for Testing and Materials (ASTM) has included five carefully defined volatility classes in its D439 Standard Specification for Automotive Gasoline. The ASTM then divides the United States into distribution areas—states or portions of states—specifying which volatility class is appropriate for each area for each month of the year. The volatility class applies to all the grades of gasoline.

Octane

The second main performance feature is the anti-knock factor, which is where the octane number and the grading of gasolines come into play. If you're not chummy with carburetors, "knocking" may mean no more to you than an annoying noise. Knocking—or pinging, or whatever—is much more than that, and there is good reason why oil companies push the anti-knock qualities of their gasolines. Here is what's happening: In normal combustion, a spark ignites the air/fuel mixture in the cylinder and the flame travels smoothly across the combustion chamber, with no abrupt change in pressure. (See *Motorcycles*, page 171, for information on pistons and cylinders.) If any of the fuel ignites spontaneously or from another source like a hot spot, pressure builds up and the shock waves cause the knocking sound. A little knocking doesn't hurt much, but heavy or prolonged knocking can affect power, overheat engine parts, or even cause engine damage.

How to stop this? Although knocking may be caused by other factors, a higher-octane gasoline is often the cure. What does the octane number mean? Take this typical gasoline pump label:

Minimum Octane Rating
(R+M)/2 METHOD
87

Note that the 87 is the octane *rating*, not an actual amount of anything. The mysterious (R+M)/2 Method explains this. There are two methods for testing the anti-knock performance of a gasoline: the Research Method (R) and the Motor Method (M), resulting in two numbers: the Research Octane Number (RON), which predicts performance at low speeds, and the Motor Octane Number (MON), which predicts performance at higher speeds and temperatures and is usually higher than the RON. When these two numbers are averaged—added and divided by 2 ([R+M]/2)—you get the octane rating on the label.

So what is octane? Octane, like butane or methane, is one of the numerous kinds of hydrocarbons contained in crude oil. An isomer* of octane, called isooctane, is an extremely high-performance fuel (a gasoline with only normal octane molecules in it would detonate so severely that it would ruin an engine). It would be far too expensive to run cars on pure isooctane, however; the octane number is an attempt to compare the performance of a given blend of gasoline with pure isooctane. An octane rating of 92 tells you that gasoline behaves as a mixture of 92 percent isooctane and 8 percent heptane (a low-performance fuel) would behave, even though that gasoline might not have an ounce of octane in it.

How does an oil company raise or lower the octane rating? In the early days of gasoline production, around the 1900s, refining gasoline from crude oil was fairly straightforward, without much variation in the product. But today gasoline is a blend of more than 200 hydrocarbons—molecules with different patterns of hydrogen and carbon atoms. As developing technology allowed the industry to "crack" large, heavy hydrocarbon molecules into smaller, lighter ones, the volatility of gasoline could be controlled. And to improve the anti-knock quality of gasoline, tetraethyl lead (TEL) was added; it was first used commercially in 1927. In 1960 tetramethyl lead (TML) was introduced. Today hydrocarbons are "cracked" and the smaller hydrocarbons are put back together in a shape that improves the anti-knock quality of the gasoline. This processing is more expensive than just stirring in a lead compound.

What octane rating should you use? As a rule of thumb, use the lowest-octane gasoline your car will run on without knocking. If, for example, your car hums along on regular, to use premium is just a waste of money, not to mention the extra resources required to produce the higher grade of gasoline. Your

---

*An isomer of a certain molecule has the same number of atoms, but they are arranged differently. Isomers of octane have 8 carbon and 18 hydrogen atoms, but the atoms have been rearranged.

car, however, does not always run best on one particular octane rating. The seasons, the place, and the altitude can change the octane rating requirements of your car. The octane ratings in mountainous regions, for example, may be several numbers below those at sea level.

Gasoline is graded according to octane level—unleaded premium, which commonly boasts an octane rating of 91, averages about four numbers higher than unleaded regular, which is often found with an 87 rating. Leaded regular often has a slightly higher rating than unleaded regular.

Pricing

Here's a question unrelated to gasoline performance that you may have pondered: why is gasoline priced to the last $9/10$ of a cent? Isn't a per-gallon gas price of $1.39$9/10$ ridiculous? Most people who comparison shop for gasoline will buy the cheapest—the decimal columns that matter do change and those are the ones everyone reads. This system of dividing the last penny into ten parts has been used for over fifty years because most oil companies still believe that even an infinitesimally lower price sells more gasoline.

A Barrel of Oil

Have you ever wondered how many gallons of gasoline can be squeezed from a barrel of crude oil? From the 42 U.S. gallons of crude oil in a barrel, most processing combinations yield 8 to 25 gallons of gasoline—although 0 to 42 gallons are possible—with the balance relinquished to other petroleum products.

▶ For information on alternative fuels, including ethanol, go to the Alternative Fuels Data Center (AFDC) at the DOE, http://www.afdc.doe.gov. For another explanation of gasoline octane, go to Marshall Brain's website at http://www.howstuffworks.com/question90.

GLOVES

••

NUMBERED GLOVE SIZES make sense—isn't that refreshing? With your hand held flat, wrap a tape measure around your knuckles, or the widest part of your hand between fingers and thumb (don't include the thumb). That number—in inches—is your glove size. Better gloves are frequently offered in exactly these numerical sizes, by inch and half inch. Many gloves, however, are sized by the Small (S), Medium (M), Large (L), and Extra Large (XL) method. These groupings, which are sometimes expanded with extra X's at either end, have received such varied interpretations from different glove companies that it's advised to either try on the pair you want or check the size chart on their website. Your best bet for fit of an unseen product, of course, is the inch size.

Here are the glove sizes used by some glove companies:

Glove Sizes

Sizes	Men	Women
Small (S)	7" to 7$\frac{1}{2}$"	6" to 6$\frac{1}{2}$"
Medium (M)	8" to 8$\frac{1}{2}$"	7" to 7$\frac{1}{2}$"
Large (L)	9" to 9$\frac{1}{2}$"	8" to 8$\frac{1}{2}$"
Extra Large (XL)	10" to 10$\frac{1}{2}$"	

GOLD
••

THE KARAT SYSTEM is confusing, for one, because it's spelled with a "c" when referring to precious stones, but with a "k" when applied to gold. The two systems are not the same—while a one-carat diamond is fairly respectable, one-karat gold is not. When applied to gold, a karat represents a ratio of gold to alloy (other metals): 100 percent gold is 24k, 14k gold is 14 parts pure gold and 10 parts alloy, and so on.

Why 24 parts? Why not 16 or a hundred? Centuries ago, gold was weighed using the troy weight system, in which a pound equaled 12 ounces (see *Weight*, page 269). A karat was used to describe $1/2$ ounce of pure gold, or $1/24$ of a troy pound.

Gold has some interesting properties that, in addition to its deep yellow color and scarcity, account for its unusual value over the centuries. Although gold, with a specific gravity of 19.33, is heavier than iron (SG 7.8) or silver (SG 10.7), it's only 2 on the Mohs' 1 to 10 hardness scale (see page 169), making it softer than most other metals. Gold is so malleable that it can be hammered into a thin sheet or drawn into fine wire.

At 24k (100 percent), gold is too soft to be made into jewelry. In the United States most gold jewelry is 14k gold—14 parts gold to 10 parts other metals—although 18k gold jewelry is also popular. By U.S. law, gold jewelry must contain at least 10 karats of gold to be labeled as karat gold. "Gold-filled" jewelry is jewelry made from a base metal with a thin layer of gold bonded to it. (It would make more sense to call this "metal-filled gold.") If gold-filled jewelry is made with better than 10k gold (the minimum required for gold-filled jewelry), it is marked something like 14*kgf*—meaning 14 karat gold-filled. Items marked *hge*, meaning "hard gold electroplate," are usually inexpensive.

Gold can also be electroplated to metal and used in costume jewelry; by U.S. law, the layer on electroplated jewelry must be at least seven millionths of an inch thick. Jewelry sold as gold in the United States must be marked with a karat or fineness of at least 10k. The legal standard differs from country to country, however:

Canada and England require 9k, for example, and France and Italy require 18k. 22k gold jewelry is not uncommon in the Far East. European countries, instead of using karats, prefer a *"Fineness"* marking to describe the number of parts of gold per thousand.

U.S. Markings	Parts Gold	Percent Gold	European Markings
24k	24/24	100.0	1000 or 999
22k	22/24	91.7	916 or 917
18k	18/24	75.0	750
14k	14/24	58.3	.583 or .585
10k	10/24	41.7	417

Gold is weighed by the U.S. troy weight system (see page 269).

▶ **For more gold facts, go to http://www.petersjewelers.com/ petersjewelers/goldinformation.**

GREENWICH MEAN TIME
· ·

THE U.S. MILITARY calls it "Zulu Time," pilots call it "Zebra Time," while most of the world calls it Greenwich Mean Time—the time in the Zero (also labeled "Z") Time Zone, which runs through Greenwich, England (see *Time Zones,* page 246). Greenwich Mean Time, or GMT, is a handy way to deal with time for any group— such as the military or an airline—that works internationally and must coordinate activities spread over many time zones. GMT will always be as many hours later as the number assigned to your own personal U.S. Standard Time Zone: +8 for Pacific, +7 for Mountain, +6 for Central, and +5 for Eastern. So if it's 8 A.M. Pacific Standard Time, add 8 hours to get 4 P.M. in Greenwich. (As Greenwich Mean Time uses the 24-hour clock, it would be written as 1600 hours—see *Military Time,* page 168.) To get from GMT to your local U.S. time, subtract 5 to 8 hours from GMT, depending on which time zone you're in; if you're on daylight saving time, subtract another hour from your total.

▶ **To find the exact Greenwich Mean Time, as well as the time anywhere in the world, go to http://www.greenwichmeantime.com.**

GROSS DOMESTIC PRODUCT (GDP)
•••

IN 1991 THE *gross domestic product (GDP)* replaced the *gross national product (GNP)* as a widely reported economic statistic. Reported quarterly by the Bureau of Economic Analysis (BEA), with annual summaries, *both present the total market value of all final goods and services produced in the United States (similar data is available for other countries) in a given quarter or year, but the gross national product (GNP) also includes income accruing to U.S. citizens as a result of investments abroad.*

Even a smidgen of curiosity will help you through the gross domestic product. Basically, the GDP is the dollar value of all the goods and services produced in America during a specified period. The figures are reported monthly by the Department of Commerce's Bureau of Economic Analysis, with annual summaries. We're not discussing profit here; we're talking product. If you ran a lemonade stand for the month of July, at the end of the month you could find your gross personal product (the value of all the lemonade you sold) two ways: (1) you could calculate your *flow-of-product* by counting your take—all the money that people spent to buy your product—say $100.00; or (2) you could add your *costs* (say, $40.00, for sugar, lemons, paper cups, advertising) to your *earnings* (whatever was left after your costs, which would be $60.00), which would also equal $100.00.

The gross domestic product does the same thing for the nation. As with the lemonade stand, there are two ways of reaching the final figure: (1) the *flow-of-product method*, which adds up all the money spent to buy goods and services, or (2) *the earnings and cost method*, which adds up how much it cost to produce all the goods and services, plus the profit from their sale. Each method will add up to the same figure.

Here's what is included in the gross domestic product:

1. Consumer spending on goods and services
2. Business outlays on investments and consumer outlays for new housing
3. All government spending on goods and services (figures are broken down for federal government and state/local governments, with the federal figures divided into defense and nondefense figures)
4. Net exports (how much more or less we sell abroad than we buy)

It's important to note that the GDP counts only the price of final goods and services. Consider lasagna: the GDP is interested only in the price on the box you pull from your grocer's freezer; it does not count the price paid to the mill for the flour or the price paid to the farmer for the tomatoes, or the wholesale price paid to the factory by the grocer. The GDP counts everything only once, in the final product.

That's the good news. The bad news is that, in addition to the GNP, there are at least two GDPs: the *Current Dollar GDP* and the *Real Dollar GDP*, not to mention an index of *Implicit Price Deflators*. If you want to make sense of GDP figures and charts, it helps to know what these things mean.

It's the job of the GDP to measure the growth of the economy—the economy's performance as compared with an earlier time. In 2002, the year chosen with which to compare current figures was 1996. The Current Dollar GDP reports exactly what was paid in actual present-day dollars. But the dollar changes in value from year to year (inflation), so the Current Dollar GDP can exaggerate actual growth—when the figures rise, how do you know if we are really producing more or if the prices are simply higher? So

**Gross Domestic Product 1995–2001
(In billions of dollars)**

Year	Current $ GDP	Implicit Price Deflator	Real $ GDP
		(Base year = 1996)	(1996 dollars)
1995	7,400.5	98.1	7,743.8
1996	**7,813.2**	**100.0**	**7,813.2**
1997	8,318.4	101.9	8,159.5
1998	8,781.5	103.2	8,508.9
1999	9,268.6	104.7	8,856.5
2000	9,872.9	106.9	9,224.0
2001	10,208.1	109.3	9,333.8

the Department of Commerce also reports how much the GNP would be in 1996 dollars. To do this, it measures how much prices increased (or decreased) since 1996, which is reported as Implicit Price Deflators (IPDs). An implicit price deflator is a measure of inflation—an index that works like any other financial index (see *Financial Indexes*, page 101), with a base year (in this case 1996) equal to 100. If prices go down, the IPD dips below 100. If prices rise, as they usually do, the IPD will be over 100. These figures can be off-putting, since the percentage symbol is not used and one doesn't normally deal with percentages over 100. But all you really need to do is subtract 100 from the figures over 100; for example, the implicit price deflator for the 2000 GDP was 106.9, showing that prices had risen overall 6.9 percent since 1996.

One last word here: people sometimes confuse the gross domestic product with "gross domestic profit." The GDP is the retail price paid for everything. When you deduct what it cost to produce the goods and services, you get the *net domestic product*, which is basically gross domestic *profit*. It is net domestic product that interests economists in the long run, but it takes longer to collect the cost data than it does the price data, so they make do with the

GDP for the short run, knowing that the NDP is usually a predictable amount less than the GDP.

> ▶ For a wealth of BEA information, go to http://www.bea.doc.gov. For an excellent summary of the past six years, go to the Political Reference Almanac at http://www.polisci.com/almanac/economics/rgdp.htm.

HATS

WHY MIGHT A MAN with a largish head wear a size 8 hat, while a small-headed woman would be apt to wear a size 21? Both numbers represent inches, but a man's hat size measures the hat, while a woman's measures the head. Here's how it works.

If you took the oval formed by the inside band of a man's hat, pushed it into a circle and then measured that circle's diameter, you would get the man's hat size. The perfectly round hat blocks used until about 1800 can be blamed for this awkward system— before that time, men's hats were made perfectly round, and men used special devices called hat screws to force their hats into a more comfortable oval before wearing them. Today men's hats are head-shaped, but the sizing system remains, in increments of $1/8$ inch, the most common size being $7\frac{1}{8}$.

Women's hats, on the other hand, are a measure of the circumference of the head that hat is designed to fit, with the measuring tape pulled just under the curve of the skull in back and across the forehead in front. Using this method, the measure of a woman's head is usually somewhere between 20 inches and $23\frac{1}{2}$ inches, the most common being 22. These measures translate directly into women's hat sizes, and sometimes into men's as well.

HEART RATE

···

YOUR HEART HAS plenty of work to do, its task being to pump blood through about a hundred thousand miles of blood vessels. To accomplish this, the average man's heart beats 70 to 80 times per minute, which (using the 70 figure) adds up to about 4,200 times an hour, more than 100,000 times a day. But the resting heartbeat of a normal human being changes from birth to old age, looking something like this:

Age	Normal pulse/minute
Newborn	As high as 110 to 160
7-year-old	About 90
Adult	60 to 80
Older people	50 to 65 not unusual

For the normal adult, the slower the resting heart rate, the stronger and more efficient the heart is considered to be, processing more oxygen with less work. You should also know your optimum heart rate, at which many health experts recommend exercising at least three times a week for 20 to 30 minutes, especially if you are concerned about putting too much stress on your heart during particularly aerobic activities such as jogging, tennis, and other sports. Use this formula to find your optimum heart rate—or close to it :

How to Establish Your Optimum Exercise Heart Rate

1. Subtract your age from the number 220.

2. Multiply that figure by .70 to get your approximate optimum exercise heart rate.

(Your optimum heart rate will be between 60 percent and 75 percent of the total of #1)

Example:

30-year-old: 220 − 30 = 190 x .70 = 133 optimum exercise heart rate

60-year-old: 220 − 60 = 160 x .70 = 112 optimum exercise heart rate

Of course, optimum heart rate is affected by factors other than your age, such as whether you are a beginner, intermediate, or advanced exerciser, your weight, and other health concerns. It's always wise to check with your health care provider in matters of the heart, to find out what he or she recommends for your optimum heart rate.

So how do you know when your heart reaches optimum excitement? You take your pulse, of course. Your pulse is caused by a stretching of the arteries that takes place after each heartbeat, most easily felt along the radial artery on your wrist. Can't find the right spot? Try this:

How to Take Your Pulse

1. Turn your left hand palm up in front of you.

2. Place the fingers of your right hand along the far side of the inside of your left arm, at the base of your thumb, just inside the outer edge of your forearm bone.

3. Press lightly until you feel your pulse.

4. Use a watch with a second hand to count the beats for 10 seconds. Multiply by 6.

▶ **For a clearly illustrated, in-depth look at the human heart, go to Marshall Brain's website at http://www.howstuffworks.com/heart. For more on target heart rates, go to the Mayo Clinic website at http://www.mayoclinic.com and do a search for "target heart rates."**

HIGHWAYS

••

THERE'S A MANUAL put out by the U.S. Department of Transportation's Federal Highway Administration called *Manual on Uniform Traffic Control Devices for Streets and Highways*. The introduction to this document emphasizes that the Secretary of Transportation is acting under congressional authority when decreeing that "traffic control devices on all streets and highways in each State shall be in substantial conformance with the standards set forth." This sounds as if there were a nationally consistent system for highway markers and signs, and if you just knew what it was, you wouldn't be confused by numbers you've never been able to make sense of.

The problem is that the federal government isn't actually responsible for highway signs. That responsibility lies with what the manual admits is "a multitude of governmental jurisdictions," beginning with state governments and extending to counties and state highway districts. Although this multitude is required to pay attention to the federal manual, the reality is that "substantial conformance" ends up meaning "sometimes but not when too inconvenient." The result has been hundreds of highway labeling systems, even though there is a move to make signs more consistent throughout the country.

There are, however, some numbers that *are* part of a system, and once you see the big picture, the numbers make sense. Here are a few of the numbered signs you might have wondered about:

DISTANCE SIGN

LAMAR 15
EADS 51
LIMON 133

Source: Federal Highway Administration, U.S. Department of Transportation

Distance Signs

When you see this sign (page 135), are you 133 miles from the *edge* of Limon or 133 miles from the *center*? The question seems worth answering, but it turns out that the Federal Highway Administration doesn't care. Each state, or some agency within the state, sets its own rules. The result is not only inconsistency among states, but inconsistency *within* states.

For example, years ago, when California's American Automobile Association was in charge of California's highway distance signs, the mileage between cities was consistently city hall to city hall. This system is so elegant, so sensible, that one yearns to believe it could still be true. When the State of California took over the job, however, it gave each of its twelve districts jurisdiction over highway signs, so now the mileage may be *from city limit to city limit* or *from city hall to city hall.*

So how do you know if you are umpteen miles from the edge of town or umpteen miles from the center? You don't.

Interstate Route Numbers

Here are some numbers that do make sense, at least much of the time. Interstate highways were originally conceived during the Eisenhower administration as a measure of national defense. Built to connect the major military installations and cities of the country (cities with a population of fifty thousand or more), the name of the interstate system was the National System of Interstate and Defense Highways. These highways were designed to carry large military equipment—overpasses had to clear sixteen feet to accommodate the largest missile anyone at that time could conceive of transporting on wheels.

In the beginning Congress limited the interstate system to 41,000 miles; later 1,500 more miles were added, bringing today's total to 42,500 miles, a figure expected to be final. Today it connects 86 percent of the major U.S. cities. Five of its routes are more than 2,000 miles in length. Three run from coast to coast (I-10, I-80, and I-90), and seven run from border to border (I-5, I-15, I-35, I-55, I-65, I-75, and I-95).

The interstate highway route numbers are posted on blue shields with red tops and white lettering. The main north-south highways are always odd numbers with one or two digits. The lowest numbers begin with the West Coast's Interstate 5, increasing as you move east and ending with the East Coast's Interstate 95. Most of these north-south routes have a "5" in the route number somewhere. For example, as you move cross-country, you find routes 5, 15, 25, 35, 45, 55, 65, 75, 85, and 95, with only a few exceptions. The east-west highways are always even numbers with one or two digits. The lowest numbers begin in the south with Florida's Route 4, increasing as you move north and ending with Interstate Route 96. Coast-to-coast (or nearly coast-to-coast) east-west interstates end with a zero; e.g., routes 10, 20, 40, 70, 80, and 90.

An interstate with three digits is either a connector to or an offshoot from the main route. The first number is followed by the interstate route number it's associated with; e.g., Interstate 580 begins and ends on Interstate 80.

INTERSTATE SIGN   **U.S. ROUTE SIGN**

Source: Federal Highway Administration, U.S. Department of Transportation

U.S. Routes

The U.S. routes are posted on the familiar black-on-white badge-shaped signs. The north-south U.S. routes are still odd-numbered, but with one to three digits.

State and County Routes

Each state chooses its own sign to indicate the route number of state highways, and counties do the same for county roads. Generally, odd-numbered routes are north-south and even-numbered routes are east-west, but don't depend on it. There are plenty of exceptions.

STATE ROUTE SIGNS

| Utah | New York | North Dakota |

Source: Federal Highway Administration, U.S. Department of Transportation

Mileposts

If you ever tried to make sense of those signs that may or may not show up every mile at the side of the road, you may have given up by now. That's okay. They're not there for you. Each state installs these markers to serve mostly as reference points, used by highway patrol officers to locate accidents, by highway departments to locate road signs, and by highway maintenance crews. The green mileposts with white numbers often are readable, however; they measure the distance from either the beginning of the route or the state line. Which state line depends on the state. Although the FHA manual suggests that the numbers begin at the junctions where routes begin or at the south and west state lines, the guidelines are not always followed.

The black-on-white mileposts are even more confusing. Put in by local counties or highway districts, they often run from county line to county line, between highway district borders, or along some strange little road that begins and ends nowhere special. Trying to understand what these signs mean may be amusing if not taken too seriously. Often they measure highway maintenance districts, or distance from a county line.

Interchanges

The Federal Highway Administration favors numbering the interchanges on large highways with mileage numbers, using the interchange's distance from the state line, the beginning of the route, the beginning of the toll road, or some other reference point. Some highway interchanges are numbered in sequence, e.g., 1, 2, 3, 4, making it awkward to add to a new one, say, between 1 and 2. Still, many highways don't number the interchanges at all.

▶ **For a website created by Robert V. Droz, passionately devoted to U.S. highways and their histories, maps, etc., go to http://www.us-highways.com. To find highway signs typical of other countries, go to a website by James Lin at http://www.ugcs.caltech.edu/~jlin/signs.**

HORSES
••

HERE'S A NEW SPIN on the decimal point: a horse that stands 16.3 hands high at the withers is not 16³/10 hands. It is 16 hands plus 3 inches high, or, one hand equaling 4 inches, a total of 67 inches. The number after the "decimal" point means, in this case, not tenths but inches, so it never goes above 3.

The *hand* dates back possibly five thousand years as a handy, portable measure for horse traders. At some point, with possible help from the ancient Egyptians, for whom the hand measure was described as five *digits* (fingers) and a palm as four digits, four inches became the accepted standard for the hand as a measure for horses.

Today only English-speaking countries, including the United States, Canada, Great Britain, and Australia, use the hand measure almost exclusively; other countries measure their horses in centimeters; e.g., 16.3 hands equals 170 centimeters. The number after a plus sign (+) that sometimes follows the centimeter figure (e.g., 170 + 3) represents the height to which a young horse is expected to grow.

Horses are measured for height at the highest point above the hips. Of the more than one hundred equine breeds, there are three major categories, differentiated, at least in part, by height:

Type of Equine	Height in Hands
Ponies	10 to 14.2
Light horses	14.2 to 17
Heavy (draft) horses	16 to 18, or 15.2 to 19 (sources differ)

▶ **For an excellent article on the history of horse measurement, see "The 'Hand' Measurement" by Greg Unger at http://www.gov.on.ca/ omafra/english/livestock/horses/facts/info_hands.htm.**

HUMIDITY

WHEN A LOCAL NEWS REPORT informs you that today's humidity is 95 percent, what does this really mean? Ninety-five percent of what? If the air were 95 percent water, you'd need an ark, and even then you couldn't breathe.

This "humidity" figure should always be called "relative humidity," because it does not refer directly to the percentage of moisture in the air, but to how close the air is to its saturation point, which changes with the air temperature. The relative humidity of 95 percent on a hot day probably translates into just under 4 percent moisture content. This 4 percent is as much moisture as the air can hold at that temperature. As the air is cooled, the relative humidity increases. At a relative humidity of 100 percent—called the *dew point*—the air must release some of its moisture as dew, clouds, or fog.

Therefore the dew point figure—the temperature at which air at a certain relative humidity will condense—is a more accurate way to measure the humidity, which explains why it is usually included in weather reports these days. Find on the chart below the dew points of air at its many combinations of temperature and relative humidity:

Dew Point Chart

Air Temp. °F	Percent Relative Humidity																		
	100	95	90	85	80	75	70	65	60	55	50	45	40	35	30	25	20	15	10
110	110	108	106	104	102	100	98	95	93	90	87	84	80	76	72	65	60	51	41
105	105	103	101	99	97	95	93	91	88	85	83	80	76	72	67	62	55	47	37
100	100	99	97	95	93	91	89	86	84	81	78	75	71	67	63	58	52	44	32
95	95	93	92	90	88	86	84	81	79	76	73	70	67	63	59	54	48	40	32
90	90	88	87	85	83	81	79	76	74	71	68	65	62	59	54	49	43	36	32
85	85	83	81	80	78	76	74	72	69	67	64	61	58	54	50	45	38	32	
80	80	78	77	75	73	71	69	67	65	62	59	56	53	50	45	40	35	32	
75	75	73	72	70	68	66	64	62	60	58	55	52	49	45	41	36	32		
70	70	68	67	65	63	61	59	57	55	53	50	47	44	40	37	32			
65	65	63	62	60	59	57	55	53	50	48	45	42	40	36	32				
60	60	58	57	55	53	52	50	48	45	43	41	38	35	32					
55	55	53	52	50	49	47	45	43	40	38	36	33	32						
50	50	48	46	45	44	42	40	38	36	34	32								
45	45	43	42	40	39	37	35	33	32										
40	40	39	37	35	34	32													
35	35	34	32																
32	32																		

The most accurate way to measure the moisture content of the air, of course, is to extract and weigh all the water from an air sample. This process is too lengthy to be useful to most meteorologists, who would like to predict the weather before it becomes yesterday's news. They depend instead on a variety of humidity-measuring instruments, called *hygrometers*. The oldest and most common of these, the hair hygrometer, uses one or more human hairs, because of their incredible sensitivity to humidity—human hair increases its length by about 2½ percent as the relative humidity increases from 0 to 100 percent, which explains why that nice springy hairdo goes limp on a humid day. (For an explanation of "humiditure," or the effects of humidity on the human body in high temperatures, see *Comfort Index*, page 56.)

▶ To find the Celsius version of the dew point chart, go to the Lamtec Corporation website at http://www.lamtec.com/dew-point-calculator.htm.

INSULATION

IF YOU WANT TO INSULATE your house and don't know your fourth R, you may want to get your feet warm, so to speak, before calling in the contractor. The language of insulation is *R-value*, a number that represents a material's *resistance* (hence the "R") *to heat flow.* An R-value (resistance to heat flow) equals the thickness in inches of a piece of material, divided by its thermal conductivity, or its ability to conduct heat. (Thermal conductivity is calculated using a formula involving hours, area in square feet, degrees Fahrenheit, and Btu's.) Nearly everything has an R-value—a piece of paper, a piece of cloth, your front door, a wall, and so on.

R-values applied to insulation are regulated by the U.S. Department of Energy (DOE). The higher the R-value, or heat resistance, of a piece of material, the more effectively it will insulate. For example, the higher the R-value of the exterior walls of your house, the less heat can escape it. An exterior wall should have a minimum R-value of 11. If there is room in the walls for only three inches of insulation, you'll need to use an insulation with an R-value of at least 3.7 per inch to give you a total R-value of about 11 (3.7 times 3 inches).

It's important to remember R-values, especially if you're discussing your home's insulating problems with a contractor. Don't talk thickness—talk R-values. Although thickness contributes to heat resistance, the R-value is actually a combination of thickness and type of material.

How to Determine Your Insulation Needs

1. *Find your zone.* Most books and pamphlets use a map with wavy lines to divide the country into insulation zones. If you're on a line or want more accurate, specific information, the Department of Energy has assigned insulation zones to ZIP codes (see URL at the end of this entry).

2. *Determine your R-value needs.* Once you know your insulation zone number, determine the minimum R-values your home may require. Your heating fuel source—gas or electricity—will also affect your choice.

3. *Choose your insulation type.* There are four main kinds of insulation:
   Blankets or batts (rock wool or fiberglass) are fitted between exposed wood-frame studs, joists, and beams; they can be used in all exposed walls, floors, and ceilings and are good for do-it-yourself jobs.
   Loose fill (rock wool, fiberglass, cellulose fiber, vermiculite, or perlite) is poured between attic joists and can be used in attic floors and hard-to-reach places. This process can also be done yourself.
   Blown fill (rock wool, fiberglass, cellulose fiber, or ureaformaldehyde foam) is blown into finished areas and can be used anywhere that the frame is covered on both sides, such as walls.
   Rigid insulation (fiberglass or extruded polystyrene board) is installed by a contractor with 1/2-inch gypsum board for fire safety; it is best for basement masonry walls.

4. *Determine the number of inches of insulation you will need of your insulation choice to reach your R-value goal.* The DOE offers all kinds of charts and instructional material, printed and online, to guide

with insulation choices and amounts. Your public library is another good source.

▶ **For a great deal of information on every aspect of home insulating, go to the Department of Energy's "Insulation Fact Sheet" at http://www.ornl.gov/roofs+walls/insulation. For more information on types of insulation, go to http://www.eren.doe.gov/consumerinfo/wx.html. To find an insulation for your home based on your ZIP code and type of heating, go to http://www.ornl.gov/~roofs/Zip/ZipHome.html.**

ISBNs

EVERY EDITION of every book is assigned a distinct ten-digit number called an ISBN, or International Standard Book Number. You can live a meaningful life without understanding ISBNs—they were once used fairly exclusively by librarians and booksellers for ordering books. But an ISBN can help you find exactly the book you want online, from a bookseller, or even in an interlibrary loan request.

THE
BACK COVER OF A
PAPERBACK BOOK

Blurb describing the
irresistible contents of this
indispensable volume!

ISBN 0-14-010654-5

The International Standard Book Number, often printed on book covers and always on the copyright page (see page 69), was adopted by American book publishers in 1967 and by the International Standards Organization in 1969 to facilitate ordering by computer.

ISBN 0-14-010654-5

0	The first digit is the area of origin. 0 means that the book was published in an English-speaking country. A 4 would indicate a Spanish-speaking country, and so on.
14	The second group represents the publisher.
01065	This third group is the book's title, assigned by the publisher.
5	The last number, called the check digit (see page 21), alerts the computer operator to errors in the previous numbers.

An ISBN is not usually required for consumer requests, but if it's handy, use it to expedite any book search. Amazon.com provides the ISBNs for its books, as does the World Catalog, available through your public or academic library.

▶ To apply for an ISBN for an independently published book, go to the R. R. Bowker ISBN application page at http://www.isbn.org/standards/home/index.asp.

KNITTING NEEDLES
••

KNITTING NEEDLES have a long history, and apparently their sizes once kind of made sense: in England, they were first based roughly on the Great Britain Standard Wire Gauges. Today, knitting needle numbers depend on what country, and sometimes what company, makes them. Knitting needles must, of course, at least somewhat correspond to knitting patterns, but while metric and U.S. sizes go up as the needles get thicker, U.K./Canadian size numbers go down. (See chart on next page.)

▶ For a complete chart of knitting needle sizes that includes "old" U.S. sizes (used in old pattern books), go to the Fiber Gypsy at http://www.fibergypsy.com/common/needles.shtml, or Yarn Forward at http://www.yarnforward.com/needleconv.html. An amusing search for knitting references in books may be found at http://www.woolworks.org/bookref.html.

Metric Sizes (mm)	U.S. Sizes	U.K./Canadian
2.0	0	14
2.25	1	13
2.75	2	12
3.0	–	11
3.25	3	10
3.5	4	–
3.75	5	9
4.0	6	8
4.5	7	7
5.0	8	6
5.5	9	5
6.0	10	4
6.5	10¹/₂	3
7.0	–	2
7.5	–	1
8.0	11	0
9.0	13	00
10.0	16	000
12.0	17	–
16.0	19	–
19.0	35	–
25.0	50	–

Source: Yarn Forward (http://www.yarnforward.com).
Used with permission.

LAND MEASURES

BEFORE THE RENAISSANCE, English property was measured in *feet, rods, furlongs, acres,* and *hides,* and it still is, sort of. The rod, also known as a *perch* or a *pole,* began as an actual 10-foot pole (for the odd history of feet, see *Length, Common Short,* page 151), but by the late 1400s it was a distance of 16¹/₂ feet, and remains that to this day. The furlong, once the width of 32 plowed rows, today equals 40 rods.

It's the acre that's most familiar, since it survives as our most popular unit for estimating the size of a nice piece of land. When the word "acre" first popped into the English language, borrowed from the Latin, it merely meant a largish piece of useful farmland. By medieval times, an acre was the amount of land that a pair of oxen could plow in one day, although in some areas an acre was measured by the amount of seed required to farm it. A *hide*, no longer used, referred to the amount an ox team could plow in a year—about 120 acres.

There were obvious problems with this—a pair of aging oxen faced with heavy soil and nasty weather plowed a much smaller acre or hide than a young, feisty pair working rich soil in the sunshine. By the 1400s the acre equaled 43,560 square feet by royal decree, a measure that has survived almost six hundred years to measure our land as well. This is how land is now measured:

Length:	$16\frac{1}{2}$ feet	= 1 rod
	40 rods	= 1 furlong (660 feet)
	8 furlongs	= 1 mile
Area:	1 acre	= 43,560 square feet (160 square rods)
	640 acres	= 1 square mile

A small plot of land, such as an average-size city lot, is usually measured in *square feet* instead of some part of an acre. Curiously, square yards are rarely used.

▶ For an area conversion calculator (e.g., to convert acres to square kilometers), go to the Go Convert website at http://www.goconvert.com/cgi-bin/area.asp. For more information on the acre and other ancient measures, go to "Mists of Antiquity" at the Baronage website, at http://www.baronage.co.uk/bphtm-02/moa-10.html.

LATITUDE AND LONGITUDE
••

IF YOU'RE AMONG the many persons alive today who think they know one thing for sure, that in 1492 Columbus discovered for the first time that the earth was round—you're wrong. Columbus did help steer the world out of the medieval period of ignorance, when scientific knowledge was suppressed, but early civilizations as far back as 5000 B.C. assumed the world was round, and by 200 B.C. talk of the equator and the Northern and Southern Hemispheres was common. A Greek librarian named Eratosthenes even measured the equator 2,200 years ago by using the sun, a well, a vertical column, and some camels. He came up with a figure of 28,700 miles, truly in the ballpark (the correct measure is 24,902 miles).

Eratosthenes is known today in mapping circles as the father of *geodesy*—the science of earth measurement. He was the first to chart the earth with parallel east-west and north-south lines, although he did not place them at regular intervals. Hipparchus of Nicaea soon did, making a grid of 360 north-south lines that went from pole to pole and 180 lines circling the earth, each parallel to the equator. (See *Circles*, page 49.) Hipparchus's north-south lines ran from the North Pole to the South Pole and were called *meridians*, a word that meant "noon," for when it is noon on one part of a line, it is noon at any other point as well. Meridians were used to measure *longitude*, or how far east or west a particular place might be, and were 70 miles apart at the equator, making the equator 25,200 miles long, only 298 miles off the mark.

The east-west lines were called *parallels*, and unlike meridians, were all parallel to each other and measured *latitude*, or how far north or south a particular place might be. There were 180 lines circling the earth, one for each degree of latitude.

The system has survived for the most part—the meridians are now about 69 miles apart at the equator and the parallels are 69 miles apart, but the lines in both directions are still separated by one degree.

The Wandering Prime Meridian

Although meridians and parallels appeared on maps for hundreds of years, there was a perplexing problem: when numbering the lines of longitude, where did one start? This was no problem for latitude—the equator was the obvious choice for 0° latitude. But where did one put the Prime Meridian, or 0° longitude?

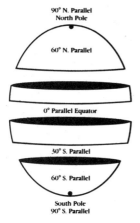

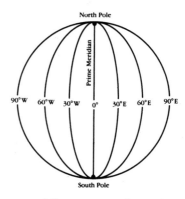

Parallels slice the earth like an onion.

Meridians section the earth like an orange.

Until an amazingly short time ago—about 120 years—the location of the Prime Meridian was a matter of patriotism: each country simply ran it through its own capital, numbering its maps accordingly. The Prime Meridian has run through Paris, Madrid, Cracow, Copenhagen, Rome, Augsburg, Beijing, St. Petersburg, Washington, and Greenwich, England. In 1884 the first International Meridian Conference finally put the Prime to rest at the Royal Observatory in Greenwich, England, where it has remained to this day. At last, time zones could be assigned to the world, impossible without an agreed-upon Prime Meridian. (See *Time Zones*, page 246.) All the lines could now be numbered the same way on all maps, and coordinates for all places in the world would be standard.

Reading Coordinates

To understand how to use coordinates, look at a globe. Longitudes east of the Prime Meridian (running through England) are numbered 1° E to 179° E (180° is the halfway point, near the International Date Line); those west are lettered 1° W to 179° W. Likewise, latitudes north of the equator are numbered 1° N to 90° (the North Pole); those south of the equator are numbered 1° S to 90° S (the South Pole). Latitudes are easy to find, as they are marked on the metal meridian. Longitudes are more difficult, usually marked along the equator. (Note that not all the meridians and parallels are put in.)

THE WESTERN WORLD BY LATITUDE AND LONGITUDE

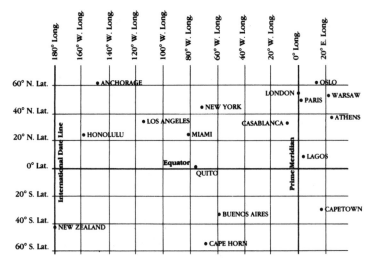

The Prime Meridian runs through Greenwich, England

Each degree of latitude or longitude is divided into 60 *minutes* and each minute can be divided into 60 *seconds*. Usually minutes are symbolized by a straight apostrophe (60') and seconds with ditto marks (60"). Sometimes, though, they're written like a decimal; however, 11.46 N, a latitude reading, is *not* a decimal, as the number after the "decimal point" indicates minutes, so it's never higher than 59. The same goes for seconds.

Coordinates are two sets of numbers, one for latitude and one for longitude; the latitude is usually written first. To find coordinates on a globe, use the longitude reading to find the correct meridian, and line it up with the metal meridian, the guide bar found on all globes. Now read the latitude on the metal bar and bingo! You're there!

▶ To find the latitude and longitude for U.S. geological features, go to the USGS at http://geonames.usgs.gov/index.html. To find the latitude and longitude of almost any U.S. ZIP code, go to the U.S. Census Bureau at http://www.census.gov/cgi-bin/gazetteer. To find the coordinates for major world cities as well as the distances (as the crow flies) between them, go to Bali & Indonesia on the Net at http://www.indo.com/distance.

LENGTH, COMMON SHORT

MOST PEOPLE ASSUME that the American system of measuring the length of everyday things is based on the foot. But exactly how long is a foot? Twelve inches, yes, but how long is an inch? One thirty-sixth of a yard? But how long is the yard? These are not stupid questions. Perfectly intelligent people have been asking them for hundreds of years, and none of the many answers has been without problems.

Two of the earliest measurements were the width of a man's thumb for the inch and the length of his foot for the foot. The tools couldn't have been handier and the system was user friendly, but people with different-sized feet couldn't do business. So in Egypt official measuring sticks the length of the king's foot were distributed. However, each new ruler changed all the measures, a frustrating custom that spread northward through Europe. Finally, in the fourteenth century, King Edward I set a standard by producing a yard based on his ample girth. Yardsticks were made and circulated. But standards continued to change (it was once changed to the distance from Queen Elizabeth I's nose to the end of her longest finger), and scientists began demanding more uniformity and precision.

At last France proposed the metric system in 1791, based on the distance of a line running from the equator, through Paris, to the North Pole. A meter, calculated to be one ten-millionth of this distance, was set into platinum and kept at Sèvres, France, at the International Bureau of Standards. By the beginning of this century, most of the world used the metric system.

But even the meter was in trouble. Truly exacting scientific measurements required something more accurate than a length of metal that could change with time and temperature. In 1960 the meter was changed to equal 1,650,763.73 wavelengths in a vacuum of the orange-red line of the spectrum of the gas krypton-86. Although the krypton-86 system was accurate to one ten-millionth of an inch, it was not useful for lengths over 8 inches, so the measure was changed again. Today's meter, official since 1983, is measured by laser and is equal to the length of the path traveled by light in a vacuum during a time interval of $1/299,792,458$ of an atomic second. This meter can be reproduced in science laboratories.

Congress based our American yardstick on the meter, so when the meter changes, our yardstick changes with it. Since 1959, the yard has been equal to 0.9144 of a meter. (See also *Metric System*, page 160.)

There is a way to spell relief from these tediously exact measures: i-n-c-h. The inch is by no means sacred, and although it's been customary for centuries to use binary (based on 2) fractions such as $1/2$, $1/4$, $1/8$, etc., there is nothing official about it and nothing special about sixteenths. However, when you're using a pocket calculator, *decimal inches* are far easier to work with than the awkward fractions presented by more traditional inch divisions. It's becoming more and more common to divide the inch into tenths, called a decimal inch. Industries usually employ the decimal inch (unless, of course, they've gone metric) and machinists routinely measure their work in thousandths of an inch, or *mils* (1 mil = $^1/_{1,000}$ of an inch). The thickness of plastic bags, for example, is measured in mils—a 2-mil garbage bag is about $^1/_{512}$ of an inch by the fractional system. *Microinches* are used to measure the roughness or smoothness of a surface.

▶ **For a time line by William B. Penzes on the definition of the meter, go to the website of the National Institute of Standards and Technology, http://www.mel.nist.gov/div821/museum/timeline.htm.**

LIGHTBULBS

UNTIL RECENTLY you probably never read the packages that incandescent lightbulbs came in except for the large-print wattage, which is how lightbulbs are sized. You put a 40-watt bulb in the closet, a 60-watt bulb in the hall, and a 100-watt bulb next to your reading chair, and that was that. Then, despite the fact that you had never complained about lightbulbs, the companies that made them began to complicate one of the few remaining simple chores in American life by offering you "improvements." Now you can buy "long-life" bulbs, "extended service" bulbs, and krypton "energy-saver" bulbs. To make the choice even more difficult, companies you never heard of are offering bargain-priced bulbs, leaving you unsure of what you're getting. If you really want to know, you have to start reading the package.

Every lightbulb package gives at least three pieces of information: wattage, lumens, and life expectancy. The *wattage* is not brightness, but a measure of the electricity you'll pay for when you use the bulb (see *Electricity,* page 82). Average *lumens* is the brightness. One standard candle produces one lumen; one standard 100-watt lightbulb usually produces about 1,600 lumens. The *life expectancy* of the bulb is given in number of hours.

Extended life lightbulbs may have a life expectancy of up to 10,000 hours, as many as fluorescents. When you compare bulbs, you'll find there are trade-offs—you may sacrifice brightness (lumens) and a bargain price to get a longer life. Bargain-priced bulbs may be so low on lumens that a 100-watt bulb may not be much brighter than a standard 75-watt bulb. Lumen for lumen, standard bulbs are probably still a better buy than long-life bulbs, no matter what the wattage of the bulb. However, the convenience of longer-lived bulbs may also be attractive—you don't need to change them as often. Bargain-priced bulbs, on the other hand, really can be a bargain if the life expectancy is not reduced and the slightly dimmer (sometimes more yellow) light is tolerable to you.

It's interesting to note how much the use of a lightbulb really costs you. A 100-watt bulb will burn for 10 hours for the price of 1 kilowatt-hour of electricity (1 kilowatt hour runs 1 watt for 1,000 hours). If it burns out after 750 hours, that bulb cost you $7.50 in power (if your electric company is charging you 10 cents per kilowatt hour) plus the cost of the bulb. Lightbulbs may use only about a penny's worth of power an hour, but the cost adds up fast.

Incandescent bulb shapes are assigned letters: A is for the typical household bulb, B looks like a Christmas tree bulb, C is a night-light bulb, and so on.

Fluorescent bulbs are an alternative for large areas, giving two to three times the lumens per watt of power than incandescent bulbs. Compact fluorescent light (CFL) bulbs, pushed hard by many environmentally conscious organizations and energy companies, have become available in shapes, sizes, and wattages to fit most lamps and light fixtures. Compact fluorescents can provide a soft warm color, cost about 75 percent less in the long run (but startlingly expensive for the initial purchase) than many incandescent bulbs, and boast a life of about 10,000 hours.

A full lightbulb education these days deserves its own book. Lightbulb companies keep offering new lightbulb choices. A recent favorite is the "blue" bulb that apparently makes colors "pop." If the colors in your home lack snap, you may not need to redecorate—just change the lightbulbs!

▶ For advice on replacing incandescent bulbs with more energy-efficient fluorescent bulbs, go to the Department of Energy's PDF file "How to Buy Energy-Efficient Compact Fluorescent Light Bulbs," at http://www.eren.doe.gov/femp/procurement/pdfs/cfl.pdf. To calculate your savings by switching to fluorescents, go to the San Diego Earth Times "High-Efficiency Fluorescent Light Cost Savings Calculator Usage," by Chris Klein, at http://www.sdearthtimes.com/ET_Lighting_Calc.html.

LUMBER

BECAUSE THERE ARE so many ways to grade lumber, depending on type, size, and/or use, few people can be expected to understand them. Redwood alone is graded by the California Redwood Association into six basic grades with more than fifty offshoots. Hardwood is graded differently from softwood, "shop" grades differ from "remanufacture" grades, which differ from construction grades, and so on. Once graded, lumber can be regraded after processing. If you're starting cold at the lumber yard, you may need more than a brief introduction.

However, there are two things that might help you when deciding what type of lumber to buy. The first is understanding the difference between *linear feet* and *board feet*. There is great variation in what kind of lumber is sold in board feet and what's sold in linear feet, but all you really need to know is how to figure each of them out.

Linear Feet. If a board is priced at $1.00 per linear foot, you will be charged $1.00 for every foot of that board that you buy, no matter what size the board is. This is as easy as it sounds. Surfaced lumber (partially finished, not rough-sawed) is often sold by the linear foot.

Board Feet (BF). Rough lumber is often sold by the board foot. A board foot is a piece of wood measuring 1 inch thick, 12 inches wide, and 12 inches long, i.e., a square foot 1 inch thick.

Most lumber sold by the board foot is not a convenient 1 inch thick and 12 inches wide, but you still need to figure out the board feet if you want to know how much the lumber will cost you. Here's the formula:

$$\frac{\text{thickness in inches} \times \text{width in inches} \times \text{length in feet}}{12}$$

This really works. Try it: you have a board 1 inch thick, 6 inches wide, and 8 feet long priced at $.50/BF. What will it cost you? Set up in the formula, it looks like this:

$$\frac{1 \text{ (thickness in inches)} \times 6 \text{ (width in inches)} \times 8 \text{ (length in feet)}}{12}$$

$$^{48}/12 = 4 \text{ board feet}$$
$$4 \text{ board feet} \times \$.50/\text{BF} = \$2.00 \text{ total cost for the board}$$

The second thing you should understand is that all lumber is measured *in the rough*, so if you buy a 2 × 4 in rough lumber, it will measure 2 inches by 4 inches. If you buy it "surfaced," it will lose some of the original wood in the finishing process, making it measure more like $1^{1}/2 \times 3^{1}/2$ inches. The rule of thumb used by many who frequent lumber yards is this: when you buy surfaced lumber, you normally lose about $^{1}/4$ inch (for 1-inch boards) to $^{1}/2$ inch (for 2-inch boards) in thickness and about $^{1}/2$ inch in width.

Now, about those grades. "Clears" are boards with no knots and are usually quite expensive. "Select" boards are of a lesser quality lumber than clears, but the defects are minor, with defects or knots under two inches.

Construction lumber is often graded as follows:

2-Inch-Thick Lumber Only	Description
No. 1 (Construction)	Many knots, all under 2 inches
No. 2 (Standard)	Many knots, up to $3^{1}/2$ inches
No. 3 (Utility)	Allows open knots, splits, pitch
No. 4 (Economy)	Lowest grade

Most other lumber is subject to a complex grading system with each type of lumber—ponderosa pine, redwood, cherry, etc.—graded differently. The "Standard Specifications for Grades of California Redwood Lumber" is over 100 pages long. It's no wonder the novice woodworker gets confused.

▶ To translate commercial lumber nominal sizes to actual sizes, go to the Engineer's Edge at http://www.engineersedge.com/commercial_lumber_sizes.htm. To convert from nominal to actual and metric dimension, go to http://www.gulfsouthforest.com/english/metricconversion.htm.

METRIC PREFIXES

BEFORE 1960, when the International System of Units, abbreviated SI (from the French Système International d'Unités) was established by the 11th General Conference on Weights and Measures, a "mega-something" was, for most people, the biggest something they could think of. And why not? *Mega-* is a prefix meaning million. Millionaires made megabucks, megahertz measured radio waves, and a megaphone impressively amplified sound. However, *mega-* can't begin to measure our galaxy, much less the universe. Today there are twenty SI prefixes, ten for big and ten for small.

Prefixes for the Astronomical

Many of these prefixes, although they sound terribly scientific, are rather charmingly based on Greek synonyms for "really large": for example, *kilo-* comes from the Greek word for "thousand," *mega-* from "great," *tera-* from "monster," and *exa-* from "beyond." Although the prefixes are used with metric measures, making teragrams and gigameters and such, it's sometimes acceptable to attach them to nonmetric measures, to make kilowatt hours and megatons. There are exceptions, especially when used with binary numbers. Metric prefixes have a slightly different meaning in the world of computers (see *Computers, Personal*, page 63).

SI Prefixes (for Large)

Prefix	Symbol	Exponent*	Number
yotta	Y	10^{24}	1,000,000,000,000,000,000,000,000
zetta	Z	10^{21}	1,000,000,000,000,000,000,000
exa	E	10^{18}	1,000,000,000,000,000,000
peta	P	10^{15}	1,000,000,000,000,000
tera	T	10^{12}	1,000,000,000,000
giga	G	10^{9}	1,000,000,000
mega	M	10^{6}	1,000,000
kilo	k	10^{3}	1,000
hecto	h	10^{2}	100
deca	da	10^{1}	10

*See *Exponents,* page 91.

Prefixes for the Minuscule

However far astronomers have peered into the universe, particle physicists have reached just as far into the minuscule. Hardly anything is more difficult to comprehend than the unseeable structure of the visible world. Still, you're probably not bothered by things "microscopic," since you *can* see them through a microscope. *Micro-*, meaning "*millionth*," for many years meant "incredibly small, about as small as you can get," with spies hiding messages on microdots and libraries reducing vast newspaper collections to microfilm. But *micro-* in today's known invisible world is a large and unwieldy prefix. Unimaginably finer prefixes are now required.

To keep from confusing these prefixes for divided numbers with those for large numbers, remember that most of the prefixes for small numbers end with "i" or "o," while, except for *hecto-* and *kilo-*, those for large numbers end with "a."

The dividing prefixes are usually applied to metric measures, like meters, grams, even seconds. One exception is the decimal inch, which can be divided into *microinches.* (See *Length, Common Short,* page 151.) Although hours are divided by sixty to make min-

SI Prefixes (Dividing)

Prefix	Symbol	Exponent*	Number
deci	d	10^{-1}	0.1
centi	c	10^{-2}	0.01
milli	m	10^{-3}	0.001
micro	μ	10^{-6}	0.0001
nano	n	10^{-9}	0.000000001
pico	p	10^{-12}	0.000000000001
femto	f	10^{-15}	0.000000000000001
atto	a	10^{-18}	0.000000000000000001
zepto	z	10^{-21}	0.000000000000000000001
yocto	y	10^{-24}	0.000000000000000000000001

*See *Exponents*, page 91.

utes and minutes are divided by sixty to make seconds, when seconds are divided, they go metric, splitting into *milliseconds, microseconds,* even *picoseconds.*

What could possibly be so small? To get an idea, make a dot by pressing the point of a pen or pencil on a piece of paper. This dot measures about 1 millimeter. It's small, but at least you can see it. Shrink the dot to 1 micrometer and you could still see it with a good optical microscope. But at .1 micrometer (100 nanometers) it would disappear, being smaller than the wavelength of visible light.

It's hard to believe that things as small as the following can be so accurately measured:

- An amoeba, which can be seen through an ordinary optical microscope, weighs about 5 micrograms.
- Wavelengths of visible light are measured in nanometers.
- A liver cell weighs about 2 nanograms.
- Subatomic particles are often measured in femtometers.
- Viruses must be measured in attometers.
- An electron weighs 0.0000000009 attogram.
- A neutrino, the smallest known mass, weighs 0.00000000000005 attogram.

So how small is small? If you have a virus that measures 1 attometer, you could sling 1,000,000,000,000,000 of those viruses across your penciled dot. Now, if you were to enlarge each of those viruses to the size of your millimeter dot and line them up end to end, they would stretch 1 billion kilometers (or 620,000,000 miles) into space, almost reaching Saturn!

▶ **For detailed information on SI prefixes, go to the "NIST Reference on Constants, Units, and Uncertainty" at http://physics.nist.gov/cuu/ Units/index.html.**

METRIC SYSTEM

LITTLE WREAKS MORE HAVOC on the average American nervous system than the threat of metrics, officially called the International System of Units (SI). You thought that the United States would never switch to the metric system, didn't you? That in the 1970s when metrics roared, grassroots America rose up and chased it off? Our holdout is hurting our wallets—more and more countries are refusing to buy our nonmetrically sized and packaged goods— and wallets usually have the last word. Whether you are aware of it or not, you have been edging, inching, even centimetering toward metrics. But it's not as bad as you think. You're already somewhat familiar with metrics. For starters, consider these things you deal with fairly automatically:

Item	Metric Measure
Electricity	Watt, volt, ampere, ohm
Radio frequencies	Hertz
Tar, nicotine, sodium, cholesterol, many vitamins and medicines	Milligram
Many tools and fasteners, blood pressure, cameras, film, binoculars	Millimeter
Engine capacity	Cubic centimeter

Actually, you've been using metrics secondhand all your life. When you measure by the yard, pound, and gallon, you are using converted meter, kilogram, and liter—by an act of Congress, our weights and measures have been based on the following metrics for over a hundred years.

Three Basic Metric Measures

Length. Although the metric system sounds modern, it's not new. The French made the first meter in 1791, calculating its length as a romantic one ten-millionth of a line running from the equator through Paris to the North Pole. A platinum meter was established with great care in a suburb of Paris at the International Bureau of Weights and Measures. Subsequently, more sophisticated measurements of the earth proved the first meter incorrect, so in 1889 a new bar, which was the length of the first but not based on any earthly measure, was substituted. But a bar can change minutely and is difficult to replicate with complete accuracy, so in 1960 scientists defined the meter as equaling the transition between the levels 2 p_{10} and 5 d_5 of the krypton-86 atom. Now the meter could be measured exactly in any properly equipped laboratory.

Today's meter, officially accepted in 1983, is equal to the length of the path traveled by light in a vacuum during the time interval of $1/299{,}792{,}458$ of a second. (See *Length, Common Short*, page 151.) Our yard has been officially defined as equal to 0.9144 meter.

Mass. What we think of as "weight" is "mass" in physics and in the U.S. Standards. The kilogram was first defined as the mass (weight) of one cubic decimeter of water at the temperature of maximum density. Scientists needing a more precise measure voted in 1875 at a General Conference on Weights and Measures to replace this with a cylinder of platinum-iridium alloy that was the same size but not based on anything, and was kept at the International Bureau of Weights and Measures. Our copy of the official kilogram, kept at the National Bureau of Standards, is the basis for our avoirdupois pound (the one you weigh yourself in), which officially equals 0.45359237 kilogram, or for general use, 0.454 kilogram.

Volume. The liter is not really a basic measure, since it is derived from the kilogram. It originally was the volume occupied by a kilogram of pure water. In 1964 the liter was redefined as a cubic decimeter of pure water, a measure that differed from the first by only 28 parts in a million. This new standard is important only in high precision measurements. The U.S. quart is equal to 1.101 liters.

The Metrification of America

The little-known truth is that the metric system has influenced U.S. measures since the year after the end of the Civil War (1866), when its use was made legal in this country. In 1893 the meter and kilogram officially became the basis of our weights and measures. Not much happened for a very long time after that until, in 1975, President Gerald Ford set up the U.S. Metric Board that was supposed to facilitate a switch from U.S. measures to metrics. That bill made the change voluntary, however, so little really happened—opposition was so heated that politicians feared for their seats. In 1982 President Reagan abolished the board. But metrics marches on. On July 25, 1991, President Bush issued Executive Order 12770, "Metric Usage in Federal Government Programs," mandating the transition to metric measurement for all federal agencies.

We are now not only the last English-speaking holdout— Britain, Australia, New Zealand, and even Canada have switched —but the only major nonmetric country in the world. Our dearly beloved system of weights and measures is becoming an international embarrassment and an economic liability.

You may feel out of control when you lose your gut feeling for the size and number of things. However, if metrics were the only system around, you'd quickly develop new gut feelings. American resistance to metrics is so passionate that you now have to cope with both systems. What could be more awkward? You have to speak metric but you think in United States. What you once figured in your head now requires a calculator. This mess is caused by our foot-dragging, and not because the metric system is difficult; in fact, nothing could be simpler.

Prefixes

Ten is the magic metric number—each power of ten is assigned a prefix, which can be attached to nearly any metric measure. This elegant simplicity, combined with the ease of metric math, has made the International System of Units the chosen system of the world. (For very high and very low metric measures, see *Metric Prefixes*, page 157.)

Prefix	Meaning	Examples
kilo-	= 1000	kilogram, kilometer, kiloliter
hecto-	= 100	hectogram, hectometer, hectoliter
deka-	= 10	dekagram, dekameter, dekaliter
(no prefix)	= 1	gram, meter, liter
deci-	= 0.1 ($1/10$)	decigram, decimeter, deciliter
centi-	= 0.01 ($1/100$)	centigram, centimeter, centiliter
milli-	= 0.001 ($1/1,000$)	milligram, millimeter, milliliter

The following common objects can help give you a feel for metric measures:

Item	Approximate Weight
A paper clip	1 gram
A dollar bill	1 gram
A dime	2 grams
A penny	3 grams
A nickel	5 grams
A quarter	6 grams
A 2-pound can of coffee	1 kilogram

Item	Approximate Length
A "fat yard" (a yard + a hand)	1 meter
The width of a paper-clip wire	1 millimeter
The width of a dime	1 millimeter
A sugar cube	1 cubic centimeter
The width of the smallest fingernail	1 centimeter

Item	Approximate Volume
A "fat quart" (1 quart + $^1/4$ cup)	1 liter

Until metric measures are the only measures used in America, however, you'll have to depend on conversion charts, like you would a foreign language dictionary. The awkward translations are probably to blame for the widespread misconception that the metric system is difficult.

U.S./Metric and Metric/U.S.

This information is included to give you a feeling for sizes; although you can use it to convert from one measure to another, the conversion factors that follow make quicker work of that chore.

1 acre	=	0.405 hectare
1 bushel	=	35.238 liters
1 centimeter (cm)	=	0.39 inch
1 foot	=	0.31 meter
1 inch	=	2.54 centimeters
1 gallon	=	3.785 liters
1 grain	=	0.0648 gram
1 gram (g)	=	0.035 ounce
1 hectare (ha)	=	2.47 acres
1 kilogram	=	2.2046 pounds
1 kilometer (km)	=	0.62 mile
1 liter (l, or L)	=	0.908 dry quart
	=	1.057 liquid quarts
1 meter (m)	=	39.37 inches

1 mile	=	1.609 kilometers
		or 1,609 meters
1 milligram (mg)	=	0.02 grain
1 milliliter (ml)	=	0.06 cubic inch
1 millimeter (mm)	=	0.04 inch
1 ounce	=	28.349 grams
1 (fluid) ounce	=	29.573 milliliters
1 (dry) pint	=	0.473 liter
1 pound	=	0.453 kilogram
1 (dry) quart	=	1.101 liters
1 (fluid) quart	=	0.946 liter
1 (long) ton	=	1.02 metric tons
1 (metric) ton	=	2,204.62 pounds
1 (short) ton (2,000 lb.)	=	0.907 metric ton
1 yard	=	0.914 meter

Conversion Factors

This fearsome chart is probably what killed metrics in the 1970s, but now you've got what it takes—a calculator (or see the end of this entry for online calculators).

When You Know This Unit	Multiply by This Number	To Get
acres	0.40	hectares
bushels	35.2	liters
centimeters	0.3937	inches
	0.03281	feet
cups	0.24	liters
cubic feet	0.028	cubic meters
cubic yards	0.765	cubic meters
cubic meters	35.3	cubic feet
	1.31	cubic yards
feet	30	centimeters
	0.3	meters
gallons	3.8	liters
grains	64.8	milligrams

When You Know This Unit	Multiply by This Number	To Get
grams	0.0353	ounces
hectares	2.47	acres
inches	2.54	centimeters
	25.4	millimeters
kilograms	2.2	pounds
kilometers	0.6	miles
kilometers per hour	0.621	miles per hour
liters	4.2	cups
	0.26	gallons
	2.1	pints
	1.0	quarts
meters	3.3	feet
	1.1	yards
	0.000621	miles
	0.00054	nautical miles
miles, statute	1.6	kilometers
	1,600	meters
miles, nautical	1,862	meters
miles per hour	1.609	kilometers/hour
milliliters	0.2	teaspoons
	0.067	tablespoons
	0.034	fluid ounces
millimeters	0.04	inches
ounces (fluid)	30	milliliters
ounces (dry)	28.3	grams
pints	0.47	liters
pounds	0.45	kilograms
quarts	0.95	liters
square centimeters	0.155	square inches
square feet	0.0929	square meters
square inches	6.45	square centimeters
square kilometers	0.4	square miles
square meters	1.2	square yards
square yards	0.836	square meters

When You Know This Unit	Multiply by This Number	To Get
tablespoons	15	milliliters
teaspoons	5	milliliters
tons, short (2,000 lb.)	0.9	metric tons
tons, metric	1.1	short tons
yards	0.9	meters

How to get rid of these annoying, terrifying, time-consuming charts? The answer is as simple as metrics itself—switch!

▶ **For excellent information on SI units, go to http://physics.nist.gov/ cuu/Units. To convert almost anything, even clothing sizes, viscosity, and more, go to http://www.onlineconversion.com. To simply calculate length, area, volume, weight, or temperature, go to the "Automated Metric Conversion Calculator" provided by Admiral Metals at http://www.admiralmetals.com/metric_conv.htm.**

MICROWAVE OVENS
••

WHEN YOU READ AN AD for a .8 cubic foot microwave oven, it's hard to visualize how big that really is—anything behind a decimal point sounds minuscule. Microwave ovens are sized by the cubic foot capacity of the interior, and a cubic foot is bigger than you may think.

What a Microwave Oven Will Hold

.4 cubic foot	a loaded salad plate
.6 cubic foot	a piled-high dinner plate
.8 cubic foot	a 5-lb. roast
1.6 cubic feet	an 18-lb. turkey

The exterior measurements vary from brand to brand:

.4 cubic foot	approx. 18" wide x 9" high x 15" deep
.6 cubic foot	approx. 18" wide x 11" high x 15" deep
1.4 to 1.6 cubic feet	approx. 25" wide x 14" high x 18" deep

The power for a microwave oven ranges from 509 watts (low) to 800 watts (high). Low-watt ovens cook more slowly than higher ones; e.g., a 500-watt oven takes about 8 minutes to bake a potato, while a 720-watt oven takes about 4 minutes. Microwave cooking times can change, depending on the power (watts) of your oven.

> ▶ To convert recipe timing from one oven wattage to another, e.g., a 700-watt recipe to an 800-watt oven (and much more good microwave oven information), go to "Conversion Charts" by Marie T. Smith at http://www.microwavecookingforone.com/chart.html.

MILITARY TIME

ONE OF THE CULTURAL SURPRISES awaiting the new military recruit is the 24-hour time system—does 1900 hours mean anything to you? Still, the 24-hour time system makes a lot more sense than ours. Times showing up twice a day can be confusing—to indicate which side of noon a time falls on, it must be followed by the clumsy "A.M." or "P.M.," which is frequently left off. That this does not cause more confusion than it does is due only to our sense of what is appropriate. If your boss invites you to his house to meet the family, saying, "Drop by at seven," you're unlikely to show up for breakfast.

The military takes time seriously, however. Not only are its operations spread over many time zones, the appropriate time for what one is called on to do may not always be obvious. So military time divides the day not into two sets of twelve hours but into one set of twenty-four hours, counting from 1:00 A.M. our time (0100, or "oh-one-hundred") to midnight (2400, or "twenty-four-hundred"). This not only gets rid of the awkward Latin qualifiers but the punctuation as well:

1:00 A.M. becomes 0100	3:00 P.M. becomes 1500
2:10 A.M. becomes 0210	6:00 P.M. becomes 1800
Noon becomes 1200	9:54 P.M. becomes 2154
1:00 P.M. becomes 1300	Midnight becomes 2400

This very sensible system might have caught on with civilians if clocks numbered 1 to 12 hadn't been around so long. In fact, official national and international time is always communicated in 24-hour time, with many other groups—pilots, for one—using it as well. It's not hard to translate 24-hour time into familiar time, though. The A.M. times are obvious. For P.M. subtract 1200 from numbers larger than 1200; e.g., 1200 from 1900 is 700, or 7 P.M. (See also *Greenwich Mean Time*, page 128.)

▶ **Find more information on military time from the U.S. Naval Observatory at http://tycho.usno.navy.mil. To find a conversion chart, go to "Military Time Conversions" at http://www.stripersurf.com/time.html.**

MINERAL HARDNESS SCALES

OF THE SEVERAL SCALES for measuring the hardness of minerals, the most common—and the least absolute—is the Mohs scale, invented by Friedrich Mohs, a German mineralogist, in 1812. Mohs' scale runs from 1 to 10, with minerals getting harder as the numbers go up. There is no defined step between numbers here: where a mineral lands on Mohs' scale depends on what can scratch it, and what it can scratch. It's almost poetic in its relativity.

It's not surprising that scientists have demanded absolute scales. There's the *Rosiwal scale*, which measures a mineral's *resistance* to abrasion; *Knoop's microhardness scale*, which measures the *depth of the scratch* from a diamond tool applied with equal force; the *Brinell hardness scale*, invented around 1900 by Swedish metallurgist Johann Brinell, which measures the area of an impression made by a chromium steel ball or cone pressed into the material; *Vickers scale*, which uses another indenter; *Rockwell*, yet another. These kinds of hardness tests measure on a macro-, micro-, and even nanoscale using, of course, fabulous equipment.

Mohs' scale may lack precision, but it's available to anybody who is trying to identify a rock. All you really need is a fingernail

(Mohs 2.5), a copper penny (Mohs 3), a penknife (Mohs 5.5), a piece of glass (Mohs 6), some quartz (Mohs 7), and a diamond (Mohs 10). To find the hardness of a beach stone, for example, you see what will scratch the stone and what the stone will scratch. Most earth stones and rocks average out at 4.5 on the Mohs scale. Gemstones are harder than glass (6) but much softer than diamond (10). No known mineral is more than a third as hard as diamonds. Gold and silver, on the other hand, unless mixed with a metal alloy, are as soft as a fingernail.

Five Common Mineral Hardness Scales

Mineral	Mohs	Rosiwal	Knoop	Brinell	Vickers
talc or graphite	1	0.03	1	3	1
gypsum or sulphur	2	1.25	32	12	3
calcite	3	4.5	135	53	9
fluorite	4	5	163	64	21
apatite	5	6.5	430	137	48
orthoclase	6	37	560	147	72
quartz	7	120	820	178	100
topaz	8	175	1,340	304	200
corundum	9	1,000	1,800	667	400
diamond	10	140,000	7,000	—	1600

▸ To find the hardness on the Mohs scale of almost any gemstone, go to the information pages provided by Chard Jewelers at http://www.24carat.co.uk/a2z.html. For a historical perspective, go to "Unforbidden Geology" at http://www.geocities.com/unforbidden_geology and click on "Rock & Mineral Hardness" for an article by Archae Solenhofen. For mineral hardness testing and equipment, go to "Material Hardness," by University of Maryland's CALCE Electronic Products and Systems Center, at http://www.calce.umd.edu/general/Facilities/Hardness_ad_.htm.

MOTORCYCLES

BECAUSE SO MANY gas-powered engines traditionally have been measured by horsepower, many people don't know that the number on a motorcycle is not a measure of horsepower—most 1000cc bikes produce less than 100 horsepower. (See *Engines*, page 87.)

The number on the side of a motorcycle means cc's, or cubic centimeters. Cubic centimeters of what? Unfortunately, although the answer does concern engine size, it's not so simple as "the volume taken up by the engine." Cubic centimeters, as applied to a motorcycle engine—or any other internal combustion engine—is a measure of the combustion space in the cylinders.

The first internal combustion engine, built in 1876 by German engineer Nicholas Otto, contained the essential parts of today's gasoline engines:

1. a *cylinder*
2. a *piston*, pumping up and down inside the cylinder
3. a *crankshaft* connected to the piston
4. *valves* to admit air and fuel into the cylinder at the beginning of the cycle and to let the exhausted gases escape at the end
5. a *device to ignite the fuel-air mixture*; e.g., a spark plug

This engine, like today's engines, worked in four strokes of the piston in the cylinder:

1. The *intake stroke:* The piston moves down, sucking the fuel-air mixture into the cylinder.
2. The *compression stroke:* The piston goes up to compress the fuel-air mixture into a small space.
3. The *power stroke:* The fuel-air mixture explodes (combusts), pushing the piston back down.
4. The *exhaust stroke:* The piston returns to the top, pushing the exhausted gases out of the cylinder.

Although Otto's engine couldn't be used for transportation—it had to be hooked up to gas lines—by 1882 another German engineer, Gottlieb Daimler, invented an ingenious device called a *carburetor*. The carburetor turned liquid gasoline into a spray so fine that the drops evaporated immediately, mixing with the air sucked up by the piston's intake stroke, and exploding easily on the compression stroke.

Today's engines, though greatly refined, work essentially the same way (although some now have a 2-stroke cycle instead of a 4-stroke). The size of an engine is measured by theoretically removing the top of a cylinder, pushing the piston all the way down, and then filling the cylinder with liquid. The cubic centimeters of liquid displaced (spilled out) when the piston is returned to its high position is the measure of the combustion area of that cylinder. If a motorcycle has four cylinders, each displacing 200 cc's, it has an 800cc engine (200 cc's times 4 cylinders).

The formula for finding the displacement in cc's in a cylinder is as simple as finding the volume of a tin can: you simply find the area of the circle at the top (see *Circles*, page 49) and multiply it by its length.

pi x $\frac{1}{2}$ bore² x the stroke = displacement

It may help to define the terms:

pi	= 3.1416
bore	= diameter of the cylinder in centimeters
stroke	= the distance the piston moves in centimeters
displacement	= volume of a cylinder in cubic centimeters (cc's)

Automobile engines are sized essentially the same way.

MOTOR OIL

LIKE MOST PEOPLE, you probably have assumed that the "w" in 10w/40 automobile engine oil stands for "weight." Wrong. Engine oil with two viscosity ratings, such as 10w/40, is simply oil that has been tested at both cold and hot temperatures. The "w" stands for "winter." Basically a car oil needs to be thin enough to flow in winter so you can start the engine, but thick enough so that when the engine gets hot (and in areas with high summer temperatures an engine can get very hot) the oil can perform its main function of keeping the metal surfaces apart. Its ability to do this is called its "film strength."

Oils with two ratings ("multigrade" oils) contain added plastics with long chain molecules called polymers. These flexible molecules allow a thick oil with good film strength in summer to remain thin enough to allow the engine to start in winter. (Oils with just one rating have been tested only at high temperatures, and would have to be changed to suit the season.) The rating numbers are arbitrary numbers assigned by the Society of Automotive Engineers ("SAE" on the oil can, bottle, or "donut" seal). The "10" isn't ten of anything; it simply stands for oil of a certain thinness when tested at 0 degrees.

Oils tested at 0 degrees are rated 5, 10, 15, or 20. Oils tested at 210 degrees are rated at 20, 30, 40, or 50. What do those numbers mean? To assign a number, the SAE times (in seconds) a 60cc sample of oil as it runs through an opening similar in size to a standard carburetor jet.

"W" ratings (oil tested at 0 degrees F):
10w oil runs half as fast as 5w oil
15w oil runs half as fast as 10w oil
20w oil runs half as fast as 15w oil

Regular ratings (number of seconds 60cc of oil takes to run through a test aperture):
20 oil takes 45 to 58 seconds
30 oil takes 58 to 70 seconds
40 oil takes 70 to 85 seconds
50 oil takes 85 to 110 seconds

How to choose the oil for your car? Check the owner's manual; most makers recommend an oil. As a rule of thumb, the lower your winter temperatures, the lower the "w" rating needs to be, and the higher the summer temperatures, the higher the regular rating. Oil recommended by the American Petroleum Institute displays a certification "starburst" and the three-part "donut" denoting the oil's performance level, viscosity, and whether it has demonstrated energy-conserving properties in a standard test in comparison with a reference oil.

If you change your own engine's oil yourself, naturally you will recycle the used oil. Use the information at the website below to help locate a recycle center in your area.

> ▶ For clear instructions on how to check engine oil levels, go to http://www.2pass.co.uk/oil.htm. For information on used engine oil recycling, go to the American Petroleum Institute page at http://www.recycleoil.org. To find the oil recycling center nearest you, go to http://www.recycleoil.org/backup/usedoil_collectioncenters.htm.

NAILS
....

THE SIZING OF COMMON NAILS is one of those deliciously archaic systems that has survived miraculously intact, with today's sizes running from 2d to 60d. The "d" is the British symbol for pence, which is why a 2d nail is called a "2-penny" nail. In 1400, a 2-penny nail was a size that sold 100 nails for 2 pence, or 2d. Likewise, 100 3-penny nails sold for 3d, 100 16-penny nails for 16d, and so on. Today most commonly used nails are sold by the pound (weight), not by the count, but they are still called "penny" nails. The most commonly used household nails are common nails (large, flat head), box nails (like common nails but thinner), casing nails (cone-shaped head), and finishing nails (small head and thinner than casing nails), all of which come in penny sizes.

Other nails are often sized simply by length in inches. Brads and "wire nails" (most nails are made of wire but not all of them are called that) have bigger heads and are sized by length and wire gauge (see *Wire*, page 274).

Although standards sometimes vary, the following chart provides fairly good guidelines for the length for the sixteen most popular nail sizes. Note that the lengths increase a quarter inch for each size under 16d and a half inch for each size over 16d.

Size	Length	Size	Length
2d	1"	10d	3"
3d	1 1/4"	12d	3 1/4"
4d	1 1/2"	16d	3 1/2"
5d	1 3/4"	20d	4"
6d	2"	30d	4 1/2"
7d	2 1/4"	40d	5"
8d	2 1/2"	50d	5 1/2"
9d	2 3/4"	60d	6"

The gauge, or the diameter of the nail, doesn't usually concern users of the penny nails, as it simply increases with the length of the nail. Technically, however, nails use a 15-1 gauge system, the diameter of the nail increasing as the gauge numbers go down (a 10-gauge nail is thicker than a 12-gauge nail). This odd system is loosely related to wire gauges, as most nails are cut from wire—the thickness of wire also increases as the gauge numbers decrease, running from the largest at 00000 (1/2-inch diameter) to a small 40 (.007 inch) (see *Wire*, page 274). Confusion reigns, of course, because the nail gauge system also works the opposite way from the screw system, in which the screw width increases as the gauge numbers go up (see *Screws and Bolts*, page 215).

How do you choose a nail size? A rule of thumb used for many purposes is that a nail driven through the thickest part of two pieces of wood should be long enough to go through both, less 3/16 of an inch. When edge-nailing—driving a nail lengthwise along a board—the nail should be three times longer than the thickness of the first piece. Although there are plenty of exceptions to the rule, it's a place to start if you're an amateur staring glassily at the nail bins.

An interesting bit of nail history is that until 1800, nails were made by hand. The first ones were probably made from bone and wood, and when the Iron Age came along, from metal. The wooden nails—called treenails—stuck around, however, used even in Colonial America, when metal nails were so precious that it was not uncommon for people to burn their houses when they moved, in order to have enough nails to build the next one! Nails were hoarded, with old ones being straightened to use again. George III insisted that nails be imported from England, where they were still being made by hand—making wrought-iron nails had become a household industry in order to fill the incredible demand. By 1740, some 60,000 people were making nails in the English town of Birmingham alone! The American habit of self-reliance dealt such a blow to the English economy that in 1750 the English passed the Iron Act, forbidding Americans to build their own ironworks; we couldn't even make our own nails. Shortly after, the Revolutionary War broke out. By 1800, our factories were making cut nails. The "French nail"—the nail made from wire—soon replaced cut nails and persists to this day.

Cut nails were cut from sheet metal and were rectangular or square—you can still buy square nails, but they tend to be a specialty item. Today's more common round shape became widely used when machines began making the nails from wire.

▶ To calculate how many pounds of nails you will need for your project, go to http://www.onlineconversion.com. Click on "Miscellaneous," then click on "Nails." To find an excellent introduction to the home workshop, go to "Sawdust Making 101" at http://www.sawdustmaking.com. For information on nail guns, go to http://www.howstuffworks.com/nail-gun.htm.

NAUTICAL DISTANCE

THERE DOESN'T SEEM TO BE any good reason for sailors to talk differently and measure differently from the rest of us. Still, while that may be true about much of the sailor talk, the measures—those knots and nautical miles and such—actually do make sense.

A look at the origins of the mile we use on land illustrates this. The Romans measured the first land mile as 1,000 paces (*milia passuum* in Latin, hence our word "mile"), with each pace equaling two marching steps. This mile, at 1,618 of our yards, was a little short of today's mile. After centuries of variation, Elizabeth I assigned the mile today's familiar 1,760 yards, or 5,280 feet, calling it a *statute mile*, a term that has endured with the length. Walking to establish distance, however, just doesn't work on water, and the nautical mile had been around long before the Romans came along anyway.

The *nautical mile* is not based on human measures but on the circumference of the earth, which has for centuries been divided into 360 degrees, with each degree divided into 60 minutes. Ancient Chaldean astronomers are believed to have established the first nautical mile based on degrees before 600 B.C., and for most of history sailors have charted their course, progress, and position by degrees of latitude and—later—longitude (see *Latitude and Longitude*, page 148). To measure distance by degree made sense. Like other measures, however, the actual length of the nautical mile varied a great deal through the centuries, with different countries dividing each degree into 10, 12, 15, or 60 parts.

Even in the twentieth century there has been wide disagreement on the precise measure of the nautical mile. The British and the Americans, for example, made the nautical mile equal to a minute ($1/60$) of a degree, but the British nautical mile measured 6,080 British feet, while the U.S. nautical mile measured 6,080.20 U.S. feet (1,853.248 meters). The British foot is $1/400,000$ smaller than the U.S. foot, which sounds silly to mention but is actually quite important for precise measurements. In 1929 a large number of countries adopted the *international nautical mile*, defined as 1,852 meters, but the United States, the U.S.S.R., and Great Britain abstained. Only in 1954 did the United States finally adopt the international nautical mile of 1,852 meters.

Today's nautical measures of distance are as follows:

U.S. Nautical Measures of Distance

6 feet (exactly)	= 1 fathom
120 fathoms	= 1 cable
	= 720 feet
8.44 cables	= 1 international nautical mile
	= 1.852 kilometers
	= 6,076.115 international feet

An imprecise but occasionally useful rule of thumb for estimating nautical miles is this: 7 nautical miles = 8 statute miles. Another quick way to roughly go from nautical miles to statute miles and back again is this:

statute miles x .87 = nautical miles
nautical miles x 1.15 = statute miles

Knots are simply nautical miles per hour: 1 knot = 1.852 kilometers, 1.151 statute miles, or 6,076.115 international feet per hour. Knots and nautical miles are not limited to seafarers—commercial and private pilots have been using them for years.

PAPER

• •

IN MOST OF THE WORLD, commercial paper sizes are based on the ISO (International Standards Organization) paper size system, in which all paper has the same aspect ratio: the height-to-width ratio of the square root of two, or 1:1.4142 (see *Aspect Ratio*, page 16). This incredibly handy system lets you halve any size paper and get the next size smaller. It's great for copy machines: you can enlarge or reduce to the next size paper and the copy will fit perfectly. A size A4 sheet of letterhead will fold and fit perfectly into a size C4 envelope.

International paper sizes fall into three formats: A (0 to 10) for office papers, B (0 to 10) for card and poster weights, and C (0 to 10) for envelopes. *The larger the ISO (metric) size number, the smaller the sheet of paper.*

American/Canadian paper sizes have been at odds with international sizes ever since metrics took over most of the world. Although letters are assigned to some of our paper sizes, we don't usually think of letters; we think of names and measurements:

American Commercial Paper Sizes	*Somewhat Equivalent ISO Sizes*
Business cards (2 x 3 1/2 inches)	A8
Index cards (3 x 5 inches)	A7
Large index cards (5 x 8 inches)	A5
Office paper (8 1/2 x 11 inches)	A4
Legal paper (8 1/2 x 14 inches)	
Double size paper (11 x 17 inches)	A3

What does "20-pound" mean when applied to paper? And 500 sheets of 8½ × 11-inch stock is a ream, isn't it? There are many types of commercial paper: When a *ream* (using a stack of 500 sheets of paper measuring 2 feet by 3 feet) weighs 20 pounds at a temperature of 70 degrees and a humidity of 50 percent, it's called 20-pound paper. This is how some commercial paper is sized. The heavier the weight, of course, the thicker the paper usually is, but the pound designation always applies to that oversized stack, not the 500 8½ × 11-inch sheets you buy at the stationer's. A ream is not always 500 sheets—sometimes it's 480 sheets. And the size of the sheet is not always 2 feet by 3 feet—sometimes it's 17 inches by 22 inches. Usually you can get 2,000 letterhead sheets out of a ream, but not always.

It's usually at the printer's that you have to choose the weight of your paper. Despite the confusion of size and number of sheets in a ream, here are a few general guidelines:

Some Common U.S. Commercial Paper Weights

9 lb.	onionskin
16 lb.	copy paper
20 lb.	standard typing and computer printer paper
24 lb.	standard letterhead paper
60 lb.	good for printing on both sides
65 lb.	business cards, postcards
100 lb.	magazine paper (coated stock)
80 to 110 lb.	index card stock
120 lb.	poster board

A recent marketing twist has produced yet another number used especially for ink-jet and laser printer paper: a brightness rating, usually ranging between 80 and 95. A device measures a beam of light of fixed size as it's reflected from the paper at a 45-degree angle. The intensity of reflected light is rated on a comparative fixed scale of 1 to 100, intensity increasing with the number. A paper with a higher brightness rating may produce brighter, sharper images than paper with a low rating. Brightness, however, is not whiteness. How white a paper looks to the human eye is influenced by how warm (red or cream shades) or cool (blue shades) the white is; blue-white usually looks whitest.

Art paper is also weighed, but it is sized by a different standard. The size of the sheets in the stack to be weighed (again, 480 to 500 sheets) depends on what the paper is for. The standard size for watercolor paper is 22 inches by 30 inches, but other art papers may not be the same:

Some Common Art Paper Weights

8 to 48 lb.	tracing papers
13 to 20 lb.	bond papers
28 to 32 lb.	ledger papers
65 to 80 lb.	cover papers (commercial weight)
90 to 400 lb.	watercolor papers

▶ **For a look at international paper sizes, go to an article by Markus Kuhn at http://www.cl.cam.ac.uk/~mgk25/iso-paper.html, or see "Guide to International Paper Sizes" at the EDS website at http://www.twics.com/~eds/paper/papersize.html. For a list of art supply companies, click on "Supplies" at http://www.artcafe.net.**

PAPER CLIPS

PAPER CLIP SIZES are a snap, but require some explanation, as the size numbers appear to be backward—the bigger the number, the smaller the clip—and the biggest has no number at all. Size #3 is smallest, #2 is medium, #1 large, and "jumbo" is biggest. "Gem clips" is the standard name for the familiar U-shaped wire, but today you also can buy vinyl-coated and plastic paper clips in entertaining patterns and colors.

One would think that is pretty much all there is to say about paper clips, but there are entire chapters of respectable length in two readable, entertaining books by Henry Petroski, a professor of civil engineering and history at Duke University: *The Evolution of Useful Things* and *Invention by Design: How Engineers Get from Thought to Thing.* Apparently, the feat of finding a reproducible design that combined an effective bend of the wire with just-right springiness—it had to bend, but not too far, and snap back to original form—eluded inventors for decades.

The design that won out was never patented, but the machine that produced it was, by William Middlebrook in 1899. Middlebrook's paper clip machine could crank out clips in enough volume and at a competitive enough price to challenge the reign of pins, which up until then had been used to hold most everybody's papers together, if not their lives, and were already being made by machine. After a century, Middlebrook's design is still in common use.

▶ For more information on the history of paper clips and other office equipment, go to the Office Museum, http://www.officemuseum.com/paper_clips.htm.

PENCILS

YOU'D THINK THAT THE PENCIL would just fade away, what with keyboards and ballpoint pens. Pencil popularity, however, seems here to stay—more than 2$^{1/2}$ billion pencils are produced in America every year. The U.S. government uses 45 million of them a year, and the New York Stock Exchange more than a million. Perhaps it's because the pencil's an old-fashioned hard worker—one standard pencil can leave a 35-mile trail, or about 45,000 words. At least forty materials from twenty-eight countries go into one.

What does the "No. 2" on the pencil signify? It's a measure of hardness. About 1800 a Frenchman named Nicolas Jacques Conté mixed clay and water with powdered graphite, rolled thin the result, and baked it in a 1,900-degree kiln. He encased the dried vermicelli-like "leads" in a wood sandwich, inventing the first modern pencil.

Today numbers and letters indicate the hardness or softness of a pencil lead, or, to put it another way, how much clay is mixed with the graphite to produce the lead—the more clay in the mixture, the harder the lead. Sizing pencils would be a simple matter, except that there are several kinds of pencils: art pencils, writing pencils, and mechanical pencils, and each kind uses a different system.

Art Pencils

Art pencils have a wide range of hardnesses to accommodate the many creative purposes pencils serve, from drawing to drafting. The scale goes from the soft end, 8B, to the hard end, 10H. Sizes 8B through F are often used for artwork, while 3H through 10H are preferred for drafting. It works like this: "B," which stands for "black," means "soft"; the higher the number that precedes "B," the softer the pencil, and the wider and darker the line produced.

"H" means hard; the higher the number that precedes "H," the harder the pencil, and the thinner and lighter the line produced. "F" means fine, but not as fine as the H numbers. Observe:

8B-7B-6B-5B-4B-3B-2B-B HB-F-H 2H-3H-4H-5H-6H-7H-8H-9H-10H
Softest <<<<<<< Softer Middling Harder>>>>>>>>>>>>>> Hardest

Writing Pencils

Writing pencils don't require such a wide range as art pencils and tend to fill that gap in the middle. Writing pencils use numbers 1 through 4 to indicate hardness, which relate directly to the art pencil system:

Writing Pencil		Art Pencil
1	=	3B
2	=	B
2.5	=	F
3	=	2H
4	=	3H

Mechanical Pencils

You don't have to sharpen a mechanical pencil, and often you can choose the kind of lead you'd like. However, there isn't much choice. Measured in millimeters (diameters), the most available sizes are 0.3 mm, 0.5 mm, 0.7 mm, and 0.9 mm. Hardnesses follow the art pencil system.

▶ **For everything you ever wanted to know about pencils, go to http://www.pencils.com/history.html.**

pH

. . . .

FROM TIME TO TIME you may run into a pH value, a number that indicates how acid or alkaline something is. On a scale of 0 to 14, pH values are applied to soils, "acid rain," waste, paper, fruits, soaps, and so on. The scale, though not difficult, is not particularly obvious. For example, you might assume that the lower the pH, the weaker the acid; instead, the opposite is true—*the lower the pH, the more acidic the solution.*

Technically, "pH" ("potential of hydrogen") describes the concentration of free hydrogen ions in a solution. You don't have to know about hydrogen ions to use the pH scale, but for the curious, here it is: the pH number is not a count of ions, but a "gram-equivalent," or weight in grams per liter of solution. As it happens, the concentration of hydrogen ions in a liter of solution can range from a 1 gram-equivalent to a .00000000000001 (10^{-14}) gram-equivalent. In 1909 a Danish scientist named Søren Sørensen used this natural spread to come up with a 0 to 14 scale. On the scale 0 was the most acid, or the strongest concentration of hydrogen ions (1 gram–equivalent), 7 (pure water) was neutral (10^{-7} gram–equivalent), and 14 had the lowest concentration of hydrogen ions, making it the most alkaline at 10^{-14} gram–equivalent.

How much stronger is beer at a pH of 4.0 than black coffee at 5.0? The pH scale is logarithmic—each whole number represents a concentration ten times stronger than the next higher number. So the beer would contain ten times the number of hydrogen ions as the coffee. To demonstrate further: a lime with a pH of 2.0 is ten times more acidic than an apple with a pH value of 3.0, which is in turn ten times more acidic than a tomato with a pH of 4.0 (making the lime one hundred times more acidic than the tomato), and so on.

The pH Scale

pH Value	Hydrogen Ion Gram Equivalent	Relative Acidity or Alkalinity	Example
0	1	10,000,000 Most acid	0.1 hydrochloric acid 0.3 sulfuric acid
1	10^{-1}	1,000,000	1.0 to 3.0 stomach acid 1.6 limes (fruit)
2	10^{-2}	100,000	2.0 to 5.6 acid rain 2.0 to 4.0 soft drinks 2.3 lemons 2.4 to 3.4 vinegar 2.8 to 3.8 wines 2.9 to 3.3 apples
3	10^{-3}	10,000	3.0 to 3.3 grapefruit
4	10^{-4}	1,000	4.0 to 5.0 beers 4.5 to 5.5 human hair 4.5 to 4.7 bananas
5	10^{-5}	100 More acid	5.0 black coffee 5.0 to 7.0 human urine 5.6 to 6.0 normal rain
6	10^{-6}	10 Acid	6.3 to 6.6 most drinking water
7	10^{-7}	1 Neutral	7.0 pure water 7.3 to 7.5 human blood 7.6 to 8.0 chicken eggs
8	10^{-8}	10 Alkaline	8.0 seawater 8.4 sodium bicarbonate (0.1 normal)
9	10^{-9}	100 More alkaline	9.0 toilet soap
10	10^{-10}	1,000	10.6 to 11.6 ammonia
11	10^{-11}	10,000	

(continued)

The pH Scale (continued)

pH Value	Hydrogen Ion Gram Equivalent	Relative Acidity or Alkalinity	Example
12	10^{-12}	100,000	
13	10^{-13}	1,000,000	
14	10^{-14}	10,000,000 Most alkaline	14.0 drain cleaner

These approximate pH ranges for things in daily life may hold some surprises. Were you aware, for example, that apples are as acidic as grapefruit? Most of our food and our body products, for that matter, with the exception of our blood, is on the acidic side. Gardeners are particularly interested in the pH values of their soil, since plants can be very sensitive to too much acid or alkaline (see *Soil, Garden*, page 228).

▶ To find information on acid rain, go to http://www.epa.gov/airmarkets and under "Environmental Issues" click on "acid rain."

PINS
....

IF YOU SEW A LOT, you probably vacuum up plenty of pins to prevent one from lodging itself in a family foot. Before the early 1800s, however, the heads of pins were attached by hand, an expensive process, so losing one in the carpet would have been unthinkable. In fact, in the 1100s pins were so valuable that the English Parliament passed a law allowing them to be sold only on the First and Second of January of any year.

Even in Colonial America, pins were scarce. Workers cut the pins from brass wire and crimped on the heads separately from a finer piece of wire, using a foot-powered drop hammer. Not surprisingly, the heads were prone to fall off, and elaborate measures were taken to keep pins from getting lost. By 1860, however, pins were made by machine at the incredible rate of 1,600 per hour, not much by today's standards, perhaps, but enough to change everyone's attitude toward them for good.

Today most pins are made of stainless steel with brass or nickel coating. Pins appear to be the simplest of sewing accessories until you are presented with a bewildering array of them. Pins are even used in banking to hold securities and tissue-thin receipts. Although even the people who sell pins don't seem to know too much about them, it's worth getting the right ones for the job.

Pin Types

Widths of pins vary not so much by length but according to their intended use, from extra-fine silk pins to sturdy quilting pins. Some pins have plastic or glass heads to make handling easier. Although these pins work well for pinning patterns, they often get hit by sewing machine needles. If you pin fabric for sewing with ball-headed pins, pull them as you sew.

Some Common Pin Types

Type of Pin	Size	Width	Use
Satin	16–18	Fine to medium	All-around pin for fabrics that handle easily
Silk	24	Extra-fine	For silks and other slippery fabrics
Pleating	28	Large	Strong pin for holding thick or many-layered fabrics, pile
Quilting	16	Fine	Holds set pleats for sewing without breaking machine needles

Pin Sizes

Pins are sized by the sixteenth of an inch. A pin measuring one inch, for example, is a size 16, or $^{16}/_{16}$ of an inch. A $1^{1}/_{4}$-inch pin is a size 20, or $^{20}/_{16}$. On the small end, a size 6 pin is $^{6}/_{16}$ of an inch, or $^{3}/_{8}$ inch.

Common Pin Sizes

Size	Length	Size	Length
6	3/8"	20	1 1/4"
8	1/2"	24	1 1/2"
14	7/8"	28	1 3/4"
16	1"	32	2"
17	11/16"		

PLYWOOD

ALTHOUGH MOST PEOPLE think of plywood as a fairly modern invention, it was actually first used by the ancient Egyptians who, around 2800 B.C., fastened plies of wood together with wooden pegs. There is a difference, however: wood was rare in Egypt, but today plywood is common and found in many types and grades. Plywood is constructed from three to seven layers of veneer sheets peeled from either hardwood or softwood logs, trimmed to size, and glued together at right angles.

Plywood sizes and grading are fairly straightforward compared to many other types of lumber. The thicknesses are measured in fractions of an inch, and the sizes of the panels are measured in feet. Unlike surfaced lumber, for example, a 1/4-inch-thick 4- by 6-foot panel actually measures 1/4 inch thick, 4 feet wide, and 6 feet long—and plywood is priced by the panel, so no elaborate figuring is required. You want to buy the least expensive plywood to do the job right, however, so you need to know the letters.

The letters you see most often applied to plywood—A, B, C, or D—refer to its "grade," or quality, but other letters are sometimes found. Keep in mind that, unlike exterior grades, the adhesive used to bind the layers of the interior grades of plywood are not water resistant.

A   knots are plugged and sanded
B   larger knots, but plugged and sanded
C   open knots
D   larger open knots
G   good side (for finishing)
I   for interior use*
S   side
SH   sheathing (rough on both sides)
WB   wallboard (sound face, utility back)
U   underlayment (for floors), sometimes "UL"
X   for exterior use

*The I is often omitted; if it isn't marked for exterior use (X), it's intended for interior use.

These letters are combined with each other or with numbers. For example:

G1S   one good side, one utility side
G2S   both sides good
ACI   one side A, one side C, for interior use
BCX   one side B, one side C, for exterior use

▶ For information on other types of board products, go to "Selecting Plywood for Home Projects," by House and Home, at http://www.houseandhomesite.com/article1007.html.

POINTS, MORTGAGE

IT GOES WITHOUT SAYING that when you shop for a mortgage, you look for low interest rates; but when the subject of points is raised you may very well draw a blank.

Actually, it's a fairly simple system—the points on a loan are *prepaid interest*. Each point will cost you 1 percent of your mortgage amount, so a mortgage for $80,000 with 2 points will cost you an extra $1,600 ($800 per point). You may pay this amount when you sign for the loan, or it may be added to the total amount of the mortgage. Points are not always charged to the buyer, however;

they can be negotiated so the seller pays some or all of the points. In the case of VA or FHA loans, the buyer can be charged only 1 point—the seller pays any remaining points.

How you choose between a loan at, say, $7^1/2$ percent interest costing 2 points or a loan at $7^3/4$ percent interest costing 1 point depends on how long you intend to keep the property. Each point effectively raises your interest $^1/8$ of 1 percent on a thirty-year mortgage, so the first loan will raise the effective interest rate to $7^3/4$ percent, a lower rate than the $7^7/8$ percent of the second loan. If you plan to keep the property for a long time, the first loan will cost you less in the long run, because your total interest rate is lower. However, if you intend to keep the property only a short time, you don't want to pay any more interest up front than you have to, so the 1-point loan might be a better choice.

Points can fluctuate so fast that a few days can cost you a bundle. Why? Because money is a commodity and is as volatile as the stock market. When money is in short supply and the economy is weak, points go up so that banks will have more available money up front. To keep borrowers from being scared off by high interest rates, lenders may "discount" (charge points on) a loan—the interest will be lower, but the points ensure the lender gets a good "yield," or profit. A loan with no points, called a *par loan*—is likely to carry a fairly frightening interest rate.

> ▶ To calculate various loan rates and possibilities, go to "Mortgage Calculators" at http://www.interest.com/calculators, or go to http://nt.mortgage101.com and click on "Calculators," then click on "Should I Pay Points?"

POLLEN COUNTS

WHETHER OR NOT a plant will aggravate allergies has much to do with how it is pollinated. The poor maligned goldenrod, often blamed for allergic reactions, produces such alluring blooms that insects cannot resist seeing to its pollination. Ragweed, on the other hand, not nearly so attractive, must rely on the wind. Wind pollination is not very effective, so to make sure that enough pollen reaches a productive destination, ragweed produces huge amounts of pollen. Grasses, too, are wind pollinated, as are many trees, the most irritating of which seem to be birch, mountain cedar, oak, willow, and pine. It's this wind-born pollen that accounts for allergies, and it can travel for hundreds of miles.

Allergy sufferers have a new alert system these days: pollen counts reported seasonally during weather reports and available for most U.S. and Canadian cities on the Internet. Spores are collected at certified pollen counting stations all over the country and the grains are counted and measured per cubic foot of air. Most pollen counts represent measures taken during the previous twenty-four hours, but they do help warn people if their particular irritant is on the loose. Pollen counts tend to be higher on warm, windy days, lower on chilly, wet ones.

Although pollen counts are often reported in a word—low, medium, high, or very high—the type of pollen isn't always made clear. Type of pollen is as important, however, as levels of pollen, as most people are not allergic to everything, and could be kept needlessly indoors on a quite fabulous warm, windy, pine-pollen day if what they're really allergic to is ragweed.

▶ For a current pollen count in cities in the United States or Canada, go to http://www.pollen.com. For information on actual grain counts per cubic meter, go to the American Academy of Allergy, Asthma & Immunology at http://aaaai.org/nab/reading_charts.stm.

POSTAL RATES
· ·

THE U.S. POSTAL SERVICE no longer classes mail from first class through fourth, a system that implied that the higher the number, the less the cost (not always so). Postal rates change so often that those quoted here may already be out of date, but they are included to give you a sense of the differences in rates for different services and how quickly the rates go up. As of June 30, 2002, most common domestic mail was classed (and charged for) as follows:

U.S. Postal Service Domestic Rates and Fees as of June 30, 2002

First-Class Mail	.37 for the first ounce
	.23 each additional ounce
Postcard	.23
Priority (two-day service)	starts at $3.85 for the first pound
Express Mail (overnight service)	Starts at $13.65 for the first 8 ounces
Parcel Post (up to 5 pounds)	Depends on distance (zone) mailed

It's worth asking before you pay, or, better yet, get the free flyer that the Postal Service calls "Postal Rates, Fees and Information" that charts the rates in detail, or find current rates on the U.S. Postal Service website.

Although postal rates do seem to be getting very high, until 1851 (the Second Continental Congress appointed the first Postmaster General, Benjamin Franklin, in 1775), the cost of sending a single-sheet letter 40 miles was either 6 cents or 8 cents. To send it 400 miles cost 25 cents. These prices were doubled or tripled or more with each additional sheet of paper (which could easily be counted, since envelopes were not used and the sheets were simply folded with the address on the outside sheet—see *Envelopes,* page 89). Mail had to be picked up from the local post office—it cost extra to have it delivered. No packages were delivered until 1912 when parcel post became law.

Those delivery prices were expensive for the early days, but with few roads and slow transportation, it was no easy task to transport a letter to its proper destination. As the post office expanded, however, the rates came down. They didn't reach 25 cents per letter until 1988, although one stamp could send more than one sheet of paper.

History of First-Class Mail Rates

Year	Cents per First Ounce	Year	Cents per First Ounce
1885	2	1978	18
1917	3	1981	20
1919	2	1985	22
1932	3	1988	25
1958	4	1992	29
1963	5	1995	32
1968	6	1999	33
1971	8	2000	34
1974	10	2002	37
1975	13		

▶ For current postage rates, go to the official website for the U.S. Postal Service at http://usps.com and click on "Postage Rates & Fees." At the same site, to find almost thirty articles on U.S. postal history, enter "history" in the search box.

PRECIOUS STONES

PRECIOUS STONES are measured in *carats* (for *karats*, used for gold, see page 127), a metric measure of weight that today equals 0.2 grams, about $1/142$ of an ounce. The word *carat* comes from the Arabic *qirat*, the seed of the carob tree once used to weigh gems and gold. Like so many other measures, the exact weight of the carat varied from country to country until its present value was established in 1913. A 1-carat diamond would be about the size of a dried pea, although most diamonds sold in jewelry stores are not that large. Smaller diamonds are referred to as a 0.50 diamond (one-half carat), or 0.25 (one-quarter carat), which may also be called a "25-pointer," as each one-hundredth of a karat is called a *point*. Sometimes a piece of jewelry containing pearls or gemstones might be labeled with a *ctw number,* for example, "ctw 1.35." The ctw (carat weight) number does not refer to the weight of any one stone, but to the *combined weight* of all the stones.

PRIME RATE
···

IN TIMES OF ECONOMIC EXCITEMENT, news of prime interest rate changes—say from 4.75 percent to 5.00 percent—jumps from the business page to the front page of many newspapers. One quarter of one percent may not sound like much, but the repercussions roll quickly—sometimes within hours—across the country. You probably know that when the prime rate goes up or down, other interest rates, including home mortgages, usually go up or down with it, involving on a national scale enormous amounts of money.

The prime rate is the lowest rate of interest commercial banks offer—it's the rate charged for short-term loans to customers with impeccable credit ratings. Unless you're worth millions, you're unlikely to get anywhere close to these rates. Rates for mere home mortgages or small business loans will always be higher.

Why is there just one prime rate when there are so many banks? Although all banks may not always offer the same prime rate, the prime rate tends to become standard across the banking industry. When one major bank lowers its rate, the others often follow so quickly that you wonder how such enormous organizations can move that fast. Because the cost of nearly everyone's money can move up and down with it, the action is tracked by small investors as well as very large ones.

Since 1971 the prime rate has changed frequently—sometimes weekly—from a low of 1.5 percent in early 1933 to 21.5 percent in late 1980. The prime rate did not always change so much. Before 1971 the prime rate was administratively fixed. It was the First National City Bank of New York that led a move to a flexible, or floating, rate that reflects what's happening in the money market and at the Federal Reserve, where commercial banks, large corporations, and other wealthy borrowers get their short-term loans, usually at lower interest than the prime rate. So although mortgages and smaller loans are not directly tied to the prime rate, they tend to follow its ups and downs.

▶ **For recent, present, and forecasted prime rates, go to the Financial Forecast Center at http://www.forecasts.org and click on "Prime Interest Rate." Then, for a history of prime rate changes, click on "Prime Interest Rate Historical Data by Month."**

PRINTERS (FOR PCs)

ALL PRINTERS CAN START looking alike in a computer store or catalog, so before you take the printer plunge, you might give some thought to what you really need. *Resolution, speed, color quality, size,* and *price* are considerations that apply to most kinds of computer printers.

First, decide on what *type* of printer will work best for you. To date, *laser* printers are considered fastest, sharpest, and most efficient for one-color, or *monochrome*, printing, while ink-jet printers, which spray ink directly onto the paper, do the best and most efficient job with color. Most ink-jets use a three-colors-in-one ink cartridge, but some have more and others offer single-color ink cartridges. There are also specialty ink-jet printers for photographs, although the all-purpose ink-jet printers are so good these days that often they print photographs quite well.

Resolution

The *resolution* of a printer is expressed as *dots per inch*, usually referred to as *dpi*. The higher the resolution capability, the sharper your printed image can be. Most printers offer a resolution of at least 1200 × 600 dpi, but it's not uncommon (at the time of this writing) to see printers at reasonable prices with 2400 × 1200 resolution.

New users of color printers may discover that an image on a computer monitor that seems in perfect focus may print out fuzzy. This is not the fault of the printer. *Ppi* (pixels per inch; see page 44), which describes the resolution of the *virtual image* on a monitor, can be translated directly into *dpi* (dots per inch), which describes the sharpness of a *printed* image. An image of 72 ppi is also a 72 dpi image and will not print well no matter how good it looks on the screen. The higher the resolution, the sharper your image.

Other things can affect image sharpness. Smooth paper, for example, with a high brightness rating (see *Paper*, page 179) may provide sharper copies than a rough paper that diffuses the light. Also, smaller dots make sharper images (some ads for ink-jet printers boast ink drops no bigger than 4 picoliters, about the size of a protozoal cell invisible to the unaided eye!).

Speed

How fast a printer prints is described as *ppm*, or *pages per minute*. If speed is important and color isn't, a laser printer, which can often print 15 ppm (low end) to 25 ppm (higher end) may be your answer. Ink-jet printers are catching up, offering several quality settings—low quality prints faster than high quality—but some may be amazingly slow at high quality. It's a good idea to check exactly how many pages per minute it can actually produce at high quality no matter what the catalog copy claims. At this writing, most ink-jet printers costing up to $400 boasted around 12 ppm black and 10 ppm color, but some printers may take up to 15 minutes to print a high-quality large photograph.

Color Quality

Although resolution affects color quality, the size of the dot sprayed on the paper can also affect color blends. Color quality is affected by many complex factors, so it's a good idea to check reviews in publications such as *Consumer Reports* or online at websites such as the one offered at the end of this section.

Size

Printers vary a great deal in size, so if your available space is limited, or if it needs to travel, check for dimensions, which are not always apparent in the descriptive copy.

Price

Here's the rub: printers may be inexpensive considering the phenomenal technological advantages they offer, but manufacturers make it up later in ink costs. It is not unusual for a three-color ink cartridge to cost as much as $35. Alternative cartridge companies have thrived in this atmosphere of seemingly inflated prices and some of their cartridges work fine. Ask someone who has experience—bad ink can gum things up but a good alternative can save hundreds of dollars. Using refill kits is reported to invite performance problems.

NEEDLESS TO SAY, reporting on price and performance of any techno-toy these days is chancy. The competition for better speed, quality, and resolution per dollar goes on, and innovations never cease.

▶ **For reviews of ink-jet and laser printers and other computer-related equipment, go to http://www.computingreview.com and click on "Reviews."**

PRODUCE

••

MANY KINDS OF PRODUCE are sized by how many items fit into the shipping box. All you really need to know about produce sizes is this: *the bigger the produce size number, the smaller the actual size will be.* This means that size 60 avocados are shipped to the market 60 to an avocado box; thus, size 60 avocados are quite small. Size 18 artichokes, on the other hand, come only 18 to a box, so they will be large. Some produce may be sized by letter—a size A red potato is bigger than a size B, even though the smaller size B potato may cost more, as small potatoes are often considered more desirable. The smallest red potatoes, called "creamers," may be most expensive of all.

There are too many variables for one number to stand for small, medium, or large. Although the box size is the same for the same kind of produce—apple boxes are always the same size and orange boxes are always the same size—it may differ from other kinds: an apple box is not quite the same size as an orange box. (Boxes are often sized to carry fifty pounds of produce.) Then, apples need packing material to keep them from bruising but oranges usually don't. Finally, there's the obvious difference in fruit sizes—a medium-sized avocado is about the size of a small artichoke.

Here are a few examples of produce sizes to give you an idea of how the sizes work (sizes can vary widely, of course):

Some Estimated Produce Sizes

Type of Produce	Small	Medium	Large
Apples and oranges	120	80–88	56–64
Artichokes	48	36	18
Avocados	60	48	24
Potatoes		100	70–80
Tomatoes		48	24

PROPERTY

• •

SURVEYORS' LEGAL DESCRIPTIONS of the exact whereabouts and boundaries of property, or "parcels," often found on deeds, appraisals, contracts of sale, and in county records, can be intimidating. It may help, however, to know some early surveyor's measures, as many older property descriptions still remain:

7.92 inches	=	1 link				
25 links	=	1 rod	=	16½ feet		
4 rods	=	1 chain	=	66 feet		
10 chains	=	1 furlong	=	220 yards		
8 furlongs	=	1 mile	=	1,760 yards	=	5,280 feet

These odd units are based on Gunther's chain, a seventeenth-century English surveyor's tool that was 66 feet long and was composed of 100 links joined by small rings. The 66 feet fit in neatly with the rod and furlong measures used for centuries in England. More primitive materials were also used for surveying—rope, leather, even hair, twisted, stretched, and dried, was popular in early American days. The steel surveyor's tape, first made in Massachusetts from ladies' hoopskirt wire about a hundred years ago, succeeded the chain—and the hair—for most purposes. Today sophisticated compasses and sighting instruments find and measure the boundaries of property, while most of the old measures have given way to *decimal feet:* the foot is divided into *tenths* instead of inches (twelfths).

Unfortunately, there are at least three ways to survey property, all of them legal and all of them still in use. A property description may use the *Metes and Bounds* method, the *Rectangular* system, or the *Lot and Block* system, but it's not unusual to find two or more in the same description.

Metes and Bounds

This system is the oldest, most commonly used, and tedious to read. The property is located by its proximity to local landmarks and neighboring property (bounds) to find a place of beginning—

often using another survey method to do so. From there, the surveyor walks the perimeter of the property, measuring angles in degrees and minutes and the distances between them. The following property description finds the point of beginning by using the Rectangular survey system (explanation follows), then proceeds with Metes and Bounds.

Commencing at the Northwest corner of Section 12 thence South along the Section line 21 feet; thence East 10 feet for a place of beginning; thence continuing East 34 feet; thence South 62 degrees, 30 minutes East 32 feet; thence Southeasterly along a line forming an angle of 8 degrees, 04 minutes to the right with a prolongation of the last described course 29 feet; thence South 13 degrees, 0 minutes to the left with a prolongation of the last described line a distance of 49 feet; thence East to a line parallel with the West line of said Section and 180 feet distant therefrom; thence South on the last described line a distance of 65 feet; thence due West a dis-

METES AND BOUNDS SURVEY

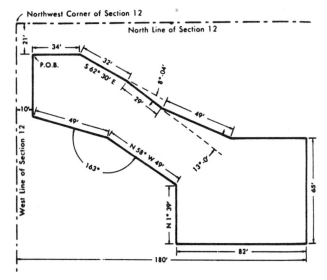

Used with permission from *The Appraisal of Real Estate,* 9th edition.
© 1987 by the American Institute of Real Estate Appraisers, Chicago.

tance of 82 feet; thence North 1 degree West 39 feet; thence North 58 degrees West a distance of 49 feet; thence Northwesterly along a line forming an angle of 163 degrees as measured from right to left with the last described line a distance of 49 feet; thence North to the place of beginning.

The Rectangular System

The Rectangular system was adopted by the Second Continental Congress when it needed to sell off parts of its huge land acquisitions quickly—staking out each perimeter with a chain and compass would have held up the much needed revenue. To avoid this, the U.S. General Land Office established reference points: true east-west lines, individually named, called *base lines*, and north-south lines, also individually named, called *principal meridians.*

Land to be surveyed was, and still is, divided by north-south lines, six miles apart, called *range lines*, and east-west lines, also six miles apart, called *township lines.* Range lines are numbered east and west from the principal meridian, and township lines are numbered north and south from the base line. When lines intersect, they make 36 square-mile *townships.* Each township is divided into 36 *sections*, each a mile square, or about 640 acres. (Due to the curvature of the earth, adjustment lines also run every 24 miles, making some sections inexact.)

A legal description of a 20-acre parcel located in the highlighted section on page 202 begins with the site and ends where the principal meridian and base lines intersect: the west half of the northeast quarter of the southeast quarter of Section 10, Township 4 North, Range 3 East, Mount Diablo Base and Meridian.

The Lot and Block System

This method is often used by land developers to subdivide a parcel. Usually a surveyor lays out the streets; then lot lines are

RECTANGULAR SURVEY

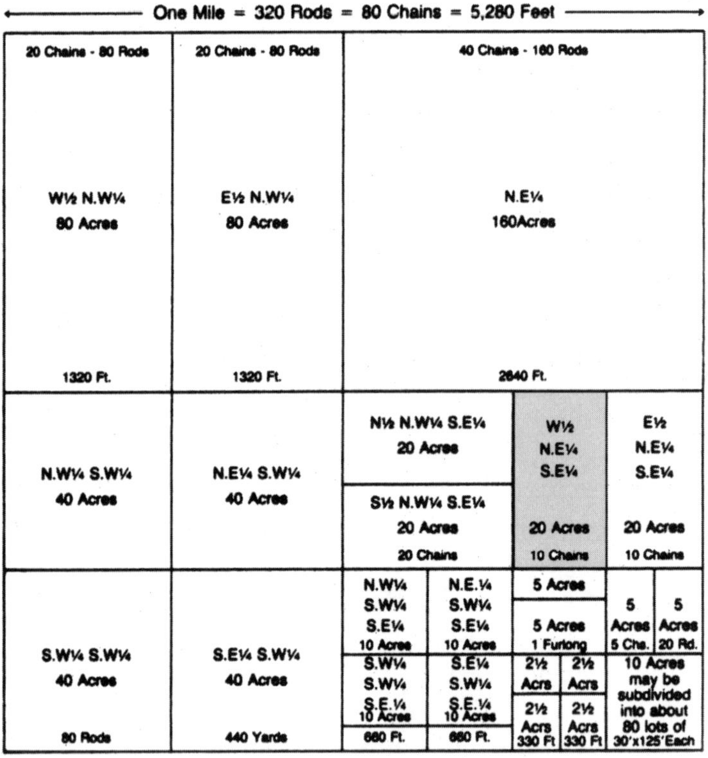
One Mile = 320 Rods = 80 Chains = 5,280 Feet
20 Chains - 80 Rods
20 Chains - 80 Rods
40 Chains - 160 Rods
W½ N.W¼
80 Acres
E½ N.W¼
80 Acres
N.E¼
160Acres
1320 Ft.
1320 Ft.
2640 Ft.
N.W¼ S.W¼
40 Acres
N.E¼ S.W¼
40 Acres
N½ N.W¼ S.E¼
20 Acres
S½ N.W¼ S.E¼
20 Acres
20 Chains
W½
N.E¼
S.E¼
20 Acres
10 Chains
E½
N.E¼
S.E¼
20 Acres
10 Chains
S.W¼ S.W¼
40 Acres
80 Rods
S.E¼ S.W¼
40 Acres
440 Yards
N.W¼
S.W¼
S.E¼
10 Acres
N.E.¼
S.W¼
S.E¼
10 Acres
S.W¼
S.W¼
S.E.¼
10 Acres
S.E¼
S.W¼
S.E.¼
10 Acres
660 Ft.
660 Ft.
5 Acres
5 Acres
1 Furlong
5
Acres
5 Chs.
5
Acres
20 Rd.
2½
Acrs
2½
Acrs
2½
Acrs
330 Ft
2½
Acrs
330 Ft
10 Acres
may be
subdivided
into about
80 lots of
30'x125' Each

Used with permission from *The Appraisal of Real Estate,* 9th edition.
© 1987 by the American Institute of Real Estate Appraisers, Chicago.

agreed upon by the owners, each lot being assigned a number. Three systems can be at work here: the parcel being developed might be located by the Rectangular system, the lots identified by the Lot and Block system, and the exact property lines might be further established by Metes and Bounds.

Is this confusing? You bet. And there are things that can affect a description, such as a meandering stream and government lots. Still, though you may not be able to write a legal description, it's

LOT AND BLOCK SURVEY

Used with permission from *The Appraisal of Real Estate,* 9th edition.
© 1987 by the American Institute of Real Estate Appraisers, Chicago.

nice to know what's generally going on when you sign those intimidating documents for your dream house.

▶ **For more information on land descriptions, go to the Moore & Warner
website at http://www.moore-warner.com and click on "Farm and
Food Facts," then on "Important Facts About Land Descriptions."**

RADIO WAVES

• •

DID YOU EVER WONDER WHY the AM numbers on your radio dial are
bigger than the FM numbers? Or what the difference is between
VHF television channels and UHF channels? Or why you sometimes hear a CB radio in the middle of your favorite rerun? In fact,
what do these things, plus electricity, microwaves, infrared waves,
light waves, X rays, and gamma rays, have in common? All are electromagnetic waves, all of which travel at the same speed—the
speed of light—and each of which vibrates at a constant rate.

What makes one electromagnetic wave different from another
is how fast it's vibrating, or the *frequency* (number) of the waves,
called *cycles,* that go by per second. Frequency is measured in *hertz:*
1 hertz = 1 cycle per second. Very low frequency waves with long
wavelengths, like electricity (AC power), vibrate at only a few cycles per second: 60 hertz is common in the United States. Radio
waves begin at about 15,000 hertz. Compared to electricity, that
sounds high, but it's nothing compared to X rays, which vibrate at
about 1,000,000,000,000,000,000 cycles per second (10^{18} hertz) or
gamma rays at more than 10^{24} hertz (see *Exponents,* page 91). Hertz
are also referred to in larger, more easily used units:

Hertz

1 cycle per second	= 1 hertz (Hz)		
1,000 hertz	= 1 kilohertz (KHz)		
1,000 kilohertz	= 1 megahertz (MHz)	= 1,000,000 hertz	
1,000 megahertz	= 1 gigahertz (GHz)	= 1,000,000,000 hertz	

How does this translate to your radio dial? The AM side, usually numbered from 550 to 1600 (some dials remove the last zero,
leaving it 55 to 160), stand for kilohertz, although today's AM
band extends from 525 to 1,700 kilohertz, or 525,000 to 1,700,000
cycles per second. The FM side of your dial is usually numbered
from 88 to 108, which stands for megahertz. FM numbers are
lower than AM numbers, but the frequencies are much higher—
88,000,000 to 108,000,000 cycles per second. The frequencies of
FM stations are sandwiched between channel six and seven,

while television stations are assigned frequencies according to channel: VHF (very high frequency) channels 2 through 6 broadcast at 54 to 88 megahertz, below the FM frequencies, while channels 7 to 13, broadcasting at 174 to 216 megahertz, and the UHF (ultrahigh frequency) channels (14 to 83), broadcasting at 470 to 890 megahertz, are above the FM channels. CB radio uses two bands, one of which is in 460 to 470, right under the UHF band, which accounts for its occasional television interference.

Whatever it's broadcasting, each station is assigned its frequency by the Federal Communications Commission (FCC), which has been regulating American broadcasting since 1934, to keep stations from interfering with each other. Each station operates strictly within its assigned channel, whose size depends on the type of broadcast. AM channels require only a 10 kilohertz band, while FM channels are closer to 200 kilohertz and television channels require 6,000 kilohertz each.

So how big is a radio wave? The length of a wave (cycle) is measured from crest to crest, or from the tip of one wave to the tip of the next. Very low frequency waves (lower than 30 kilohertz) can measure over 10,000 yards—more than six miles—from crest to crest. Medium frequency waves—AM broadcasting waves fall in here—are about 1,000 to 100 yards each. VHF waves, used for FM and television broadcasting, measure 10 yards to 1 yard. UHF waves are from about a yard to half an inch. Extremely high frequency waves, such as X rays, are so small that they are measured in angstroms (one ten-billionth, or 0.00000000001, of a meter): light rays are approximately 3,900 to 7,700 angstroms wide, while an X ray might measure 1 angstrom, and gamma rays can be smaller than 0.000001 angstrom.

It's the size of the electromagnetic wave, related to its frequency, that is really what makes a light wave (which you can see) different from an electrical wave, or a radio wave, or an X ray. The range is phenomenal—frequencies run from 1 to more than 1,000,000,000,000,000,000,000,000 hertz, with wavelengths measuring from several miles to far smaller than 0.0000000000000001 meter.

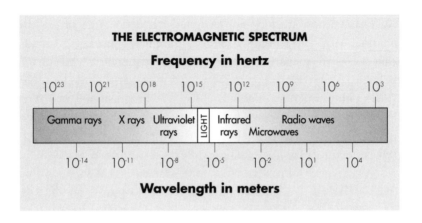

THE ELECTROMAGNETIC SPECTRUM

Frequency in hertz

> ▶ To find out more about radio waves, go to "The Electromagnetic Spectrum" at http://imagers.gsfc.nasa.gov/ems/radio.html. For information on microwaves, click on "Next Shorter Wave Length." For a chart of the electromagnetic spectrum in color, go to http://www.lbl.gov/MicroWorlds/ALSTool/EMSpec/EMSpec2.html.

RAILFALL

RAINFALL

THERE IS HARDLY A MORE MISUNDERSTOOD weather forecast than the prediction of rain. If you read that there's a 50 percent chance of rain for today, it sounds as if the weather people were guessing that there's half a chance that the area covered by the forecast (yours) will get rained on, as if they were betting 50-50 odds. Although there seems to be a difference of opinion among forecasters, the National Weather Service insists that the forecast percentage is a *probability*, not the percentage of your forecast area that will be wet by the end of the day. One could argue that odds are still 50-50 that you won't need your umbrella.

Forecasts unaccompanied by precise definitions can add to the confusion. This is what they usually mean:

Rainfall Descriptions

Light rain	Trace to 0.10 inches per hour
Moderate rain	0.11 to 0.30 inches per hour
Heavy rain	Over 0.30 inches per hour

Cloudiness Descriptions

Partly sunny or partly cloudy	Clouds will cover 30 to 70 percent of sky
Cloudy	Clouds will cover 90 percent of sky
Fair	Clouds will cover less than 40 percent of sky, with no fog anticipated

Rain reports—the measure of rainfall in inches—represent the amount of rain that would have remained on the ground if it did not run off or soak in. To calculate this, *rain gauges*—straight-sided containers 8 inches in diameter—are scattered throughout the forecast area, each one often representing many square miles. In the Midwest the average gauge represents 250 square miles, although the U.S. average is one per 100 square miles. The intensity of rainfall can also be measured by weight in bucketlike devices. Measurements of rain collected in rain gauges are taken daily, either by hand or by electronic devices. Since rain rarely falls evenly, this method of calculating rainfall might be likened to measuring the height of one meteorologist in each state and then saying that Missouri meteorologists are taller than Maryland meteorologists. To help fill in the gaps, a huge network of private weather stations operated by volunteers called Cooperative Weather Observers collects weather information in up to ten thousand sites around the country and reports it to the U.S. Weather Service.

A rain gauge is accurate for one place: your house, for example, or your garden or farm. You can make a rain gauge from any straight-sided, flat-bottomed container, such as a large juice can. Ideally, it's set 3 feet above the ground and away from buildings, trees, or other interferences. (See URL at the end of this entry for instructions.)

Radar

Since 1957, meteorologists have depended on a dedicated national grid of weather radar stations called WSR-57 (Weather Surveillance Radar) authorized by Congress after hurricanes devastated the U.S. East Coast in the mid-fifties. The last of these was replaced in the mid-nineties by the more powerful and sensitive NEXRAD (Next Generation Weather Radar). When the news media weather reports announce Doppler weather data, they're referring to NEXRAD's Doppler radars, which bounce microwaves off raindrops and measure the difference between transmitted and received frequencies. In addition to precipitation speed and intensity, Doppler radars can measure, to some extent, wind intensity and direction, and detect the low pressure swirls that can result in tornadoes, something the old system could not do.

▶ **To look up rainfall measurements around the country, go to http://www.ccrfcd.org/raingage.htm. For a large variety of weather information, go to the National Oceanic and Atmospheric Administration at http://www.noaa.gov or the National Weather Service at http://www.nws.noaa.gov. To make your own rain gauge, go to http://www.miamisci.org/hurricane/rainmeasure.html.**

ROMAN NUMERALS
• •

LIKE DRACULA, Roman numerals rise from their coffin in the dead of night and stamp themselves onto buildings, slip into books, number chapters, and force themselves into student outlines. Decoding Roman numerals isn't really difficult though, and might even be an amusing pastime.

Here are the letters used to symbolize numbers in the Roman numeral system:

I	=	1	C	=	100
V	=	5	D	=	500
X	=	10	M	=	1,000
L	=	50	There is no zero.		

To read a number, you can simply add up the numbers from left to right, *if* they appear in descending order, large numbers to small ones:

Roman Numbers	Arabic Numerals
II	1 + 1 = 2
III	1 + 1 + 1 = 3
VIII = V + III	8 = 5 + 3
XXVII = XX + V + II	27 = 20 + 5 + 2
LXXXVI = L + XXX + V + I	86 = 50 + 30 + 5 + 1
CCLI = CC + L + I	251 = 200 + 50 + 1
MMMCCCVI = MMM + CCC + V + I	3,306 = 3,000 + 300 + 5 + 1

The Romans, much like the rest of us, were always looking for a better way to do things, and so after a while, subtraction was introduced to shorten the bulkier numbers. The subtracting involves only the numbers 4 and 9 wherever they occur, including 14 and 19, 24 and 29, as well as 40 and 90, 400 and 900, and 4,000 (technically, Roman numerals can count only to 4,999). So you subtract smaller numerals that precede larger ones: instead of writing MMMMCCCCXXXXIIII (4,000 + 400 + 40 + 4 = 4,444), you can shorten it to MMMMCDXLIV (4,000 + [500 − 100] + [50 − 10] + [5 − 1]). Here are some easier examples:

IV	V − I = 4	XL	L − X = 40
IX	X − I = 9	XCIX	(C − X) + (X − I) = 99
XIV	X + (V − I) = 14		

Adding and subtracting Roman numerals—much less multiplying and dividing them—is quite literally unthinkable. Hence, their demise.

▶ **For a Roman numeral translator, date translator, and an entertaining quiz, go to a website by Stephanus Gibbs at http://www.guernsey.net/ ~sgibbs/roman.html.**

RUBBER BANDS

RUBBER BANDS ARE SPEEDY, reusable, fun to shoot, and cheap. The National Office Products Association claims that if a rubber band saves one second of working time, it pays for itself. But wait— what do those strange size numbers mean? Rubber band sizes are confusing, because the size numbers are arbitrary, not being of anything, but representing a length-width combination. Furthermore, as you will see, a larger number doesn't always mean a longer rubber band. There is some method to the madness, however: with the exception of size 8, all the sizes in the same decade,

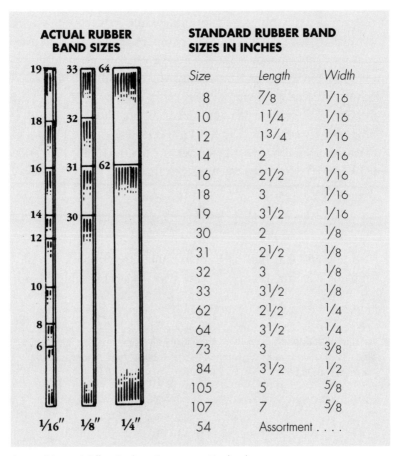

Size	Length	Width
8	7/8	1/16
10	1 1/4	1/16
12	1 3/4	1/16
14	2	1/16
16	2 1/2	1/16
18	3	1/16
19	3 1/2	1/16
30	2	1/8
31	2 1/2	1/8
32	3	1/8
33	3 1/2	1/8
62	2 1/2	1/4
64	3 1/2	1/4
73	3	3/8
84	3 1/2	1/2
105	5	5/8
107	7	5/8
54	Assortment	

ACTUAL RUBBER BAND SIZES

STANDARD RUBBER BAND SIZES IN INCHES

Source: National Office Products Association. Used with permission.

such as teens, twenties, and so on, are the same width, and the widths do increase as the tens get higher; for example, a size in the teens is always 1/16 inch wide, while a size in the 30s is always 1/4 inch wide, etc. The higher the number within a decade, the longer the rubber band.

▶ **For more extensive rubber band size list, go to Allsup Consulting "Non-Engineering Data" at http://www.dhc.net/~allsup/misc.htm.**

SANDPAPER

SANDPAPER ISN'T REALLY SANDPAPER anymore—it's "coated abrasive." The original material was paper covered with grains of flint, which was inexpensive but didn't last long and made slow progress. Today, although flint is still available, other abrasives are more popular. Garnet is the hardest natural abrasive used in sandpaper, and it lasts five times longer than flint. Synthetic papers are even more popular—aluminum oxide is widely used as an all-around paper, and silicon carbide is the hardest of all the synthetics. There are other "abrasives," as they are called now, as well.

The old system for grading grits on abrasive papers was a 1 to 12 system, with the low numbers being coarse and the high numbers leading to finest. Today that system has been replaced with a 12 to 600 system, which also goes from low numbers for coarse to high for incredibly fine. The numbers refer to the size of the grit on the paper, not the number of grits per square inch, although the numbers probably do refer to the number of grits that could fit in a defined area. The amount of grit on sandpaper, however, can vary: "open coat" sandpaper has fewer grits, cutting faster and cleaning more easily than "closed coat" sandpaper, on which the grits are closer together.

There are usually 22 grades of abrasive paper, not 600 as the numbers seem to imply: 12, 16, 20, 24, 30, 36, 40, 50, 60, 80, 100, 120, 150, 180, 220, 240, 280, 320, 360, 400, 500, 600. The papers are also marked with an A, C, or D (there is no B) to indicate the weight of the backing: A is the lightest. As with many hardware items, the adjectives applied to the various grades are not always the same—one company's "fine" may be between 100 and 120, while another's may be as coarse as 80. The important thing is the number.

Sandpaper Grades

240–600	Extra fine
150–220	Very fine
100–120	Fine
60–80	Medium
30–50	Coarse

Which sandpaper do you use for what? It really depends on a number of factors, but these suggestions from several heavy users of sandpaper serve as a "rough" guide:

40 or 50	De-rusting metals Stripping house paint Getting rid of a lot of wood fast for shaping
60	Coarse sanding for wood shaping Stripping wood floors Grinding welding joints Rough metal work
80	General joint alignment in woodworking Rough metal finishing Stripping painted furniture Flattening board laminations
100	General medium woodworking Smoothing joints Auto body finishing
120	Final prepainting finish for furniture
220	Fine sanding for wood (higher is polishing)
220–400	Smoothing paints on wood or metal
400–600	Metal polishing Polishing glass edges

▶ **Find more on sandpaper at http://www.woodzone.com/articles/ sandpaper or go to http://www.sawdustmaking.com, scroll down, and click on "Sandpaper."**

SCANNERS (FLATBED)

A FLATBED SCANNER records printed images or characters to a computer monitor, appearing to work pretty much like a photocopier. However, if you own a computer but not a scanner, perhaps you're waiting to understand the numbers that describe potential scanners before risking a purchase. This is quite understandable; a scanner, although often sitting next to a printer and often used in conjunction with one, does not speak printer language. It's easy to get confused. Here are some things to consider.

Type of Scanner

You can choose from several kinds of scanners, but the most common and versatile is the flatbed scanner. A sheetfed scanner works like a fax machine and can only take single sheets. A photo scanner works only for photos; a slide scanner scans only slides. Many flatbed scanners can do all this and more: they can scan single sheets, color or black-and-white photographs, slides (with a special attachment), line drawings, pages from books and magazines, and objects placed upon the bed. Using OCR (optical character recognition), most scanners can also scan print so it can be edited.

Resolution

A scanner's image sharpness, as in printer resolution (see *Printers*, page 195), is given in *dpi*, or *dots per inch*: at this writing, 1200 × 2400 dpi is common for a scanner intended for home use, although higher is available. If you're concerned that this will not be enough, consult someone who is already using a scanner as you plan to use yours.

Bit Color Depth

A scanner may claim a *bit depth* of 24, 30, 42, or 48. The higher the number, the more colors the scanner will pick up. Here's how it works:

What is described as dots per inch (dpi) for printed material is described as *pixels per inch (ppi)* on a monitor. A computer screen is made up of rows and rows of tiny square *pixels*. Each pixel on a 24-bit color monitor is made up of at least 24 *bits*, eight bits for red, eight bits for green, and eight bits for blue, offering a total of over sixteen million color combinations. A 30-bit scanner has ten bits per color, a 42-bit scanner fourteen, and so on. The more colors a scanner can record, the greater the depth of color.

Dynamic Range

Dynamic range, similar to color depth, measures the *tone range* of colors from 0.0 (white, or no colors) to 4.0 (perfect black); the rating is sometimes referred to as a *Dmax* number. Dmax 3.6 is excellent; so far no scanner rates a perfect 0.4. Many scanner tags do not offer this information.

Size and Speed

Most scanners record an image with a CCD (charged-coupled device) that passes a light source over a 9- × 12-inch or 14-inch area. Scanners with larger scanning areas are available but tend to be quite expensive. Speed is not always reported, so if it's important to you, you might have to test an actual model. Fifteen ppm (pages per minute) is presently considered quite fast for black ink only; twelve ppm for color. Speed can vary with the quality setting.

Color Photo Scanning

The software that runs most scanners is called Twain. Twain offers several settings, including color photo, black-and-white photo (called *grayscale*), line (true black and white), and OCR (optical character recognition), which allows scanned text to be edited. The most commonly used is color photo.

Unless you're familiar with scanners, you may not realize that scanners and printers do not speak the same color language. Color as we have always understood it operates quite differently in the digital world of computer monitors and television screens than in the analog world of printed material. If you scan an image to the computer and then print it out on a printer, the printer must translate the scanner/computer colors to printer colors. The result can often include startling changes. Here's why:

Light from a computer monitor or television screen shoots straight in your eyes instead of bouncing off objects and *then* into your eyes, as from objects in the real world. This direct light mixes differently than reflected light to make colors. Computer monitors and television screens use the *RGB (Red, Green, Blue) color system,* meaning that red, green, and blue are mixed to make all the colors. In the RGB virtual color world, red plus green makes yellow!

A printer, however, uses the *CMYK (Cyan, Magenta, Yellow, and usually blacK) color system,* in which yellow plus blue (Cyan) makes green. So while the numbers of pixels per inch can be directly translated to dots per inch, the colors that make up the pixels are not the same as the colors that make up the dots.

▶ For a scanning education, go to a website by Wayne Fulton at http://www.scantips.com.

SCREWS AND BOLTS

FEW THINGS ARE AS BAFFLING to the uninitiated as the huge variety of threaded products—and their associated numbers—in a hardware screw and bolt department. The first problem is deciding what's a screw and what's not. There is some energetic difference of opinion about this—one authority insists that a screw comes to a point and a bolt ends flat and requires a nut or hole with mating threads. Another, confronted with the nontapering machine screw, feels strongly that any threaded fastener is a screw until you put a nut on it, in which case, it's a bolt. The truth is, it doesn't really matter—screws and bolts are sized pretty much the same way.

Then there is the dazzling array of screws. If you want to buy a screw, you need to know the size, the material it's made of and/or the material you're screwing it into, and the kind of head. FH is a flat head screw; RH is a round head. There are also hex head, pan head, and Phillips, not to mention lag screws, sheet metal screws, square drive screws, and machine screws.

Then, there is the problem of the screw size. There are often three numbers sizing screws, usually written something like this: 4–40 × $\frac{1}{2}$, sometimes written 4/40 × $\frac{1}{2}$.

The first number—in this case, the 4—is the *size*. The American Society of Mechanical Engineers (ASME), responsible for most screw and bolt sizing, uses one system for small screws and another for larger screws. Screws with a diameter under $\frac{1}{4}$ inch are commonly numbered from 000 to 12. The smaller the number, the smaller the diameter of the screw as measured just under the head. Screws $\frac{1}{4}$ inch in diameter or larger are usually sized by the fraction of an inch. So instead of a 0 or 6, you'll see a fraction, like $\frac{3}{8}$ or $\frac{5}{16}$ or $\frac{1}{2}$.

The second number, which usually comes after a hyphen or slash, is the *pitch*—the number of threads per inch.

Some Common Size/Pitch Combinations for Screws

2–56	8–32	$\frac{1}{4}$–20
4–40	10–24	$\frac{1}{4}$–28
6–32	10–32	$\frac{1}{4}$–32

The number after the "×" is the length of the screw in inches. Size and thread pitch combinations, such as those above, come in various lengths. A size 4/40 × $\frac{1}{2}$ is a size 4 screw with 40 threads to the inch and $\frac{1}{2}$ inch long. Although some boxes of screws are labeled with the length first, coming before the "×," it's not hard to know whether the length is first or last—one of the numbers will correspond to the length you're looking at. You also have to contend with metric screws; metric measures are usually preceded with an "M," and these screws are found in a special section.

There was a time when threaded fasteners were handmade and there was no standardization at all. Each nut had to be carefully paired with its bolt, for no other would fit it. As better lathes were developed for cutting the threads, the nuts and bolts from one shop would be interchangeable, but not with those from another shop. Coming up with standard screw, nut, and bolt sizes kept machinists, inventors, and governments busy for hundreds of years. It was in about 1800 that David Wilkinson invented the screw-cutting lathe in America that could cut precision screws and bolts that matched. Today, in a process called thread-rolling, blanks are re-formed using threaded dies. Nothing is cut away.

The standardization of screw threads was a longer battle, however, continuing between the Americans and the British right into World War II, when most of the parts for war equipment from Great Britain and the United States were interchangeable— except the screws needed to put them together! The problem was that the British had proposed the first standards for screw threads in 1841, which set the angle between the sides of the threads at 55 degrees. Then in 1864 the United States had decided to set its own standard of 60 degrees, finding it stronger and easier to gauge than the British 55-degree angle. Each country held stubbornly to its own idea of the perfect screw until 1960, when the 60-degree angle was accepted by both, along with a standard of diameters and threads-per-inch for each.

It was about this time that the world was pushing metrics in every possible area of measurement. The International Organization for Standardization began work on a worldwide standard screw thread system in 1964 that would somehow bring the metric screw system and the United Thread System (the U.S.-U.K. system) together. They are still working at it. For most purposes, metric threaded fasteners must still be purchased specifically for metric equipment.

▶ For details on the ongoing search for metric agreement, go to Think and Go Metric, "How ISO Metric Standards Cut Manufacturing Costs," http://www.kok.com/pr02.htm.

SHIPS

● ●

ALTHOUGH MOST RECREATIONAL WATERCRAFT are described in terms of length (feet), large commercial vessels have outgrown this description and today often are described in terms of *tons*. "Tonnage," when applied to a ship, can have either of two meanings—it can refer to the volume of available space or it can refer to weight—but a book or magazine describing a "20,000-ton ship" as often as not will fail to explain which kind of ton it's referring to. And there is a big difference.

Gross Tonnage

Gross tonnage, also called *gross register tonnage*, or *gross weight*, is not weight at all. *Gross tonnage is the total cubic capacity of a ship* (all enclosed space, less a few spaces such as hatchways) as expressed in *register tons*, with 1 register ton equaling 100 cubic feet. Gross tonnage is a measure of *volume*, even if it is sometimes referred to as "weight." A ship of 20,000 gross tons has 2,000,000 cubic feet of enclosed space. Although most often applied to passenger ships, it's not unusual to see it used with other ships as well.

This use of tonnage to measure volume began back in the thirteenth century when merchant ships frequently carried wine in giant casks called *tuns;* a ship's carrying capacity came to be measured by the number of tuns she could carry. By the fifteenth century England had established a standard wine-filled tun of 250 gallons weighing 2,240 pounds. The 100-cubic-foot ton, which replaced it in the nineteenth century, remains the most common comparative measure of ship size. The 1969 International Convention on Tonnage Measurement of Ships set international standards for both gross and net tonnage, retaining the 100-cubic-foot ton. (*Net tonnage*, not often encountered in general sources, is actual carrying capacity: the gross tonnage less specified spaces unavailable for cargo, such as the engine room, crew's quarters, etc.)

How do gross tons translate into ship size? Columbus's *Santa Maria* is said to have been about 150 tons, the *Mayflower* 180 tons, the average clipper ship about 1,000 tons, and nineteenth-century sailing ships reach up to 5,000 tons. The British steamship *Great Eastern*, launched in 1859, was almost 19,000 gross register tons and for nearly fifty years was the biggest ship in the world. But passenger ships got bigger and bigger—the *Titanic*, which sank on her 1912 maiden voyage, was 46,000 tons—culminating in the 1930s with the three biggest: the *Queen Mary* at 81,000 gross tons and the *Queen Elizabeth* and the French *Normandie* at 83,000 gross tons each. These huge ships proved less efficient than smaller passenger ships, however; today the average cruise ship is about 20,000 gross register tons.

Displacement Tonnage

Displacement tonnage does refer to weight, but not the actual weight of the ship. *Displacement tonnage is the weight of the water displaced by the ship.* Because physically weighing a ship would be awkward, if not impossible, the submerged area of the ship is calculated in cubic feet. A floating object always displaces an amount of water equal to the volume under the water, so the number of cubic feet of water displaced will be the same as the number of submerged cubic feet of ship. Multiply this figure by the weight of a cubic foot of water and you have the weight of water displaced. This figure is expressed using the *long ton* of 2,240 pounds (the 2,000-pound *short ton* is rarely used in the shipping business).

Although this may seem an odd way to weigh something, the system works well enough. Sometimes that's not enough to know, however; you may also need to know which type of displacement weight is being referred to.

Loaded displacement tonnage is the weight of the water displaced when a ship is carrying its normal fuel, crew, and cargo load. When a ship is described in "displacement tons," this usually refers to loaded displacement tons. Most naval ships are described in displacement tons. The full load displacement weight of a battleship can be up to 59,000 tons; an aircraft carrier about 80,000 tons.

Light displacement tonnage is the weight of the water displaced by the unloaded ship.

Deadweight tonnage (dwt) is the difference between the first two, which amounts to the weight of cargo, stores, water, fuel, crew, and passengers (in terms of the weight of water displaced) that the ship can carry. Freighters and tankers are usually described in terms of deadweight tons. A typical cargo vessel of 9,200 gross tons (cubic foot capacity) may average about 21,000 tons displacement (meaning loaded displacement) and 13,500 tons deadweight.

Twenty-foot Equivalent Units (TEU) are sometimes used to describe the shipping capacity of vessels called *container* ships, which carry cargo in easily managed, portable metal boxes. One TEU equals one 20-foot ISO (International Standards Organization) container measuring 20 × 8 × (usually) 8 feet high. The *Regina Maersk*, one of the largest container ships to call at a North American port, is described as a 6,000 TEU vessel. Ports are sometimes described by how many TEU they can handle. The Port of Long Beach, California, for example, reports moving 4,462,967 TEUs in 2001.

To get a sense of today's ship sizes, consider the *Titanic*, with a gross tonnage of 46,329 and an overall length of 882.5 feet. Today's cruise ship *Grand Princess* (Princess Cruises), although not much longer, has more than twice the gross tonnage, at 109,000. The *Regina Maersk* may be the largest container ship at a length of 1,043 feet. The largest supertanker in operation is probably the *Jahre Viking* at 564,763 gross tons and 1,504 feet.

The trend toward bigger and bigger oil tankers came to a halt in 1989 when the midsize *Exxon Valdez* ran aground and spilled nearly 11 million gallons of oil into Alaska's Prince William Sound. The U.S. Congress quickly passed the U.S. Oil Pollution Act of 1990 outlawing single-hull oil tankers in U.S. waters and requiring all crude oil supertankers to have double hulls by 2015. Old tankers are being renovated and new ones are being built. The first, *Polar Endeavour*, at 125,000 gross tons, sailed in 2001. The third, *Polar Discovery*, was christened in April 2002.

Although the *Exxon Valdez* disaster changed the way crude oil is shipped, it wasn't the world's biggest oil spill disaster. In 1979 the *Atlantic Empress* and the *Aegean Captain* collided off the coast of Trinidad, spilling 88.5 million gallons of crude oil into the Caribbean Sea.

▶ For more on merchant shipping, go to http://www.navis.gr. For ship sizes and oil tankers, click on "Miscellaneous," then on "Ships and Shipping." For information on oil tanker spills, go to the Trade Environment Database at http://www.american.edu/TED/EXXON.htm.

SHOES

SHOE SIZES IN THIS COUNTRY really make no sense at all, and maybe the reason for this is that they've been based on *barleycorns* since the seventh century. This system became more or less official when, in 1324, King Edward II decreed the inch to be the length of three barleycorns. Shoemakers determined that the longest normal foot around was as long as 39 barleycorns in a row, which was exactly 13 inches. Thus 13 became the largest shoe size, with full sizes equaling one barleycorn ($^{1}/_{3}$ inch) each. So a size 12 is 38 barleycorns, a size 11 is 37 barleycorns, a size 10 is 36 barleycorns, and so on. This system found its way to America, and in 1880 Edwin B. Simpson of New York introduced the first universally adopted system for shoe sizing, which remains to this day, adjusted only slightly: the insole measurement of American shoes has decreased by $^{1}/_{12}$ inch and half sizes are available, equaling half a barleycorn ($^{1}/_{6}$ inch). Today, of course, size 13 is no longer the biggest size.

Unfortunately, American women's shoe sizes do not correspond to men's—a man's size 8 is about a woman's size $9^{1}/_{2}$. Perhaps Mr. Simpson introduced this confusion. Children's shoe sizes are also odd, because the width of the hand (about 4 inches) was used to determine the smallest size, and the length of the hand (about 9 inches) the largest size. So children's sizes run from 0 (4 inches) to 13 (9 inches).

European shoe sizes are understandably unrelated to this complicated system. Their unit is still based on thirds, though: each European size equals 2/3 of a centimeter, with the biggest size usually a 50 (the equivalent of an American 14). Most of the world uses this metric shoe-sizing system, which doesn't require half sizes and applies to both male and female feet.

A new metric shoe-sizing system called Mondopoint has been introduced by SATRA, a British shoe research organization, which would solve the shoe confusion worldwide. However, although most countries say the shoe fits, Americans are not ready to give their comfortable barleycorns the boot.

▶ **For an international shoe size conversion chart, including American (men and women), British, European, and Japanese sizes, go to the All About Dance website at http://www.allaboutdance.com. Under "Sizing and Color Charts" click on "Shoe Size Conversions."**

SNOWFALL

IF YOU'VE JUST LIVED THROUGH a blizzard that meteorologists report dropped 16 inches of snow on your sidewalk, just how much actual precipitation is that? Snow, in its melted form, is figured into the annual precipitation figures. The rule of thumb for estimating this is that 10 inches of snow equals 1 inch of water. But anyone who has shoveled a few sidewalks knows that there's snow and there's snow—10 inches of light fluffy stuff is less heavy and contains less water than the wet, backbreaking kind. So measuring snow depth won't work for the statistical record. It might in fact take 40 inches of particularly dry snow to make a liquid inch.

You'd think the new fancy radar systems and weather satellites could practically count snowflakes, but not so. Snowfall resists automated measuring systems. Meteorologists still collect snow in rain gauges—straight-sided 8-inch containers—and in snow gauges, which are slightly larger and measure not only the snowfall but the amount of water generated when it melts.

In mountainous areas where the snowpack (deep layers of accumulated snowfalls) is an important source of water, the snow depth is not only measured, but core samples are taken to see what kind of snow is involved. Snow that melts or is rained on does not always run off immediately; the water can filter to the bottom and freeze into ice, as much as doubling the snow/water ratio. This kind of information is important not just to skiers, but to water- and flood-control agencies.

▶ For more information on snow and ice, go to the National Snow and Ice Data Center (NSIDC) at http://www.nsidc.colorado.edu. For NOAA's "Snow Measurement Guidelines," go to http://www.wrds.uwyo.edu/wrds/wsc/reference/snowmeas.html. For U.S. snowfall distribution maps from The Snow Booklet, by Nolan J. Doesken and Arthur Judson, go to http://ulysses.atmos.colostate.edu/~odie/snowtxt.html and click on "U.S. Snowfall Patterns."

SOCIAL SECURITY NUMBERS

IF YOU WANT A JOB in the United States, you have to apply for a Social Security Number, used to identify you for tax and, of course, Social Security pension purposes. At least, that was the original purpose. Today it is used more and more as a national identity number. If you've ever wondered whether your Social Security number gives away secrets to people in the know, you can stop worrying. However, the number can be used to access a great deal of information about you, and even to "steal" your identity. The Social Security Administration has begun cautioning people against giving out their social security numbers. Despite all this, and despite the fact that you are the only person holding your particular Social Security number, your Social Security number by itself reveals little about you.

Where Social Security Numbers Are Assigned

001–003	New Hampshire	449–467	Texas
004–007	Maine	468–477	Minnesota
008–009	Vermont	478–485	Iowa
010–034	Massachusetts	486–500	Missouri
035–039	Rhode Island	501–502	North Dakota
040–049	Connecticut	503–504	South Dakota
050–134	New York	505–508	Nebraska
135–158	New Jersey	509–515	Kansas
159–211	Pennsylvania	516–517	Montana
212–220	Maryland	518–519	Idaho
221–222	Delaware	520	Wyoming
223–231	Virginia	521–524	Colorado
232–236	West Virginia	525–585	New Mexico
232 and		526–527	
237–246	North Carolina	and	
247–251	South Carolina	600–601	Arizona
252–260	Georgia	528–529	Utah
261–267		530	Nevada
and		531–539	Washington
589–595	Florida	540–544	Oregon
268–302	Ohio	545–573	
303–317	Indiana	and	
318–361	Illinois	602–626	California
362–386	Michigan	574	Alaska
387–399	Wisconsin	575–576	Hawaii
400–407	Kentucky	577–579	District of Columbia
408–415	Tennessee	580	Virgin Islands
416–424	Alabama	580–584	
425–428		and	
and		596–599	Puerto Rico
587–588	Mississippi	586	Guam
429–432	Arkansas	586	American Samoa
433–439	Louisiana	586	Philippine Islands
440–448	Oklahoma	700–728*	Railroad Board

*700–728 was reserved for railroad employees. New number issuance in 700-series was discontinued in 1963.

Note: Some numbers are shown more than once because either they have been transferred from one state to another or they have been divided for use among certain geographic locations.

Source: Social Security Administration, U.S. Department of Health and Human Services

Social Security numbers are divided into three parts. Before 1972 the first three digits simply established the state where the card was issued. Today the first three digits are determined by— but are not the same as—the ZIP code of the state where you resided at the time of application.

The second group of numbers is the Social Security Administration's code number for the year the card was issued, beginning with 01 and proceeding in a set pattern—not necessarily in sequence—from there. Number 385-42-0000, for example, does not mean that the card was issued in 1942—42 has been issued in different years by different states, depending on how quickly each of their three-digit state codes worked through the sequence. A very low number, such as 01 or 02, probably means that the card was issued about fifty years ago, when numbers were first assigned. However, that is not always true.

The third group—four digits—is, taken with the others, your personal number, assigned at random.

▶ **To read about Social Security numbers and privacy issues, go to the Electronic Privacy Information Center at http://www.epic.org/ privacy/ssn.**

SOCKS
•••

YOU HAVE IT from the sock authority of the United States of America, the president of the National Association of Hosiery Manufacturers (NAHM): sock sizes correspond approximately to the actual length of your foot, in inches. If your foot is 10 inches long, your sock size is probably also 10. How did such a sensible system begin? One can only assume that it was first applied to men's socks, men's clothing being the only area of apparel in which sizes are based on real measurements.

Before the 1940s socks were made of natural fibers such as cotton, wool, and silk. Natural fibers are rigid, so socks had to be sized to the last half-inch. Each pair of socks had a specific size, such as 9, 9¹/2, 10, 10¹/2, and on up. A size 9 sock fit a foot measuring 9 inches, and so on.

Then, in 1939, nylon, the first synthetic fiber, was invented, and by the early 1950s yarn producers had figured out how to make it stretch and, much like a telephone cord, snap back to its original shape. This stretchiness was God's gift to the sock people, who could now put a wide range of foot sizes into the same-size sock. Not only did this save lots of money; the sock actually fit better, clinging to whatever foot it surrounded. So today, if your foot is 10 inches, you wear a size 9–11 sock. Fortunately, you don't really need to know how long your foot is; you probably have known your sock size for quite a while.

However, socks for little feet—infants' and children's—correspond more to their shoe size than the actual foot measurement; the hosiery industry is predicting that all sock sizes someday may be designed to approximate shoe sizes more closely.

SODIUM (SALT)

WHEN YOU READ the sodium content on a food label, how do you know whether or not to be shocked? How much sodium should you—or shouldn't you—consume? The recommended amount for adults is under 3,300 mg per day. The 6,000 to 12,000 mg consumed daily by the average American is too much. But how much is that?

Consider this: 1 teaspoon of salt contains about 2,000 mg of sodium (1,938 to be exact), meaning that 1¹/2 teaspoons (close to 3,000 mg) per day is about right. If you average 8,000 mg daily, you are consuming 1¹/3 tablespoons of salt daily, the equivalent of 2 cups of salt every month. Unfortunately, you can't always tell the amount of sodium in food by taste. According to McDonald's May 2002 figures, a small order of French fries (135 mg) contains about the same amount of sodium as a glass of milk (135 mg), but their Quarter Pounder with Cheese may contain almost ten times that much (about 1,310 mg).

About one-third of the sodium you eat occurs naturally in fresh foods; the rest is added during processing, cooking, and at the table. Processed and fast foods are some of the worst sodium offenders. The easiest way to cut your sodium intake is to avoid them and go light on the shaker. To gauge how heavy your hand is on the shaker, sprinkle a piece of paper as you normally do a plate of food; then measure the salt in a measuring spoon.

Some Sodium Comparisons Per Serving

Low-Sodium Foods	mg	High-Sodium Foods	mg
1/4-lb. hamburger and bun	222	McDonald's Quarter Pounder	840
1/4-lb. (Cheddar) cheeseburger & bun	544	McDonald's Quarter Pounder with cheese	1,310
1 fillet halibut, broiled in butter	168	McDonald's Filet-O-Fish	890
Homemade chili with ground beef & canned low-salt tomatoes & kidney beans	370	Canned chili con carne with beans	531
		Bouillon cube	960
7 oz. chunk tuna, water pack	75	7 oz. chunk tuna, oil pack	800
Homemade chicken or beef broth (no salt added)	50	Many canned soups	1,000 to 2,000
1 cup boiled carrots	50	1 cup canned carrots	581

Source: McDonald's figures from "Nutrition Facts," May 2002, at the McDonald's Corporation website at http://www.mcdonalds.com/countries/usa/food/nutrient_breakdown /media/breakdown.pdf. All other figures from Nutritive Value of American Foods, by Catherine F. Adams, United States Department of Agriculture.

Although companies are beginning to provide alternatives for health-conscious customers, fast and processed foods can sometimes use amazing amounts of sodium. Many of Schlotzsky's sandwiches test out at almost 4,000 mg sodium and even more. If you're hooked on a fast food favorite, it's worth checking it out.

▶ **To check the nutrition content of a fast food restaurant, go to http://www.olen.com/food. For an eye-popping look at the sodium, fat, calorie and other nutritional content of the major fast food chains, go to "Fast Food Facts" by Ken Kuhl at http://www.kenkuhl.com/ fastfood and click on "Fast Facts." To find out the sodium content of common foods, go to "Sodium Content of Your Food" at http:// www.midwestear.com/sodium.htm.**

SOIL, GARDEN
••

EVEN IF YOU'RE AN AVID GARDENER who reads about soil pH with some frequency, you may still be among the many who are confused about the subject. In fact, if you're serious about gardening, you've probably had your soil tested. That's often a good idea—many garden soils are too acid, meaning that the pH is too low (see *pH*, page 184). As a rule of thumb, the more rain you get, the more acidic your soil is likely to be; soils in a dry climate tend to be alkaline, containing chalk, lime, or other such substances.

Why should you be concerned about pH? The pH of soil affects the plants' ability to use the nutrients from organic matter in the soil as well as the fertilizer you may add. If the pH is too low or too high, a nutrient may not remain soluble long enough to reach the roots. The pH also affects the number of microorganisms in the soil, which help change organic nitrogen to a form that the plants can use.

The best pH for most gardens (flower and vegetable) is 6.5, a level at which nearly any plant except "acid-loving" plants can grow. The chart on page 229 offers general guidelines to the pH level most plants prefer, but there are always exceptions to every rule. (The pH of most ready-mixed soils you buy at a garden shop is printed right on the bag.) Public libraries, bookstores, and the Internet can provide more detailed information.

Soil Testing

If you're curious about the pH of your garden soil, have it tested. It rarely costs very much and serves a dual purpose, for the experts who do the testing are often the same ones who will tell you what to do if your soil pH is too low or too high. How to find the testing agency? Call your public library or find it online.

Once you get your pH results, be sure to get expert advice before you try to correct your soil. Each type of soil (sandy, loam, and clay) requires a different treatment—the more clay in acid soil,

A Garden of pHs

Range or Average pH	Example
2.7 to 3.4	Swamp peat
4.0 to 8.0	Survival range for most plants
4.5 to 5.5	Rhododendrons and azaleas
4.5 to 4.7	Average soil
5.5 to 6.5	Woodland ferns
5.5 to 7.2	Reasonable pH for most plants
Under 6.0	Considered to be "acid soil"
6.0 to 6.8	Most annuals
6.0 to 7.0	Best for vegetables*
6.0 to 7.0	Best pH for most plants
6.0 to 7.0	Best for lawns
6.5 to 7.0	Most perennials and vines
9.0 to 11.0	Desert soils
9.4	Lime (calcium carbonate)

*Some vegetables that will grow in 5.5 soil (as well as in the optimum 6.0 to 7.0 soil) are cucumbers, eggplants, onions, peppers, potatoes, pumpkins, rhubarb, sweet potatoes, tomatoes, and turnips. Potatoes, both white and sweet, are especially fond of acid soil.

the more lime will be needed to neutralize it. It can take years to correct the soil down to the root zone, so if your soil is quite a bit off, get it tested every year for a while to see how it's progressing.

▶ Find your cooperative extension office online at http://www.urbanext.uiuc.edu/netlinks/ces.html. For how to correct your soil, go to Smart Gardening at http://www.smartgardening.com and click on "Soil pH."

SOUND
•••

A SOUND IS A VIBRATION that travels in waves through the air or some other medium. But what does sound sound like and how is it measured? This is determined through pitch, loudness, and speed.

Pitch

The pitch of a sound—how high or low it sounds—depends on the frequency of its waves, or how fast the waves pass a particular point. High-pitched tones are produced by quickly vibrating, high-frequency waves; low tones by more relaxed, low-frequency waves. This frequency is measured in *hertz* (see *Radio Waves*, page 204), the number of waves (or cycles) per second. The lowest note on a piano, for example, has a frequency of 27 Hz, while the highest note is measured at 4,000 Hz. Humans with normal hearing can hear sounds even higher than that—up to 20,000 Hz. Sounds too low for human hearing (those below 20 Hz) are called *infrasonic*; those too high (over 20,000 Hz), *ultrasonic*. It's not unusual for animals to have infrasonic and/or ultrasonic hearing:

Humans	20 to 20,000 Hz
Dogs	15 to 50,000 Hz
Cats	60 to 65,000 Hz
Bats	1,000 to 120,000 Hz
Dolphins	150 to 150,000 Hz

Loudness

Most of us have assumed that loudness is measured in *decibels*. Technically, this is not true—loudness is measured in *phons*, a combination of decibels and hertz. The decibel is a level of a sound's energy, or power, or intensity. This energy can be measured in watts per square meter, but sound generates so little energy (the sound energy generated by a rock band might barely power a 100-watt lightbulb) that these numbers are awkward; for example, 10 decibels equals .000000000001 watt per square meter. Decibels are much easier to use.

The decibel is not an actual unit of measurement, but a comparison between one sound and another. In 1935–36, the U.S. government tested 5,000 people for the softest sound they could hear. This sound level became the reference point, or 0 decibels (dB), representing minimum human hearing. Thus 0 decibels is not an absence of sound, but the softest sound audible to the human ear. Here's how some sounds measure in decibels:

Decibels of Some Common Sounds

Decibels	Effect on Human Hearing	Example
0	Hearing begins	
10	Just audible	Leaves rustling
30	Very quiet	Ticking clock at 1 yard, library, whisper
40		Quiet office, bedroom
50	Quiet	Light auto traffic
60	Intrusive	Air-conditioning unit at 20 feet
70		Freeway traffic, noisy restaurant (conversation is difficult)
80	Annoying	Motorcycle, hair dryer, alarm clock
85 and over	Can damage hearing	You must raise your voice to be heard
90	Very annoying	Heavy truck, city traffic, lawn mower
100		Inside a subway, auto horn, chain saw
110		Amplified rock music, nightclub

(continued)

Decibels of Some Common Sounds (continued)

Decibels	Effect on Human Hearing	Example
115		Jet aircraft engine at 20 feet
120	Uncomfortable	Very close thunder clap
130	Pain threshold	Air raid siren
140–150	Painful	Jet taking off

What do those numbers actually mean? Is a motorcycle (at 80 decibels) only twice as loud as your bedroom (at 40 decibels)? Hardly. The decibel scale is logarithmic, similar to the Richter scale (see *Earthquakes*, page 80). Although to the human ear a 10-decibel increase doubles the loudness, a 3-decibel increase (approximately) doubles the actual intensity of the sound. In other words, if the noise made by one jet engine measures 115 dB, two jet engines would measure 118 dB. It works out like this:

The Decibel Scale

Decibels	Intensity (read "loudness" if you like)
0	minimum human hearing
10	10 times more than 0
20	100 times more than 0
30	1,000 times more than 0
40	10,000 times more than 0
50	100,000 times more than 0
60	1,000,000 times more than 0
70	10,000,000 times more than 0
80	100,000,000 times more than 0
90	1,000,000,000 times more than 0
100	10,000,000,000 times more than 0
110	100,000,000,000 times more than 0

Speed

How fast sound travels depends on what it's moving through. Although sound moves through air at about 750 miles per hour at sea level and 32 degrees Fahrenheit, it can zip through water at about 3,204 miles per hour, through brick at 8,114 miles per hour, and steel at 11,181 miles per hour.

Aircraft that fly faster than the speed of sound fly at *supersonic* speeds. *Mach 1* is the speed of sound, *Mach 2* is twice the speed of sound, and so on. The Mach numbers are used because the speed of sound depends on the altitude and temperature, and is found by dividing the speed of the aircraft by the speed of sound at that altitude. A plane flying 740 miles per hour at 40,000 feet, where sound travels at 660 miles per hour, would be 740 divided by 660, or Mach 1.12.

▶ To find out more about decibels and the effects of loud sounds on human hearing, go to http://www.music-injury.com/html/prevent_loss.html.

STAPLES

IN THE 1800s, staples were cut from tin with a mallet. It wasn't until the early 1900s that staples were made of wire and preformed into their familiar shape. They were packed loose in a box—imagine trying to load up a stapler with individual staples. Today preformed wire staples are held with glue in handy strips of exactly 210 staples each for standard staplers and half strips of 105 for smaller staplers. These are usually packed 24 to a box, or just over 5,000 staples.

Standard office staples are usually made of round, galvanized wire .019 inch thick, are 1/2 inch wide, and have 1/4 inch "legs." Flat staples for staple guns use heavier wire—staples using wire .024 inch thick or more are considered heavy duty. Both are sized by length, which refers to the length of the legs, in fractions of an inch, from $^5/_{32}$ inch to $^1/_2$ inch for round staples, and from $^{11}/_{64}$ inch to $^9/_{16}$ inch for flat staples.

> ▶ **For an illustrated history of staplers, go to "Antique Staplers & Other Paper Fasteners" at http://www.officemuseum.com/staplers.htm.**

STEEL WOOL
••

ALL BRANDS OF STEEL WOOL are sized in much the same way, although the markings may be dissimilar. For example, #3/0 is the same as #000 (not #3). Sometimes the descriptions vary, too, but *the smaller the number (or the more zeros there are) the finer the steel wool.*

Steel Wool Sizes						
#3	*#2*	*#1*	*#0*	*#00 or #2/0*	*#000 or #3/0*	*#0000 or #4/0*
coarse	medium	medium coarse	fine or medium fine	very fine or fine	extra fine	finest

STREET ADDRESSES

HOUSE NUMBERS tend to be odd on one side of the street and even on the other. You can count on it. But even after years in a town, you may not know which side of the street to squint at in order to locate odd-numbered 735 Prospect Street. Why is that? It's because you never know. It's easy to assume that a sensible system is at work because there are numbers involved and numbers imply order. There probably *is* a sensible system, but frequently several different systems apply in the same town. During the early growth of many cities and towns, small, widely separated areas often developed workable systems for themselves that years later clashed when the areas grew together and the systems bumped into each other. So while you might find the odd numbers on most streets in your town on the south or west side, they may occasionally pop up on the north and east sides.

Surprisingly, only in the last ten or twenty years have most cities, towns, and townships made a serious effort to make sense of a hundred, possibly two hundred years of individual and community whims and official fancies. This late response to the street name and number question is probably because, before computers became common, it was all just too intimidating. Now, however, sensible numbering and nonduplication of street names are crucial to prompt emergency help: police, fire, and ambulance services are usually the first to be consulted by city planning commissions, and most 911 calls are responded to with the help of computerized address information. Planners usually work closely with the U.S. Postal Service as well.

SUNSCREEN

••

HOW MANY TIMES have you stared at sunscreen lotions, puzzling over whether to buy one labeled 6, 15, or 45? What do those numbers mean?

The number on a sunscreen is called SPF (sun protection factor), a standard established and recognized by the Food and Drug Administration. The SPF is a multiplier for the length of time you can withstand exposure to the sun longer than you normally would. If you usually burn after a half-hour exposure to the sun, you can lengthen your time before sunburning to three hours by using a number 6 sunscreen ($^1/_2$ hour × 6), or to $7^1/_2$ hours by using a number 15 sunscreen.

Although at the moment the FDA recognizes SPF ratings only up to 15, the numbers are getting higher—sunscreens with an SPF as high as 45 can be purchased. Effectiveness apparently does not increase much with SPFs over 15; furthermore, authorities recommend frequent reapplication of sunscreen no matter what the SPF.

Thanks to the thinning atmospheric ozone layer, more ultraviolet rays are getting through, and the occurrence of skin cancers is increasing; some skin cancers can take as long as twenty years or more to show up. The Environmental Protection Agency, together with the National Weather Service, now reports a *UV Index (Ultraviolet Index)* for many U.S. cities.

UV Index Number	Exposure Level
0 to 2	Minimal
3 to 4	Low
5 to 6	Moderate
7 to 9	High
10+	Very High

About a million new cases of skin cancer are diagnosed each year, and some of them can kill. What should you do to protect yourself and your children? Here are the EPA guidelines:

Exposure Category	UV Index	Protective Actions
Minimal	0, 1, 2	Apply SPF15 sunscreen
Low	3, 4	SPF15 and protective clothing (hat)
Moderate	5, 6	SPF15, protective clothing, and UV-A&B sunglasses*
High	7, 8, 9	SPF15, protective clothing, sunglasses, and make attempts to avoid the sun between 10 A.M. and 4 P.M.
Very High	10+	SPF15, protective clothing, sunglasses, and avoid being in the sun between 10 A.M. and 4 P.M.

*Sunglasses that block 99–100% of both UV-A and UV-B rays.

▶ **To find the current ultraviolet (UV) reading for your area, go to the Environmental Protection Agency website at http://www.epa.gov/ sunwise/uvindex.html and enter your ZIP code.**

TEMPERATURE
•••

THE NOTION OF SWITCHING from familiar Fahrenheit readings to those of Celsius—or is it Centigrade?—is very disorienting. Exclaiming about a 38-degree day doesn't have the same impact as the Fahrenheit equivalent of over 100 degrees, and "below-zero" Fahrenheit weather makes zero Celsius look tepid by comparison. Why all these annoying temperature scales?

The temperature scale Americans love so well has been in existence since 1714 and was devised by German physicist Gabriel Daniel Fahrenheit. To establish a scale, one needs a fixed cold point and a fixed hot point. Fahrenheit chose a mixture of table salt and ice—the coldest temperature he could devise and then thought to be the coldest possible—as his cold point, and, curiously, body temperature, which he established as 96 degrees, as his hot point, dividing the space between into 96 parts. (He was wrong about body temperature—it was later established at 98.6 degrees.) On Fahrenheit's scale, water froze at 32 degrees and boiled at 212 degrees.

Only twenty-eight years later, Anders Celsius, a Swedish scientist, introduced another scale, which he felt was more sensibly based on the freezing and boiling points of water and was also metrically sound. He set the freezing point of water at 0 degrees and its boiling point at 100 degrees, dividing the space between into a tidy 100 parts. (Celsius degrees are 1.8 times bigger than Fahrenheit degrees.) Countries using the metric system and scientists worldwide, who have always preferred metric measurements, adopted the Celsius scale without hesitation. Degrees were called "centigrade" until 1948, when the name was officially changed to Celsius by an international conference to honor its inventor. ("Centigrade" is still commonly used in the United States, however.)

To translate Fahrenheit degrees to Celsius: subtract 32 and divide by 1.8, or ($^\circ$F − 32) ÷ 1.8. To go from Celsius degrees to Fahrenheit: multiply by 1.8 and add 32, or ($^\circ$C × 1.8) + 32. Although most thermometers today are marked with both scales, most Americans still may not know how many degrees Celsius makes for a nice spring day.

F and C Temperatures You Live By

Degrees Fahrenheit	Approx. Degrees Centigrade (Celsius)	Conditions
212.0	100	Water boils
104.0	40	Heat wave conditions
98.6	37	Normal body temperature
98.6	37	Very hot day
86.0	30	Very warm day
68.0	20	Mild spring day
50.0	10	Warm winter day
32.0	0	Freezing point of water
32.0	0	Cold day
20.0	−7	Very cold day
0.0	−18	Extremely cold day

Even Celsius had its drawbacks, however. It seemed silly, certainly unscientific, to have "minus" degrees, since temperature is a measure of heat. In 1948 British physicist William Thomson, Baron Kelvin, introduced a new scale that put 0 degrees at absolute zero—the coldest possible temperature, at which molecules stop moving and gases vanish—and used Celsius degrees to measure up from there. The Kelvin scale does not use the superscript degree symbol (°). On the Kelvin scale, water freezes at 273.15 kelvins (the preferred usage is "kelvins" or "K" not "degrees kelvin") and boils at 373.15 kelvins, exactly 100 degrees higher. This makes it easy to go back and forth from Celsius (C) to Kelvin (K)—since 0 degrees C is 273.15 K, you add 273.15 to Celsius degrees to get kelvins and subtract it from kelvins to get Celsius. Kelvin's scale is not only accepted by the scientific community; it is the final authority. Celsius and Fahrenheit are now both defined in terms of kelvins, much as the yard is defined by the meter.

▶ Find temperature conversion tables at http://www.infrared-thermography.com/tempchart-4.htm or an interactive temperature converter at http://www.convert-me.com.

TIDE TABLES
• •

EVEN IF YOU DON'T LIVE near the coast, you probably know that the tide comes in and the tide goes out in a fairly predictable manner. You may even know that it does this, for the most part, twice a day. Possibly you've heard that each high tide happens about 12 hours and 25 minutes after the last one, a correct average but a dangerous assumption. And that's where you stop. You'd think that if there were two tides a day, they'd be a tidy 12 hours apart, occurring at the same time daily. It's that extra 25 minutes that confuses you.

You can blame this inconvenience on the moon. The rhythmic rise and fall of ocean waters is caused by the moon's gravitational pull on the earth (although the sun's gravitational pull, the whirl of the earth, and the weather all play a part). Unfortunately, the lunar day is not in sync with the 24-hour solar day—it's about 50 minutes longer—making tide prediction a scheduling nightmare. Furthermore, the tides are so affected by the coastline and other geographical factors that high tide in one bay may be different from that in the next. This is why it's best, if you're planning a coastal outing—fishing, swimming, tide-pooling, clamming, or whatever—not to make any assumptions about tides but to consult the tide tables.

Where to find them? Coastal newspapers publish the tide heights and times for the day; almanacs have them for the bigger stations; most places that issue fishing licenses offer a whole year's tide tables for the local area in a little booklet, often free; and, of course, there's always the Internet (see end of entry for address). These tide table publications are based on the National Oceanic and Atmospheric Administration's (NOAA) careful figures and predictions, which are in turn based on careful observations and comparisons with a sample nineteen-year period.

A warning, though: officials at NOAA complain about the lack of accuracy in some of these booklets, which, though based on NOAA figures, may not actually be published by NOAA and are occasionally "full of typos and printing errors." For serious planning, you might venture to a library's reference section to consult Tide Tables (current year), West (or East) Coast of North and South America, issued by NOAA. Even these figures are estimates, however; tides can be influenced by weather even as distant as a storm off the coast of Japan.

Local tide table formats vary, but they still function the same way. The tables give the high and low tide times and heights for one main area for one year. Only a few pages are then required to list the "corrections"—how those times and tide heights differ from the main tables—for the other nearby areas. Fortunately, these differences never change, so only one set of figures needs to be listed for each place.

Local booklets usually account for daylight saving time, but always check—NOAA does not. Also, tide tables use decimal feet, dividing feet into tenths instead of inches. Some questions still arise, however. Not only is sea level different from place to place, but due to melting glaciers, it's rising. So a 0.4 foot figure tells you not how much higher the water is than sea level, but the mean lower low tide (which is simply the average of the lower of the two daily low tides over a certain 19-year period). On the East Coast, water heights are based on the mean low tide (the average of all the low tides). The tide tables do not tell you the actual depth of the water, only the differences from the base.

Few tides are exactly 12 hours and 25 minutes apart. Because there are other strong influences on tide times, it could be dangerous to try to time the next high or low tide by adding 12 hours and 25 minutes to the last one—you don't want to be trapped on rocks or a rugged beach during a swift incoming tide.

If you're visiting the coast and don't want to sound like an inlander, here are a few terms for you:

Ebb current	The movement of water away from the shore
Flood current	The movement of water toward the shore
Neap tide	A slow tide, in which the difference between high and low water is less than usual
Spring tide	A fast tide, in which the difference between high and low water is more extreme than usual (this happens when the moon is extreme—new or full—not just in the spring)

▶ **To find the entire year's tide tables for any of 3,000 coastal stations, go to http://co-ops.nos.noaa.gov/tp4days.html. To find the water temperature and levels on many U.S. ocean beaches, go to http:// www.nodc .noaa.gov/dsdt/cwtg.**

TIME

∙∙∙

ASKING SOMEONE for the time sounds like a simple request, and it is, usually. But if you start digging around into who actually determines what time it is, the answers—there's more than one—get complicated. Telling time accurately, and keeping the world on the same time, has stumped early time tellers as well as modern day scientists. If you start to ask what time it is, you can run into apparent solar time, mean solar time, sidereal time, astronomical time, atomic time, Universal Time, U.S. Standard Time, and Greenwich Mean Time, to mention just a few. If you set a clock for each of these times, the settings will not all be exactly the same.

Apparent solar time is sundial time, noon determined by the moment when the sun is highest (it's rarely exactly overhead). This means that noon in the next town east or west will be several minutes earlier or later than noon in your town, so that the time is not the same in even nearby locations. Still, apparent solar time was used in this country until the railroads came along (see *Time Zones,* page 246).

Mean solar time bases time on the length of an average day. Because the earth does not spin at a uniform speed, day lengths in a year are not exactly the same.

Sidereal time tells time by the position of the stars, also called *astronomical time.* Sidereal time is tracked by a telescope—in the United States, the Photographic Zenith Tube at the U.S. Naval Observatory in Washington, D.C.—in which the same stars appear at the same time every day. The mean sidereal day is 23 hours, 56 minutes, 4.09 seconds; the sun rises nearly 4 minutes later every day when measured by the stars. Because the earth's rotation can vary in speed, sidereal time is not perfectly uniform.

Atomic time is U.S. Bureau of Standards time, kept by atomic clocks (see *Time Units,* page 244). Atomic clocks are incredibly accurate, based on the behavior of cesium atoms, not on the behavior of the earth or the heavens; a second must be added to the end of every other year or so to keep atomic time in sync with the stars.

Universal Time (UT) is also known as *Greenwich Mean Time*. In 1972 key international groups concerned with time decided to keep laboratory clocks on atomic time, adding or subtracting "leap seconds" to the last minute of the year when needed and reporting to the Bureau International de l'Heure (BIH) in Paris, which has the last word in establishing Universal Time, also called BIH Time. Today the BIH fields information from all over the world via a U.S. satellite and other channels, which it processes to help standardize time throughout the world. The whole world is not on exactly the same time. Even though a second can be timed to the billionth, getting everyone on the same nanosecond everywhere remains a challenge. (See also *Greenwich Mean Time*, page 128; *Military Time*, page 168; and *Time Zones*, page 246.)

Coordinated Universal Time (UTC) is Universal Time coordinated with the National Bureau of Standards' atomic clocks and the U.S. Naval Observatory's sidereal time. It is this time that is broadcast on the National Bureau of Standards' radio station WWV. If you call WWV—(303) 499-7111—you will get the exact time in Greenwich, England, using the 24-hour time system: the seconds are ticked off and the exact time is given every minute. (The military, by the way, relies on a different time signal, broadcast by the U.S. Naval Observatory.)

U.S. Standard Time is based on Coordinated Universal Time (UTC): Universal Time is simply translated into the correct time for your U.S. Standard Time Zone. (See *Time Zones*, page 246.) If you call "Time"—it's in your phone book—this is the time you'll get. It's usually based on WWV broadcasts.

Daylight saving time is U.S. Standard Time plus 1 hour, first introduced during World War I in 1916. The reasoning behind this system is this: if everyone gets up an hour earlier in spring and summer, when the sun rises earlier and sets later, much energy used for nighttime lighting is saved. However, because adopting daylight saving time was up to local communities, confusion reigned: some used it; some didn't. As of 1987, all states adopting daylight saving time begin it at 2 A.M. on the first Sunday in April and end it at 2 A.M. on the last Sunday in October. A few states and territories—Arizona (excepting the Navajo Indian Reservation), Hawaii, parts of Indiana, American Samoa, Guam, Puerto Rico, and the Virgin Islands—still don't use it.

The Global Positioning System (GPS) is synchronized to UTC and is not adjusted for leap seconds (see *Time Units*, following this entry).

▶ For more on timekeeping, go to the U.S. Navy website "Tycho" at http://tycho.usno.navy.mil. To find the official U.S. time, go to the WWV station at http://nist.time.gov and click on your location. For more on daylight saving time, go to "Daylight Saving Time" at http://webexhibits.org/daylightsaving.

TIME UNITS
· ·

DO YOU KNOW HOW LONG a second is? You might say "one-sixtieth of a minute." Or maybe you'd push it further: "There are 60 seconds in a minute, 60 minutes in an hour, and 24 hours in a day, making 86,400 seconds in 24 hours [$60 \times 60 \times 24 = 86,400$]. Therefore a second is $1/86,400$ of a day."

This perfectly sensible answer was the accepted measure of the second until 1820, when a committee of French scientists pointed out that the length of one day may vary a few thousandths of a second from another. So they measured a year of days and defined the second as $1/86,400$ of an *average* day, not just any day.

Then in 1956, scientists noticed that the earth's rotation was slowing down a bit—each day is about 20 microseconds longer than the corresponding day in the prior year, adding up to 7.3 milliseconds per year. Strangely enough, while the day is getting longer, the year is getting shorter—the earth's orbital period is 5.3 milliseconds less each year. In order to account for this, scientists decided to base the second on an average year. The official second, called the *ephemeris second*, became $^{1}/_{31,556,925.9747}$ of the year 1900, which was chosen as the *mean solar year.* But it's tough to remeasure the year 1900 in the laboratory. Furthermore, despite the impressive number of digits, the ephemeris second could be divided only into millionths, which was just not precise enough.

Since 1967 the second has been based on the absolutely predictable behavior of the cesium atom. In vastly oversimplified terms, the outer electron in the cesium atom flips when exposed to a radio signal of exactly 9,192,631,770 Hz. The quartz oscillator producing this signal is automatically adjusted to keep those electrons jumping, and its frequency, divided by 9,192,631,770 is defined as one second. This definition will probably remain for a while, as scientists can now split seconds into completely accurate *microseconds* (millionths of a second), *nanoseconds* (billionths), *picoseconds* (trillionths), and beyond.

The day is no longer our basic unit of time, divided into smaller units, nor is the year. Instead the tiny second, controlled by the U.S. Bureau of Standards, is multiplied to define our days and years. We now live on atomic time, kept by atomic cesium clocks that measure time in nanoseconds. Even this isn't perfect, though. Now and then a second has to be added at the end of a year to keep us in sync with the stars—at the end of January 1, 1999, the twenty-second "leap-second" since 1972 was added. None was added in 2000, 2001, or 2002.

▶ **To hear an atomic second tick by, and for the exact Coordinated Universal Time, call WWV at 303-499-7111, or sister station WWVH at 808-335-4363 in Hawaii. (Neither call is toll free.)**

TIME ZONES

• •

TIME ZONES ARE ESSENTIAL to keeping the world sunny-side up and making today's complex airline schedules possible. Before the late 1800s, however, no one gave much thought to schedules. Each town ran on sundial time, considering noon to be the moment when the sun was (more or less) directly overhead. Even a good horse took so long to get from one town to another that exact time hardly mattered. It was not essential for time to be precise until trains began traveling across the country. In part, standardized time and time zones resulted when people became regularly inconvenienced by the erratic time clock—there's hardly a more irate person than the one who's just missed a chosen mode of travel. The railroads tried to make schedules, but the railroad clocks had to be changed around so much that the schedules weren't very efficient—Michigan and Illinois each had 27 different local times, Indiana had 23, and Wisconsin had 38, just for starters.

Finally, in 1883, the railroad companies adopted a time zone system that had been suggested by a teacher, Charles Gowd, which divided the United States into four time zones: Eastern, Central, Mountain, and Pacific. The width of each zone was the distance it took the sun to travel one hour, or 15 degrees between longitude lines that run from pole to pole (see *Latitude and Longitude*, page 148). After quite a bit of controversy the country adopted the railroad system, although the government didn't make it official until 1918. Other countries were immediately interested, however. In 1884 an international conference in Washington, D.C., divided the globe into twenty-four time zones, using the zero degree longitude line that runs through Greenwich, England, as the base line, and the 180 degree longitude line as the International Date Line.

Today the time zone lines zig and zag to avoid splitting towns and smaller countries into different zones and other awkwardness. Zones to the east of the Greenwich base line are numbered +1 to +11, each an hour later. Zones to the west are numbered −1 to −11, each an hour earlier. The zones meet at an imaginary line

WORLD MAP OF TIME ZONES

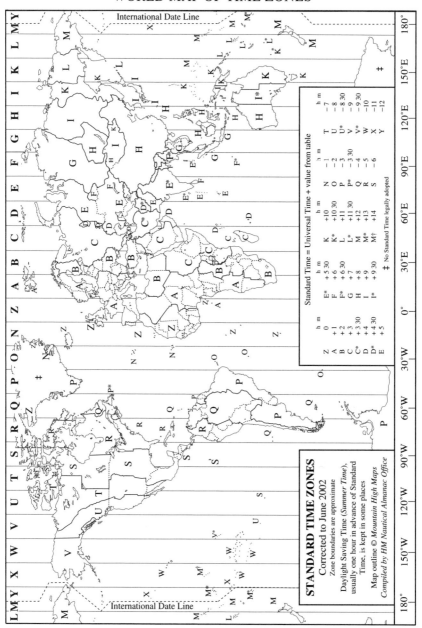

STANDARD TIME ZONES

Corrected to June 2002

Zone boundaries are approximate

Daylight Saving Time (*Summer Time*), usually one hour in advance of Standard Time, is kept in some places

Map outline © *Mountain High Maps*

Compiled by HM Nautical Almanac Office

Standard Time = Universal Time + value from table

	h m		h m		h m
Z	0	E*	+ 5 30	K	+10
A	+ 1	F	+ 6	K*	+10 30
B	+ 2	F*	+ 6 30	L	+11
C	+ 3	G	+ 7	L*	+11 30
C*	+ 3 30	H	+ 8	M	+12
D	+ 4	I	+ 9	M*	+13
D*	+ 4 30	I*	+ 9 30	M†	+14
E	+ 5				

	h m		h m
N	− 1	T	− 7
O	− 2	U	− 8
P	− 3	U*	− 8 30
P*	− 3 30	V	− 9
Q	− 4	V*	− 9 30
R	− 5	W	−10
S	− 6	X	−11
		Y	−12

† No Standard Time legally adopted

Source: Supplied by HM Nautical Almanac Office © copyright Council for the Central Laboratory of the Research Councils

called the International Date Line, which is divided into two half-zones, +12 and −12. This makes the U.S. time zones −5 for Eastern Standard Time, −6 for Central Standard Time, −7 for Mountain Standard Time, and −8 for Pacific Standard Time. A few countries, like India, Australia, Afghanistan, and Iran, have split time zones.

One way to establish the time at a foreign locale is to find out its time zone number and your zone number. If the foreign zone number is larger than yours (Tokyo at +9 is larger than −5 in New York, for example), add the two numbers (5 + 9 = 14) and count the total going eastward, with time getting later. If the foreign zone number is smaller (−10 for Hawaii is a smaller number than −5 for New York), subtract (10 − 5 = 5) and count the total going west, with time getting earlier. This is to save you the headache of coping with the International Date Line. If you happen to be on daylight saving time, remember to subtract an hour from your own time to put you on Standard Time before you start.

Here's what time it is around the world, in many of the time zones.

When it is noon in London, Glasgow, or Greenwich, England, going west it is:		
Time	City	Time Zone
1 P.M.	in Berlin, Budapest, Madrid, Oslo, Paris, Rome, and Vienna	+1
2 P.M.	in Athens, Cairo, and Istanbul	+2
3 P.M.	in Moscow and Leningrad	+3
4 P.M.	in Manila, Saigon, and Shanghai	+4
5 P.M.	in Karachi	+5
5:30 P.M.	in Calcutta	+5½
7 P.M.	in Bangkok and Singapore	+7
8 P.M.	in Beijing, Hong Kong, Manila, Perth, and Taipei	+8
9 P.M.	in Seoul and Tokyo	+9
10 P.M.	in Sydney	+10
Midnight	in Wellington, New Zealand	+12

Time	City	Time Zone
	When it is noon in London, Glasgow, or Greenwich, England, going east it is:	
11 A.M.	in Ponta Delgada, Azores	−1
9 A.M.	in Buenos Aires	−3
8 A.M.	in Caracas, Halifax, and La Paz	−4
7 A.M.	in Detroit, Lima, Montreal, New York, and Washington, D.C.	−5
6 A.M.	in Chicago, Houston, Mexico City, and St. Louis	−6
5 A.M.	in Denver, Edmonton, El Paso, Phoenix, Salt Lake City	−7
4 A.M.	in Los Angeles, San Francisco, Seattle, and Vancouver	−8
3 A.M.	in Anchorage	−9
2 A.M.	in Honolulu	−10

Try it. You are in New York (Zone −5) and it is 11:00 A.M. on Sunday. You want to know what time it is in Tokyo (Zone +9). You have to go 5 zones east to reach Greenwich and 9 more east to reach Tokyo, totaling 14 hours. Remember, as you go east, you are heading toward tomorrow, which is traveling westward, so when you pass midnight, you are in the next day, in this case, 1 A.M. on Monday. For a time zone numbered lower than yours (stay in Zone −5 for a moment), e.g., Honolulu (Zone −10), subtract Hawaii's zone from your zone, count five hours going west, getting earlier, making it 6:00 A.M. in Honolulu.

Still confused? Just wait until you get to the International Date Line!

The International Date Line

The International Date Line, zigzagging through the Pacific Ocean from pole to pole just west of Alaska, looks as if it was drawn by an international committee, and it was. If you float over this line (most of it's over water) at, say, 9:00 A.M. on a Wednesday, going west, you leap twenty-four hours into the next day, to

INTERNATIONAL DATE LINE

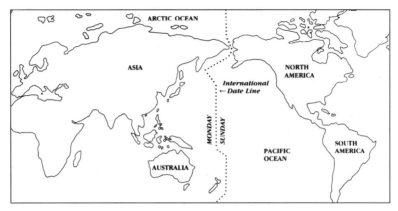

Source: Adapted from U.S. Bureau of Standards' "Standard Time Zones of the World"

9:00 A.M. on Thursday. Cross the line eastward and step into the day before. This is more than most of us can deal with.

Try this: It's Thursday at 7 A.M., you're in Denver (Zone –7), and you move west all the way around the globe, counting backwards by time zones as you go. If you do this, you'll find that it is 8 A.M. on Wednesday in Chicago, just one zone east of you. But if you move around the globe east from Denver, you'll find it's 6 A.M. on *Friday* in San Francisco!

To prevent this from happening, the International Date Line was established as the only place where there can be a day's difference between time zones. A day officially begins when it's noon in Greenwich, England, and midnight on the International Date Line. Because the earth spins eastward, when you cross the International Date Line going west toward Asia, you "lose" twenty-four hours. If you cross the International Date Line going east toward the Americas, you "gain" a day.

▶ To find the correct time nearly anywhere in the world, go to "The World Clock—Time Zones" at http://www.timeanddate.com/worldclock. For a world time zone map, go to http://aa.usno.navy.mil/faq/docs/world_tzones.

TIRES

••

IF ALL TIRES LOOK ALIKE to you, familiarity with tire language may give you a way to compare the many possibilities. There are so many different numbers stamped on tire sidewalls that one company manual requires fifteen pages just to introduce them to the sales personnel. Tire manufacture is complicated—tires are not stamped out like Lifesavers.

Passenger Car Tires Sizes

Example: P195/80R15 or just 195/80R15 Since 1976 the most widely used system for sizing tires is the *P-Metric system*, created to accommodate the tiny tires used by the then-new small economy cars. The numbers the P-Metric system uses, however up-to-date the system is supposed to be, are an unbelievable hodgepodge: a metric number, a percentage representing a ratio, inches, and sometimes even a load limit number that isn't the load limit at all but a number representing the load limit. Take our sample tire size, P195/80R15:

P   means the tire is intended for a passenger vehicle. LT would mean "light truck," which may use a different size system (see page 252). Sometimes the P is left off.

195   is the section width, sidewall to sidewall, of the properly inflated tire in millimeters.

80   is the aspect ratio of the tire, or the relationship between the tire section height and the section width. It's a percentage figure: if a tire has an aspect ratio of 80, the height is 80 percent of the width. Essentially, a low aspect ratio means the tire rides low and wide, which gives better control than a high ratio; e.g., 85, which rides higher but with more give.

R   is the type of tire, in this case, radial. A B here means "belted bias," and a D signifies "diagonal bias." Diagonal bias tires are constructed with diagonally built layers; belted tires have additional layers that run around the tire, like a belt; radial tire layers run at right angles to a similar belt layer.

15   is the rim diameter in inches of the wheel the tire fits. The most common rim sizes are 13, 14, and 15 (whole numbers), and these wheel sizes are standard throughout the auto industry.

Of the above numbers, you can select all but the rim diameter—if your car takes a 13-inch tire, you must buy a 13-inch tire. But you can change the width of the tire, or the type or aspect ratio. If the P-Metric system isn't used for the tires on your car, remember that a decimal is always decimal inches and almost always means tire width (sidewall to sidewall). If a size is preceded by a letter between A and N, it probably means load/size—the lower the letter, the smaller the size and load-carrying capacity of the tire.

Light Truck Tire Sizes

The size of a light truck tire may be expressed in at least three (and probably more) ways, but LT always means "light truck."

LT215/75R15   This number reads the same as for P tires.

7.50R15LT   The 7.50 here is the section width in inches instead of millimeters. The rest is the same as for P tires.

31 x 10.50R15LT   The 31 is the diameter of the tire (not the rim) in inches, and the 10.50 is the section width (sidewall to sidewall) in decimal inches. The rest is the same as for P tires.

Speed Rating and Load Index

Example: P195/60R15 86H Following the tire size number is sometimes another number-letter combination. The number represents the *load index*. It isn't 86 of anything but represents the maximum number of pounds the tire can safely carry when properly inflated. The load index range is 71 to 110, with the 71 representing 761 pounds and 110 representing 2,337 pounds. Here 86 represents 1,168 pounds.

The letter is the *speed rating*. Speed ratings originated in Europe, where, historically, speed limits often have been higher than ours, as high as 100 miles per hour, and sometimes even absent. Euro-peans give tires speed ratings represented by a letter.

Speed Rating	Top speed (miles per hour)	Top speed (kilometers per hour)
M	81 mph	130 kph
N	87 mph	140 kph
P	93 mph	150 kph
Q	99 mph	160 kph
R	106 mph	170 kph
S	112 mph	180 kph
T	118 mph	190 kph
U	124 mph	200 kph
H	130 mph	210 kph
V	149 mph	240 kph
ZR	168–186 mph	270–300 kph

A word of warning: although a high speed rating may tell you something about a tire, all tires with the same rating are not equal. There are too many factors involved in building a tire to rely on one rating to judge it. The speed rating usually follows the tire size, except for ZR, which may follow the aspect ratio.

Serial Number

Known as the DOT (Department of Transportation) number, the serial number is usually found on the opposite side of the tire from the size number, near the rim of the wheel. (Tires are usually mounted with the serial number facing inside, so you may not be able to see it on your vehicle's tires.) It is part of a system of tire identification that became federal law in 1971. A DOT number looks something like this: DOT MAL9 ABC032.

DOT   means that the tire meets or exceeds Department of Trans-portation safety standards.

MA   is the code number assigned by DOT to the manufacturing plant.

L9   is a code number for the tire size.

ABC   is a group of up to four symbols, optional with the manufac-
       turer, to identify the brand or other significant characteristics
       of the tire.

032   is the date of manufacture.

Federal law stipulates that tire dealers must record the buyer's name and address with serial numbers of the tires purchased.

Uniform Tire Quality Grade Labeling

Example: Traction 150 Treadwear B Heat Resistance C The government requires that tires have mileage and safety ratings stamped right on the tires. If you can't find the ratings on a tire, ask the dealer—reputable tire dealers have this information for any of their products. The system is called Uniform Tire Quality Grade Labeling (UTQGL), and is regulated by the National Highway Traffic Safety Administration of the U.S. Department of Transportation.

Note that a C rating on a tire may not make it a poor choice. Sometimes it's a trade-off—you may want open tread for good traction, but open tread heats up more easily, so you may have to settle for a heat resistance grade of C. The numbers do give you a way to begin comparing tires. Here is how the rating system works, according to the brochure called "Uniform Tire Quality Grading"* from the U.S. Department of Transportation, with some help from *The Car Book* (Jack Gillis, HarperCollins, published annually). All tests are supposed to be done on a specified government course and meet any other government specified controls.

---

*This booklet giving the quality ratings for more than 2,000 tires is available free from the U.S. Department of Transportation, National Highway Traffic Safety Administration, 400 Seventh Street SW, Washington, D.C. 20590.

Treadwear	90 to about 330	To get the expected mileage, multiply the grade times 200. For example, a tire graded 100 will last for about 20,000 miles. The higher the rating, the farther the tire is expected to roll.
Traction	A, B, or C	An A-rated tire has the best traction, C the worst, representing the tire's ability to stop on wet pavement.
Heat Resistance	A, B, or C	An A-rated tire runs cool, while a C-rated tire tends to heat up faster. Hot tires wear down faster than cool tires.

Other Sidewall News

You might also find some of the following imprinted on a tire:

1. The name of the tire company
2. The country where the tire was manufactured
3. M/S label: whether tire meets regulations for a mud and snow tire; e.g., M+S
4. Whether the tire is tubeless or tube-type (with tube)
5. Ply information for tread and sidewalls, including the tire ply composition and materials used; e.g., plies: sidewall 2 polyester, tread 2 polyester + 2 steel + 2 nylon
6. Maximum load that can be carried at maximum pressure; e.g., max load 1,250 lb. at 36 p.s.i. (pounds per square inch) max pressure
7. Safety warning, which may be stamped on the tire or found in the owner's manual

Tire Pressure

There has been growing concern that drivers are not keeping proper tabs on their tire pressure and are driving with underinflated or overinflated tires. Tires underinflated by 6 or more p.s.i. can fail and those that much over can become easily damaged. The concern is great enough that the National Highway Traffic Safety Administration is requiring all vehicles made after November 2003 to provide a low tire pressure warning system. Until then, get handy with a quality air gauge. The suggested maximum p.s.i. for a particular tire can be found imprinted on the outside wall of the tire itself, along with all the other numbers described in this entry.

▶ For general tire size and grading information, as well as links to reports on particular tires, go to the Department of Transportation website at http://www.nhtsa.dot.gov/cars, scroll down, and click on "Uniform Tire Quality Grading System."

TYPEFACES/FONTS

IN THESE DAYS OF COMPUTERS, most of us are familiar with fonts, which are the character designs in computer-generated material, and are often based on and similar to typefaces—the character design of print-shop and typewriter-generated material that used to be primarily the domain of printers and designers. Fonts and typefaces are related, as are their sizes.

It all began with a Frenchman, Pierre Fournier, who in 1735 invented the point system to size up printers' type, and another Frenchman, François Didot, who based Fournier's points on the French inch, with 72 points to the inch. In 1886 American type founders adopted the French system but based the point size on the American inch, which was, at the time, slightly shorter than the French inch. To this day, the European and American point sizes do not agree.

Points measure the tallness of type, with type sizes running from a practically microscopic 1 point (now possible with computers) to the inch-high 72-point headline. The *height* of the typeface is measured from the lowest descender (such as the bottom of a "y") to the highest ascender (such as the top of an "h"), with a little leeway at the top and the bottom. In other words, type size is not actually a measure of the type, but of the space required to accept the tallest and lowest letters.

8 or 9 point type is commonly used in newspapers.

10 point type is used for many books.

12 point type is the larger typewriter size.

18 point type works for a small headline.

The space between lines, called *leading* (pronounced "ledding"), is also measured in points. The *width* of a line of type is measured in picas, 6 picas to the inch. The width of columns—blocks of type—are measured in picas, as are the space between them and the margins, sometimes called "gutters." The pica type used on many typewriters was called that because each character was 1 pica wide ($\frac{1}{6}$ inch) and 12 points ($\frac{1}{6}$ inch) tall, and there were six lines of type to the inch. (Six lines per inch was standard for most typewriters, even those using the smaller "elite" type.)

Indentations are measured in *ems*. An em is about the size of the letter "M," hence the name, but is technically equal to the type's height. In other words, the size of an em for a 12-point typeface would be a sideways 12 points, but since points are used to measure only up and down, never sideways, the em is used to represent the sideways measure of the height. Most indentations are 1 or 2 ems.

Unfortunately, figuring a type size from the printed page is all but impossible. The problem is twofold: First, there's no standard for the amount of leeway (or shoulder) at the top and bottom of the type. A larger shoulder makes a smaller letter, and vice versa. The only way to measure type is to measure the points in a block of solid lines with no leading between them and divide by the number of lines. Since almost all print contains leading, the opportunity to do this is impractically rare. Second, the width of the type (the number of characters per pica) can vary immensely—chunky, round letters with small ascenders will look much larger than lanky letters with long ascenders. The space between characters and words also varies. Note the variation in the following 12-point typefaces:

This is 12 point Times type.

This is 12 point Bodoni Book type.

This is 12 point Goudy Old Style type.

This is 12 point Helvetica type.

This is 12 point Courier type.

This is 12 point Eurostile type.

▶ For a course in fonts and design, go to MyDesignPrimer at http://mydesignprimer.com and click on "Type." A history of the various typefaces can be found at "ABC Typography," http://abc.planet-typography.com.

UNIVERSE (DISTANCES)

THE ASTRONOMICAL UNIT, the light-year, and the parsec are the measurements used to estimate the distance between various points in the universe. These and other monstrous measurements offered by today's astronomers sound so terrifyingly huge that the mind resists them, convinced they are incomprehensible. The measures aren't hard to understand, though. They offer us a concept of how vast the universe is, as well as a healthy appreciation of size. The *astronomical unit* (A.U.) is the smallest: it's the distance between Earth and the sun, which can be measured in miles (93 million) or kilometers, or whatever you're comfortable with. The astronomical unit is useful for measuring distances in our solar system. A *light-year* takes you into the galaxy: it's the distance light travels in one year—5,880,000,000,000 (or nearly 6 trillion) miles—at about 186,000 miles per second. The *parsec* is simply 3.2 light-years.

It's interesting to note that light-years represent the age of the image as well as its distance—the light from an object a light-year away has taken a year to reach you, so you are seeing it as it was a year ago. The years you see into an object's past are numbered by its distance from you in light-years: when you look at Rigel, a star in the constellation Orion, for example, which is 900 light years away, the image you see is 900 years old. Astronomers, staring deep into the universe, are looking billions of years into the past.

How does the universe measure up? As it happens, there are almost the same number of inches in a mile (63,360) as there are astronomical units in a light-year (63,310). An inch is traditionally about the width of your thumb; if you make your thumb represent 1 astronomical unit (the distance between Earth and the sun, or 93,000,000 miles), you can use it to chart the universe. The A.U. figures given in the following chart represent how many times farther the distance is than that between Earth and the sun.

Thumb-Sketch of the Universe

Description	Distance from the Sun	Distance on Your Chart Needed to Accommodate This Scale: (1 A.U. = 1" and 1 lt-yr = 1 mi.)
Earth	A.U. 1 Miles: 93 million	1 thumb-width or 1 inch
Pluto, farthest planet from the sun	A.U. 29 Miles: 2.7 billion	29 inches
1 light-year: the distance light travels in one year	A.U. 63,310 Light-years: 1 Miles: 5.88 trillion	1 mile
1 parsec: the distance light travels in 3.2 years	A.U. 200,000 Light-years: 3.2 Miles: 19 trillion	3.2 miles
Alpha Centauri, one of our nearest stars	A.U. 270,000 Light-years: 4.3 Miles: 25 trillion	4.3 miles

(continued)

Thumb-Sketch of the Universe (continued)

Description	Distance from the Sun	Distance on Your Chart Needed to Accommodate This Scale: (1 A.U. = 1" and 1 lt-yr = 1 mi.)
Rigel, a star in the constellation Orion	A.U. 57 million Light-years: 900 Miles: 5.25 quadrillion	900 miles
M13 in Hercules, one of the farthest star groups visible to the naked eye in the N. Hemisphere	A.U. 1.7 billion Light-years: 26,700 Miles: 160 quadrillion	26,700 miles*
The center of our galaxy	A.U. 2 billion Light-years: 32,000 Miles: 190 quadrillion	32,000 miles
Nearest observed galaxies	A.U. 4.8 billion Light-years: 75,000 Miles: 450 quadrillion	75,000 miles
Andromeda, our nearest full-size galaxy	A.U. 140 billion Light-years: 2.2 million Miles 1.3 x 10^{13}**	2.2 million miles***
Nearest known quasar	A.U. 63 trillion Light-years: 1 billion Miles: 6 x 10^{21}	1 billion miles
Distant quasars	A.U. 945 trillion Light-years: 15 billion Miles: 9 x 10^{22}	15 billion miles

*Your chart must now be long enough to circle the earth.

**See *Exponents*, page 91.

***Your chart must now be 10 times longer than the distance from Earth to the moon.

▶ **Enjoy an interactive space adventure at "Astronomical Distances," http://janus.astro.umd.edu/astro/distance.**

VISION

∙∙

YOU KNOW THAT 20/20 VISION is excellent visual acuity. But what are those "20s" twenty of? The answer is *feet*. You look at an eye chart from a distance of 20 feet. If you can read the lines normal eyes can see at 20 feet, you have 20/20 vision. If you can only read the lines people with normal vision can see at 40 feet, you have 20/40 vision. If your eyesight is better than normal, you might be able to read at 20 feet what most people have to get 5 feet closer to read, giving you 20/15 eyesight. The first 20 never changes.

This twenty-slash-whatever system is sometimes confusing. It is quite sensible to assume that the first number describes one eye, while the second describes the other; however, only the second number applies to you. It can describe your vision as you use both eyes, or each eye can be tested separately—one of your eyes might have 20/20 vision while the other has 20/40. So why don't they just drop the first 20? Because there is another test for up-close acuity in which you are shown a card with lines of increasingly larger-sized characters from 14 inches away, the distance at which most people read. Normal up-close vision is described as 14/14. If you have 14/56 up-close vision, you need to get within 14 inches of reading material that a normally sighted person can see at 56 inches. So *the first number tells you whether the second number stands for your distance or your up-close acuity.*

▶ For a virtual vision acuity (VA) test, go to http://www.dada.it/eyeweb/eotto.htm. Do not use this test for diagnostic purposes.

VITAMINS AND MINERALS (RDIs)

IF YOU'VE EVER TRIED to read the ingredients and figures listed on a bottle of vitamin tablets, especially those touted as high-potency, or even "super-high potency," you'd probably welcome a chart that offers some guidelines. Unless your doctor is treating a special health problem, you may not need the impressive percentage over the U.S. RDI (U.S. Reference Daily Intake) some vitamin pills offer.

All vitamins are divided into two groups: those that are fat soluble (vitamins A, D, E, and K) and those that are water soluble (vitamins B and C). Your body stores the fat-soluble vitamins but gets rid of unused water-soluble ones, meaning that if you've been eating right, you've got a reserve of A, D, E, and K, but the C and B vitamins must be replenished every day. It's also far easier to get too much of the fat-soluble vitamins than the water-soluble ones.

It's easy to be put off by vitamin and mineral measures, which use the metric system of grams (1 gram weighs about the same as a dollar bill), milligrams (one-thousandth of a gram), and micrograms (one-millionth of a gram), as well as International Units. How much is an International Unit? There is no set value. An International Unit is the amount of a substance, such as a vitamin, that it takes to produce a certain effect when tested according to an internationally accepted biological procedure. In other words, if it takes more of one vitamin than of another to be effective, the value of one's International Unit will be higher than the other's. For example, it might take only 300 micrograms of vitamin A to produce a specified effect, but 1 whole milligram of vitamin E. The IU for that form of vitamin A equals 300 micrograms, and the IU for vitamin E equals 1 milligram.

RDIs, DRIs, RDAs, and DVs

Until recently RDIs were called RDAs (Recommended Daily Allowances). These became confused with the recommendations of the nongovernment Food and Nutrition Board of the Institute of Medicine, also called RDAs. So the names have been changed. Now

Vitamins

Vitamin	Current RDI*	New DRI†	UL‡
Vitamin A	5,000 IU	900 mcg (3,000 IU)	3,000 mcg (10,000 IU)
Vitamin C	60 mg	90 mg	2,000 mg
Vitamin D	400 IU (10 mcg)	15 mcg (600 IU)	50 mcg (2,000 IU)
Vitamin E	30 IU (20 mg)	15 mg§	1,000 mg
Vitamin K	80 mcg	120 mcg	ND
Thiamin	1.5 mg	1.2 mg	ND
Riboflavin	1.7 mg	1.3 mg	ND
Niacin	20 mg	16 mg	35 mg
Vitamin B-6	2 mg	1.7 mg	100 mg
Folate	400 mcg (0.4 mg)	400 mcg from food 200 mcg synthetic"	1,000 mcg synthetic
Vitamin B-12	6 mcg	2.4 mcg #	ND
Biotin	300 mcg	30 mcg	ND
Pantothenic acid	10 mg	5 mg	ND
Choline	Not established	550 mg	3,500 mg

* The Reference Daily Intake (RDI) is the value established by the Food and Drug Administration (FDA) for use in nutrition labeling. It was based initially on the highest 1968 Recommended Dietary Allowance (RDA) for each nutrient, to ensure that needs were met for all age groups.

† The Dietary Reference Intakes (DRI) are the most recent set of dietary recommendations established by the Food and Nutrition Board of the Institute of Medicine, 1997–2001. They replace previous RDAs, and may be the basis for eventually updating the RDIs. The value shown here is the highest DRI for each nutrient.

‡ The upper limit (UL) is the upper level of intake considered to be safe for use by adults, incorporating a safety factor. In some cases, lower ULs have been established for children.

§ Historical vitamin E conversion factors were amended in the DRI report, so that 15 mg is defined as the equivalent of 22 IU of natural vitamin E or 33 IU of synthetic vitamin E.

" It is recommended that women of childbearing age obtain 400 mcg of synthetic folic acid from fortified breakfast cereals or dietary supplements, in addition to dietary folate.

It is recommended that people over 50 meet the B-12 recommendation through fortified foods or supplements, to improve bioavailability.

ND upper limit not determined. No adverse effects observed from high intakes of the nutrient.

Source: Council for Responsible Nutrition. Used with permission.

the FDA's official recommendations for the daily intake of vitamins and minerals are called RDIs (Reference Daily Intakes) and similar recommendations by the Food and Nutrition Board, upon which the FDA's RDIs are based, are called DRIs (Dietary Reference Intakes). DVs (Daily Values) apply to the composition of foods: fats,

Minerals

Mineral	Current RDI*	New DRI†	UL‡
Calcium	1,000 mg	1,300 mg	2,500 mg
Iron	18 mg	18 mg	45 mg
Phosphorus	1,000 mg	1,250 mg	4,000 mg
Iodine	150 mcg	150 mcg	1,100 mcg
Magnesium	400 mg	420 mg	350 mg§
Zinc	15 mg	11 mg	40 mg
Selenium	70 mcg	55 mcg	400 mcg
Copper	2 mg	0.9 mg	10 mg
Manganese	2 mg	2.3 mg	11 mg
Chromium	120 mcg	35 mcg	ND
Molybdenum	75 mcg	45 mcg	2,000 mcg

* The Reference Daily Intake (RDI) is the value established by the Food and Drug Administration (FDA) for use in nutrition labeling. It was based initially on the highest 1968 Recommended Dietary Allowance (RDA) for each nutrient, to ensure that needs were met for all age groups.

† The Dietary Reference Intakes (DRI) are the most recent set of dietary recommendations established by the Food and Nutrition Board of the Institute of Medicine, 1997–2001. They replace previous RDAs, and may be the basis for eventually updating the RDIs. The value shown here is the highest DRI for each nutrient.

‡ The Upper Limit (UL) is the upper level of intake considered to be safe for use by adults, incorporating a safety factor. In some cases, lower ULs have been established for children.

§ Upper limit for magnesium applies only to intakes from dietary supplements or pharmaceutical products, not including intakes from food and water.

ND Upper limit not determined. No adverse effects observed from high intakes of the nutrient.

Source: Council for Responsible Nutrition. Used with permission.

cholesterol, carbohydrates, sodium, potassium, and protein. Apparently all these changes are supposed to clear things up.

There is a great deal of differing advice about how much of a vitamin or mineral is good for you—these days you're advised to choose your authorities and health advisors with care. The charts for vitamin and minerals as recommended by both the FDA and the Food and Nutrition Board, as well as ULs (upper limits), indicating how much is too much, might be a place to start.

VOLUME
···

THE AMERICAN METHOD of measuring volume is one of the most antiquated measuring systems around, derived from the Egyptian mouthful and the twelfth-century "Winchester bushel," the oldest official English measure of volume on record. After that time, different measures were used for different goods for more than 500 years, and measures with the same names changed sizes depending on what was being measured. Thus a gallon of wine measured 231 cubic inches while a gallon of ale would measure 282 cubic inches, and so on. The most commonly used, however, were the *Winchester bushel* and the *wine barrel*.

These measures, along with the accompanying confusion, were transported to Colonial America. The mouthful, as well as the ancient custom of doubling each measure to find the next, had found their way to the New World:

2 mouthfuls	=	1 jigger
2 jiggers	=	1 jack
2 jacks	=	1 jill
2 jills	=	1 cup
2 cups	=	1 pint
2 pints	=	1 quart
2 quarts	=	1 pottle
2 pottles	=	1 gallon

2 gallons	=	1 peck
2 pecks	=	1 pail
2 pails	=	1 bushel
2 bushels	=	1 strike
2 strikes	=	1 coomb
2 coombs	=	1 cask
2 casks	=	1 barrel
2 barrels	=	1 hogshead
2 hogsheads	=	1 pipe
2 pipes	=	1 tun

It was obvious on both sides of the Atlantic that some sort of standard was necessary. In 1824 Britain decided to change the wine gallon to the imperial gallon, with a capacity of 277.5 cubic inches, and the bushel to 8 imperial gallons, or 2,219.4 cubic inches.

The United States, however, opted for the old measures. In 1832 the U.S. Treasury officially adopted the old English wine gallon of 231 cubic inches and the even older Winchester bushel of 2,150.42 cubic inches. Even today, none of the British and U.S. measures of volume, though having the same names, have the same capacity—the British measures are slightly larger. This includes British cooking measures: their teaspoon, tablespoon, and cup are slightly larger than ours, nice to know if you're using a British cookbook. Britain has recently solved its problem of too many confusing volume measurements by adopting the metric system.

How do things stand in the United States? Although attempts are being made to edge toward metric measures (usually included on packaging along with the familiar old measures), we have two official groups of volume measures, one for wet and one for dry. Some of these measures have the same names and some do not. The smallest wet measures, like the minum and the dram, are "apothecary" measures traditionally used for measuring drugs and medicines. The largest measure, the barrel, is rather imprecise—it can be as large as anyone says it is.

Official U.S. Measures of Volume Wet*		Official U.S. Measures of Volume Dry	
60 minums	= 1 fluid dram	2 pints =	1 quart
8 fluid drams	= 1 fluid ounce	8 quarts =	1 peck
4 fluid ounces	= 1 gill	4 pecks =	1 bushel
4 gills	= 1 pint		
2 pints	= 1 quart		
4 quarts	= 1 gallon		

*The accepted volume of a barrel in the United States varies significantly, depending both on the commodity for which it is used and how it is defined in state law (varying from state to state). The barrel can measure both wet and dry volume.

Source: National Bureau of Standards, Department of Commerce.

Although the above measures are an improvement over those from Colonial times, the system is still flawed. Today's gallon and bushel are secondhand metric measures—both are defined in terms of cubic inches, which are by U.S. law defined in terms of the meter (see *Metric System*, page 160). The simple metric solution, measuring volume by the liter, has still eluded us.

▶ **To find volume measurement equivalents, go to "Convert It!" at http://microimg.com/science/volume_equiv.**

WEEK

••

OUR SEVEN-DAY WEEK is purely arbitrary. It's not based on anything in nature—not the movement of the earth or anything in the heavens. The weeks are not really a division of anything, either—you can't group them evenly into months or even a year. The week somersaults awkwardly through the calendar with no quick way to tell which weekday will land on which date.

Technically, the week was probably inspired by a need to schedule market days and religious holidays. Its length has varied: the Egyptians and Greeks had a ten-day week, the Romans an eight-day week, China a fifteen-day week, and even today weeks from four to ten days are used by some of the world's more remote communities. Our seven-day week comes from the Jewish calendar, which bases its week on the seven-day creation, in which God worked for six days and rested on the seventh. Some have tried to outlaw the week: the French tried during the French Revolution, the Soviets tried it in the 1930s, but the week always bounced back. Americans seem to love the week. It's user-friendly and scientists have refrained from trying to split the week into nanoweeks. We even increased our rest days from one day to two—the first and last day of the week—a precious, fairly recent period of time, which we cherish as the weekend.

WEIGHT

••

NOT JUST ONE but three perfectly legal U.S. weight systems involve pounds and ounces! What's the difference between a *troy pound*, an *apothecary pound*, and an *avoirdupois pound*? The answer is very old and simpler than you think.

The Grain

The seeds of our systems of weights were exactly that—seeds used with simple balances to weigh precious gems and metals and other small items. The ancient Egyptians used the grain as an official measure, in multiples of their favorite number:

Ancient Egyptian Weights

60 grains = 1 shekel
60 shekels = 1 great mina
60 great minas = 1 talent

The grain has prevailed through history, with values varying from half to a quarter of the value of today's U.S. grain, which is officially 0.0648 gram. This grain is the same for all U.S. ounce-pound systems—7,000 grains equal the familiar pound, and 5,760 equal the less familiar apothecary pound. In the beginning, though, the pound was smaller.

The Troy Pound

Ancient Egyptians have been credited with the first pound, which is said to have been 1/100 of a cubic foot of water, or about 25 percent smaller than the pound you use today—5,244 grains. The Romans adopted the Egyptian pound, called it *libra pondo* (meaning "a pound by weight," hence our abbreviation lb.), and divided it into twelve parts of 437 grains each, calling each part an *uncia* (which means "twelfth part").

The use of this 12-ounce pound spread to Europe, where the ounce was enlarged to 480 grains and the pound was called the *troy pound*, honoring the thriving French medieval trading town of Troyes. When the troy pound reached England, it became popular for weighing precious metals and gems, and was adopted as the official weight system for British currency. The colonists brought the troy pound to America, where it was later officially adopted by the U.S Mint. The troy pound continued as the accepted measure of precious gems and metals on both sides of the Atlantic (hence its nickname "jeweler's weight"). Today the 12-ounce troy pound has been all but abandoned for the metric system. It is still legal, however, and its equivalents are published by the National Institute of Standards and Technology (NIST).

U.S. Troy Weight

24 grains	=	1 pennyweight		
20 pennyweights	=	1 ounce	=	480 grains
12 ounces troy	=	1 pound troy	=	5,760 grains

The Apothecary Pound

In Europe the troy pound was also used by the medical world to measure drugs and medicines—the London College of Physicians adopted it in 1618—a custom carried on in America. Although an apothecary pound and ounce were and continue to be the same size as the troy pound and ounce, the apothecary scruple and the dram facilitated the mixing of small amounts. Although apothecary weights have been almost entirely replaced by the metric system, they are still legal in the United States and described by the National Institute of Standards and Technology (NIST):

U.S. Apothecary Weights

20 grains	=	1 scruple		
3 scruples	=	1 dram	=	60 grains
8 drams	=	1 apothecary ounce	=	480 grains
12 ounces	=	1 apothecary pound	=	5,760 grains

The Avoirdupois Pound

The everyday pound, the one you calculate your weight and your market produce in, is the *avoirdupois pound* (pronounced "a-ver-de-*poiz*"). The avoirdupois system of weights is yet another rearrangement of the troy system. When the 5,760-grain troy pound was considered by many medieval Europeans to be too small for everyday use, they added four troy-size (480 grain) ounces to make it a 16-ounce pound of 7,000 grains. (The literal meaning of "ounce" is "12th-part" even if it has become a 16th-part.) The avoirdupois pound (French for "goods of weight") became the accepted general measure of weight in both England and America.

Avoirdupois Weights

27^{11}/32 grains	=	1 dram	
16 drams	=	1 avoirdupois ounce	= 480 grains
16 ounces	=	1 pound	= 7,000 grains
100 pounds	=	1 hundredweight	
20 hundredweights	=	1 ton*	= 2,000 pounds

*The 2,000-pound ton, called the *short ton*, is the common U.S. ton. For some purposes, however, we use the British ton of 2,240 pounds avoirdupois, called the *long ton*. The increasingly used metric ton equals 2,204.623 pounds.

THE THREE SYSTEMS have many similarities. Although the troy and apothecary pounds contain 12 ounces while the avoirdupois pound contains 16, and the apothecary and avoirdupois dram-size differs, all three systems use the 0.0648-gram grain and the 480-grain ounce. They have something else in common: the metric system has, directly or indirectly, replaced them all—the U.S. avoirdupois pound has been officially defined in terms of the kilogram (equaling 0.45359237 kilogram) since 1893, while most of today's experts in medicines and precious metals and stones have replaced their drams, scruples, and pennyweights with grams and milligrams. (See *Metric System*, page 160.)

Office of Weights and Measures

The Office of Weights and Measures (OWM), one of the longest running and best known programs of the National Institute of Standards and Technology (NIST), promotes uniformity in U.S. weights and measures laws, regulations, and standards.

▶ Convert weights from one system to another on "Convert-Me" at http://www.convert-me.com. For a complete list of U.S. official measures, go to the National Institute of Standards and Technology site at http://ts.nist.gov/ts and click on "Tables of Units of Measurements."

WIND

MOST PEOPLE HAVE FIGURED OUT that when the wind direction is reported on the news, it is always the direction the wind is coming from. For example, a SW wind is blowing from the southwest (the weather vane arrow always points into the wind). Wind direction is often a good weather predictor—even Aristotle observed that in his neck of the world, winds from the northwest brought clearing weather, those from the northeast brought snow and cold, while south and east-southeast winds were hot.

Wind measurement is one of the more difficult weather phenomena. The simplest instrument for measuring wind speed, known as velocity, is an *anemometer*—Robert Hooke invented the first one in 1667—which today most commonly consists of three or four cups spinning around a vertical shaft; the wind speed is measured by the speed of the spin. The NEXRAD Doppler radar network is sensitive to wind on the ground and is useful in predicting areas that might spawn tornadoes (see page 208). Upper air wind speed is measured by weather balloons; near-surface ocean winds from an aircraft or satellite by *scatterometer*, a microwave radar sensor.

Beaufort Scale

Lacking such sophisticated instruments, most of us rely on weather news, which reports the wind speed in miles per hour, a difficult figure to translate into reality—how forceful is a 30 mph wind anyway? The answer to this very sensible question was crucial to farmers and sailors, so as early as 1806, an admiral in the

Beaufort's Wind Scale

Wind Speed in mph	Beaufort Number	Effects on Land	Official Designation
Less than 1	0	Calm; smoke rises vertically	Light
1–3	1	Smoke shows wind direction	
4–7	2	Wind felt on face; leaves rustle; wind vanes move	
8–12	3	Leaves, small twigs move; small flags extend	Gentle
13–18	4	Wind raises dust and loose paper; small branches move	Moderate
19–24	5	Small leafy trees sway; small waves crest	Fresh
25–31	6	Large branches move; umbrellas become unwieldy	Strong
32–38	7	Whole trees sway; walking into the wind is difficult	
39–46	8	Twigs break from trees; cars veer	Gale
47–54	9	Slight structural damage	
55–63	10	Trees are uprooted; a good deal of structural damage	Whole Gale
64–72	11	Widespread damage	
73 and up	12	Widespread damage	Hurricane

British Navy, Sir Francis Beaufort, devised a 1 to 12 wind scale which, only slightly revised, is still in use today.

You might assume that the force (or destructive capability) of wind increases equally with its velocity (speed). But although the speed of a 40 mph wind is twice that of a 20 mph wind, its force is equal to that two times *squared* (2 × 2), meaning that a 40 mph wind is four times more powerful than a 20 mph wind. If a 30 mph wind is three times faster than a 10 mph wind, its force is that three times squared (3 × 3) making it nine times more powerful than the 10 mph wind. This makes a 40 mph wind *sixteen* times more powerful than a 10 mph wind (4 squared, or 4 × 4).

▶ **For an online wind velocity converter, go to http://www.windsurfer .com/calculator.html. For a current U.S. severe wind map, go to http://www.nws.noaa.gov.**

WIRE
∙∙

ALTHOUGH THERE ARE ALL SORTS of wire gauge systems for the many kinds of wire that hold our world together or connect one part to another, most of them have one thing in common: except for metrically measured wire, it's measured by the decimal inch, and except for music wire, *as the size numbers go up, the wire gets thinner.* These apparently illogical sizing systems can be blamed on the production process: wire is made by pulling a metal rod through progressively smaller holes. Originally, wire pulled through just one hole was called size one; wire that required two passes was thinner and was called size two, and so on.

Although there are many wire gauge systems for various types of wire, each relates, albeit with a different decimal-inch actual measurement, to a wire size number that generally runs from 0000000 (the largest) to 40 (the smallest).

▶ **For a chart of nine types of wire gauges, go to "Wire Gauges" at http://shopswarf.orcon.net.nz/wiregage.html.**

ZIP CODES

•••

IN 1963 THE U.S. POSTAL SERVICE numbered every American post office with a 5-digit ZIP code. The numbers began with zeros at the farthest point east (00601 for Adjuntas, Puerto Rico) and worked up to nines at the farthest point west (99950 for Ketchikan, Alaska). It seemed outrageous at the time—the ZIP code's raison d'être was facility of computer sorting, and computers were not yet familiar to most Americans. In 1983 the U.S. Postal Service added four digits to the ZIP code, and as common as computers are these days, most people still don't know their 9-digit code, and those who do resist using it.

It really is a fairly efficient system, however, and why fight anything that will speed up the mail? Let's use the ZIP code 95448 for Healdsburg, California, as an example—here's what the first five digits mean:

9 The first digit represents one of ten geographical areas, usually a group of states. The numbers begin at the farthest points east (0) and end at the farthest points west (9).

54 The second two digits, in combination with the first, identify a central mail-distribution point known as a sectional center. The location of a sectional center is based on geography, transportation facilities, and population density.

48 The last two digits indicate the town, or local post office. The order is often alphabetical for towns within a delivery area—for example, towns with names beginning with "A" usually have low numbers. (This may not apply to metropolitan areas, where numbers are assigned as they become available.)

The last four digits added after a hyphen, e.g., 95448-1234, are called ZIP + 4 coding. Mail with ZIP + 4 coding benefits from cheaper bulk rates, being easier to sort with automated equipment. It's also helpful for businesses that wish to sort the recipients of their mailings by geographical location. The first two numbers of the 4-digit suffix represent a delivery sector, which may be several blocks, a group of streets, several office buildings, or a small geographical area. The last two numbers narrow the

ZIP CODE NATIONAL AREAS

The first digit of a ZIP code divides the country into 10 large groups of states numbered from 0 in the Northeast to 9 in the far west.

EXAMPLE

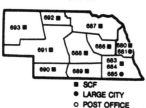

■ SCF
● LARGE CITY
○ POST OFFICE

Within these areas, each state is divided into an average of 10 smaller geographic areas, identified by the 2nd and 3rd digits of the ZIP code.

WHAT YOUR ZIP CODE MEANS

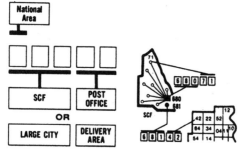

The 4th and 5th digits identify a local delivery area.

Source: U.S. Postal Service 1988 National Five-Digit ZIP Code and Post Office Directory. Used with permission.

area further: they might denote one floor of a large office building, a department in a large firm, or a group of post office boxes.

▶ **To find the ZIP + 4 code for a U.S. address, go to http://usps.com and click on "Find Zip Codes."**

Sources

Please find here some of the more important sources used to write this book. More references may be found following the appropriate subject entry.

Books, Magazines, and Newspapers

Adams, Catherine F. *Nutritive Value of American Food in Common Units.* Washington, D.C.: U.S. Department of Agriculture, 1975.

Agricultural Marketing Service. Washington, D.C.: U.S. Department of Agriculture, 1986.

American Institute of Real Estate Appraisers. *The Appraisal of Real Estate,* 8th edition. Chicago: American Institute of Real Estate Appraisers, 1983.

Asimov, Isaac. *Asimov on Numbers.* New York: Doubleday & Co, 1977.

———. *The Clock We Live On.* New York: Abelard, Schuman, 1965.

———. *Realm of Numbers.* Boston: Houghton Mifflin Co., 1959.

———. *The Universe,* revised edition. New York: Walker & Co., 1980.

Berger, Melvin. *For Good Measure.* New York: McGraw-Hill, 1971.

Bishop, Owen. *Yardsticks of the Universe.* New York: Peter Bedrick Books, 1984.

Boorstin, Daniel J. *The Discoverers.* New York: Random House, 1985.

Branley, Franklyn M. *Think Metric!* New York: Crowell, 1973.

Brondfield, Jerome. "The Marvelous Marking Stick." *Kiwanis Magazine,* February 1979.

Bureau of Labor Statistics Handbook of Methods, Volume II: The Consumer Price Index. Washington, D.C.: U.S. Department of Labor, April 1984.

Burns, Marilyn. *About Time.* Boston: Little, Brown, & Co., 1978.

Busha, Ed., et. al. *The Book of Heat.* New York: The Stephen Greene Press, 1982.

Campbell, Tim. *Do-It-Yourself Weather Book.* Birmingham, AL: Oxmoor House, 1979.

Consumer Tire Guide. Washington, D.C.: Tire Industry Safety Council, n.d.

Crockett, James Underwood. *Vegetables and Fruits.* Alexandria, VA: Time-Life Books, 1972.

Diagram Group. *Comparisons.* New York: St. Martin's Press, 1980.

———. *Measurements and Conversions.* Philadelphia: Running Press, 1994.

Dunne, Pete. "Pete's Picks," *Birder's World,* Feb. 2002.

The Economist. *Desk Companion.* New York: John Wiley and Sons, 1998.

Encyclopedia Americana, international edition. Danbury, CT: Grolier, 2002.

Forest Products Laboratory. *Wood Handbook: Wood as an Engineering Material,* revised edition. Washington, D.C.: U.S. Department of Agriculture, 1974.

Fundamental Facts About United States Money. Atlanta: Federal Reserve, 1987.

Gallant, Roy A. *Man the Measurer.* New York: Doubleday & Co., 1972.

Gillis, Jack. *The Car Book.* New York: Harper & Row, 1987.

———. *The Car Book.* Washington, D.C.: Tilden Press, 1982–1999.

Gioello, Debbie Ann. *Figure Types and Size Ranges.* New York: Fairchild Books, 1979.

Goudsmit, Samuel Abraham, and Robert Claiborne. *Time.* Alexandria, VA: Time-Life Books, 1980.

Harrison, Phil. "All You Need to Know about Binoculars." *Astronomy,* June 2001.

HELP! The Indispensable Almanac. New York: Everest House, 1986.

The Heritage of Mechanical Fasteners. Cleveland, OH: Industrial Fasteners Institute, 1974.

Highfield, Roger. "Carbon Dating Might Be Wrong by 10,000 Years." *Daily Telegraph* (London), June 30, 2001.

Hirsch, S. Carl. *Meter Means Measure.* New York: Viking Press, 1973.

Historical Statistics of the United States, Colonial Times to 1970. Washington, D.C.: U.S. Department of Commerce, 1975.

Horenstein, Henry. *Black & White Photography: A Basic Manual,* second edition, revised. New York: Little, Brown and Co., 1983.

Jespersen, James, and Jane Fitz-Randolf. *From Sundials to Atomic Clocks.* Washington, D.C.: National Bureau of Standards, U.S. Department of Commerce, 1977.

Johnstone, William D. *For Good Measure.* Chicago: NTC Publishing Group, 1998.

Judson, Lewis V. *Weights and Measures Standards of the United States,* revised edition. Washington, D.C.: U.S. Department of Commerce, 1976.

Klein, Arthur H. *The Science of Measurement.* New York: Simon & Schuster, 1974.

Lewis, Edward V. *Ships*, revised edition. Alexandria, VA: Time-Life Books, 1973.

London, Barbara, and Jim Stone. *A Short Course in Photography: An Introduction to Black-and-White Photographic Technique*, third edition. New York: HarperCollins, 1996.

London, Barbara, and John Upton. *Photography*, sixth edition. New York: Longman, 1998.

Lord, John. *Sizes*. New York: HarperPerennial, 1994.

Lyons, Walter A. *The Handy Weather Answer Book*. Detroit: Visible Ink Press, 1997.

McGraw-Hill Encyclopedia of Science and Technology, sixth edition. New York: McGraw-Hill, 1987.

Miller, Albert, et al. *Elements of Meteorology*. Columbus, OH: Charles E. Merrill, 1983.

Moroney, Rita L. *The History of the U.S. Postal Service 1775–1984*. Washington, D.C.: U.S. Postal Service, n.d.

Morris, Kenneth M., and Alan M. Siegel. *The Wall Street Journal Guide to Understanding Personal Finance*. New York: Lightbulb Press, 2000.

Motor Gasolines. Richmond, CA: Chevron Research Company, 1985.

National Committee on Prevention, Detection, Evaluation, and Treatment of High Blood Pressure. National Institutes of Health. NIH Publication No. 98-4080, November 1997.

National Institutes of Health. *Sixth Report of the Joint Committee on Prevention, Detection, Evaluation, and Treatment of High Blood Pressure*. National Institutes of Health Publication #98-4080, November 1997.

New Encyclopaedia Britannica. Chicago: Encyclopaedia Britannica, Inc., 1986 and 2002.

Osol, David C., editor. *Remington's Pharmaceutical Sciences*, sixteenth edition. Easton, PA: Mack, 1980.

Oxford English Dictionary. New York: Oxford University Press, 1971.

Paul, Henry E. *Binoculars and All-Purpose Telescopes*. Radnor, PA: Chilton Book Co., 1965.

Petroski, Henry. *The Evolution of Useful Things*. New York: Knopf, 1992.

———. *Invention by Design*. Cambridge, MA: Harvard University Press, 1996.

"Reading the Sidewall." *Modern Tire Dealer*, 1983.

Reithmaier, L. W. *Private Pilot's Guide*. Fall River, MA: Aero, 1977.

Rossi, William A. "How Shoe Sizes Grew." *Footwear News Magazine*. New York: Fairchild Publications, Summer 1988.

Saitzyk, Seven L. *Art Hardware*. New York: Watson-Guptill, 1987.

Staplers and Paper Fasteners. Alexandria, VA: National Office Products Association, 1981.

Swezey, Kenneth M. *Formulas, Methods, Tips and Data for Home and Workshop.* Albany, NY: Popular Science, 1969.

Tammeus, Bill, "Narrowing the Age of the Universe." Knight-Ridder/Tribune News Service, Feb. 20, 2001.

Thomas, Robert B. *The Old Farmer's Almanac.* Dublin, NH: Yankee Books, 1986.

Thompson, Philip D. *Weather.* New York: Time-Life Books, 1965.

Turbak, Gary. "Measuring Our Metric World (Minus America)." *Kiwanis Magazine,* October 1987.

U.S. Department of Agriculture. Agricultural Market Service. Center for Nutrition Policy and Promotion. *Dietary Guidelines for Americans,* 2000.

U.S. Department of Commerce. National Bureau of Standards. *What About Metric?* revised edition. Washington, D.C.: U.S. Department of Commerce, 1985.

————. National Bureau of Standards. *Units and Systems of Weights and Measures: Their Origin, Development and Present Status.* Washington, D.C.: U.S. Department of Commerce, 1985.

————. National Oceanic and Atmospheric Administration. *Tide Tables 1987, West Coast of North and South America.* Washington, D.C.: U.S. Department of Commerce, 1985.

————. National Oceanic and Atmospheric Administration. National Weather Service. *The Aneroid Barometer.* Washington, D.C.: U.S. Department of Commerce, n.d.

Uzes, Francois D. *Chaining the Land.* Rancho Cordova, CA: Landmark Enterprises, 1979.

Vivian, John. *Wood Heat.* Emmaus, PA: Rodale Press, 1976.

Walker, Bryce, and the Editors of Time-Life Books. *Earthquake.* Alexandria, VA: Time-Life Books, 1982.

Wilford, John Noble. *The Mapmakers.* Alfred A. Knopf, 1981.

Wood, Richard A., editor. *The Weather Almanac,* seventh edition. New York: Gale Research, 1996.

World Book Encyclopedia. Chicago: World Book, Inc., 1987.

World Book Multimedia Encyclopedia, Macintosh edition. Chicago: World Book, Inc., 1999.

Internet

American Heart Association. "Dietary Guidelines for Healthy American Adults: AHA Scientific Position." *American Heart Association.* March 12, 2002. ‹http://216.185.112.5/presenter.jhtml?identifier=4561›.

Brain, Marshall. "How Bits and Bytes Work." *Marshall Brain's HowStuff-Works.* [Feb. 25, 2002.] ‹http://www.howstuffworks.com/bytes.htm›.

———. How Stuff Works. Raleigh, NC: BYG Publishing, 2001.

———. "How UPC Bar Codes Work." *Marshall Brain's HowStuffWorks.* n.d. [Feb. 25, 2002.] ‹http://www.howstuffworks.com/upc1.htm/›.

"Calculation and Conversion Tools." *Internet Public Library.* The Regents of the University of Michigan, 2002. ‹http://www.ipl.org/ref/RR/static/ref19.00.00.html›.

Council for Responsible Nutrition. *Vitamin and Mineral Recommendations.* 2001. ‹http://www.crnusa.org/Shellscireg000002.html#HistVitamins›.

"Currency Features." *Federal Reserve Bank of Atlanta.* n.d. ‹http://frbatlanta. org›.

Dana, Peter H. "Global Positioning System Overview." *The Geographer's Craft Project,* Department of Geography, University of Colorado at Boulder, 1999, revised May 5, 2000. ‹http://www.colorado.edu/geography/gcraft/notes/gps.html›.

"Decyphering Pollen Counts." *AllerDays.* n.d. [April 26, 2002.] ‹http://www.allerdays.com/the_season_decipher.shtml›.

"Engine Oil (Lubricants)." *Energy Professional Home.* Certification Programs. American Petroleum Institute. n.d. [May 8, 2002.] ‹http://api-ec.api.org›, click "Energy Professional Home," click "Certification Programs," click "Engine Oil."

Engineer's Edge. ‹http://www.engineersedge.com/directory.shtm›.

Ernest Orlando Lawrence Berkeley National Laboratory. *Berkeley Lab.* "Electronic Spectrum." n.d. [May 31, 2002.] ‹http://www.lbl.gov/MicroWorlds/ALSTool/EMspec/EMspec2.html›.

Federal Reserve Bank of St. Louis. *Economic Research.* "Prime Commercial Loan Rate." [May 28, 2002.] ‹http://research.stlouisfed.org/fred/data/irates/prime›.

Federal Reserve Board of Governors. "Industrial Production and Capacity Utilization." Federal Reserve Statistical Release. ‹http://www.federalreserve.gov/releases/G17/Current/Table0.htm›.

Fulton, Wayne A. "A Few Scanning Tips." n.d. [June 5, 2002.] ‹http://www.scantips.com›.

"Glossary for Transport Statistic," second edition. 1997. *Organization for Economic Cooperation and Development.* Document prepared by the Inter-secretariat Working Group on Transport Statistics. ‹http://www1.oecd.org/cem/online/glossaries/glointe.pdf›.

Hibbert, Chris. "What To Do When They Ask for Your Social Security Number." *Social Security Number FAQ.* ‹http://www.faqs.org/faqs/privacy/ssn-faq›.

"History of the Lead Pencil." Early Office Museum. n.d. [May 10, 2002.] ‹http://www.officemuseum.com/pencil_history.htm›.

"How Credit Cards Work." *Marshall Brain's HowStuffWorks.* n.d. ‹http://www.howstuffworks.com/credit-card.htm›.

"International Convention on Tonnage Measurement of Ships, 1969." *International Maritime Organization.* 2002. ‹http:www.imo.org/Conventions/mainframe.asp?topic_id=259&doc_id=685›.

Kimball, Trevor. *My Design Primer.* My Design Studio. [April 5, 2002.] ‹http://mydesignprimer.com›.

Knott, Ron. "Fibonacci Numbers and the Golden Section." Home page. March 4, 2002. ‹http://www.mcs.surrey.ac.uk/Personal/R.Knott/Fibonacci/fib.html›.

Kuhn, Marcus. "International Standard Paper Sizes." *The Computer Laboratory.* University of Cambridge. n.d. [May 10, 2002.] ‹http://www.cl.cam.ac.uk/~mgk25/iso-paper.html›.

Martin, Richard. "Tankers for the New Millennium." ABC News Internet Ventures. 1999. ‹http://abcnews.go.com/sections/tech/DailyNews/tankers990322.html›.

"Material Hardness." *Calce: Electronic Products & Systems Center.* University of Maryland. n.d. [May 7, 2002.] ‹http://www.calce.umd.edu/general/Facilities/Hardness_ad_.htm›.

"NAB: Reading the Charts." *American Academy of Allergy, Asthma & Immunology.* National Allergy Bureau. n.d. [May 26, 2002.] ‹http:www.aaaai.org/nab/reading_charts.stm›.

National Institute of Standards and Technology. "General Tables of Units of Measurements." NIST Handbook 44, Appendix C: Specifications, Tolerances and Other Technical Requirements for Weighing and Measuring Devices. ‹http://ts.nist.gov/.ts/htdocs›, click "320," click "235," click "appxc," click "appxc."

———. "International System of Units (SI)." *The NIST Reference on Constants, Units, and Uncertainty.* n.d. [May 29, 2002.]

———. *Tables of Units of Measurements.* ‹http://ts.nist.gov/ts›.

———. *Technological Services Home Page.* "Fact Sheet on Metric Labeling for Consumer Packages." [Feb.19, 2002.] ‹http://ts.nist.gov/ts/htdocs›, click "230," click "235," click "metric."

The National Snow & Ice Data Center. [June 7, 2002.] ‹http://www.nsidc.colorado.edu›.

Nice, Karim, and Gerald Jay Gurevic. "Digital Cameras." *Marshall Brain's How-StuffWorks.* n.d. ‹http://www.howstuffworks.com/digital-camera.htm›.

Park, John L. "Metric Prefixes." *The ChemTeam.* n.d. [May 5, 2002.] ‹http://dbhs.wvusd.k12.ca.us/Metric/Metric-Prefixes.html›.

Pechter, Edward A. "Breast Measurement." *Bra Bustline Sizing System.* n.d. [March 5, 2002.]

"Photo Tips." *PhotoSecrets.* ‹http://www.photosecrets.com/tips.html›.

"Preventing Hearing Injury." *Music-Injury.com.* ‹http://www.music-injury.com/html/prevent_loss.html›.

"Regulations at a Glance." *Council for Responsible Nutrition.* 2001. [April 16, 2002.] ‹http://www.crnusa.org/Shellscireg000003.html›.

Tyson, Jeff. "How Computer Memory Works." *Marshall Brain's HowStuffWorks.* n.d. [April 25, 2002.] ‹http://www.howstuffworks.com/computer-memory.htm›.

———. "How Scanners Work." *Marshall Brain's HowStuffWorks.* n.d. [June 5, 2002.] ‹http://www.howstuffworks.com/scanner.htm›.

"Unfair Competition and Unlawful Practices." U.S. Code Title 27 (Intoxicating Liquors), Chapter 8 (Federal Alcohol Administration Act), Subchapter I (Federal Alcohol Administration), Section 205. ‹http://law2.house.gov/uscode-cgi/fastweb.exe?getdoc+uscview+t26t28+›.

U.S. Coast Guard. *Office of Boating Safety.* "Boating Under the Influence." October 23, 2001. ‹http://uscgboating.org/saf_bui.asp›.

U.S. Department of Agriculture. Agricultural Market Service. "How to Buy." [April 17, 2002.] ‹http://www.ams.usda.gov/howtobuy›.

———. Food Safety and Inspection Service. "Inspection and Grading," slightly revised. Consumer Education and Information. 2000. ‹http://www.fsis.usda.gov/OA/pubs/ingrade.htm›.

U.S. Department of Commerce. Bureau of Economic Analysis. *National Income and Product Accounts Tables.* "Table S.1.Summary of Percent Change from Preceding Period in Real Gross Domestic Product and Related Measures." April 28, 2002. ‹http://www.bea.doc.gov/bea/dn/nipaweb/TableViewFixed.asp#Mid›.

———. National Oceanic and Atmospheric Administration. National Weather Service. "Meteorological Tables." August 2001 press release. ‹http://www.erh.noaa.gov/er/iln/tables.htm›.

———. National Oceanic and Atmospheric Administration. National Weather Service. *Office of Meteorology.* "Snow Measurement Guidelines (10-23-96)." [June 7, 2002.] ‹http://www.wrds.uwyo.edu/wrds/wsc/reference/snowmeas.html›.

————. National Oceanic and Atmospheric Administration. Seafood Inspection Program. "Protection Through Inspection." ‹http://seafood.nmfs.gov›.

U.S. Department of Energy. Environmental Protection Agency. *Energy Star.* ‹http://www.epa.gov/nrgystar/contact_us.html›.

————. Office of Energy Efficiency and Renewable Energy. "Energy Glossary and Fact Sheets." *Consumer Energy Information.* ‹http://www.eren.doe. gov/consumerinfo/factsheet.html›.

————. Office of Energy Efficiency and Renewable Energy. "How to Buy Energy-Efficient Compact Fluorescent Light Bulbs." December 2000. *Federal Energy Management Program.* ‹http://www.eren.doe.gov/femp/ procurement/pdfs/cfl.›

U.S. Department of Labor. Bureau of Labor Statistics. *Consumer Price Indexes.* ‹http://www.bls.gov/cpi›.

————. "Frequently Asked Questions." *Consumer Price Indexes.* n.d. ‹http://www.bls.gov/cpi/cpifaq.htm›.

U.S. Department of Transportation. National Highway Traffic Safety Administration. ".08 BAC Illegal Per Se Level." *State Legislative Fact Sheets.* January 2001. ‹http://nhtsa.dot.gov/people/outreach/stateleg/ 08BACLegFactSheet00.htm›.

————. "Federal Legislative Programs Designed to Encourage Enactment of State Impaired Driving Laws." Section 408 and Section 410 Programs. [July 18, 2002.] ‹http://www.nhtsa.gov/people/injury/alcohol/limit.08/ Presinit/federal.html›.

U.S. Environmental Protection Agency. *Air Quality Index: A Guide to Air Quality and Your Health.* June 2000. ‹http://www.epa.gov/airnow/aqibroch›.

————. "What Is the UV Index?" Sept. 1999; EPA430-H-99-001. *Sunwise.* [June 9, 2002.] ‹http:www.ep.gov/sunwise/uvwhat.html›.

U.S. Food and Drug Administration. FDA home page. "Daily Reference Values (DRVs)." ‹http://www.fda.gov/fdac/special/foodlabel/drvtabl.html›.

————. "'Daily Values' Encourage Healthy Diet." By Paula Kurtzwell. n.d. [April 16, 2002.] ‹http://www.fda.gov/fdac/special/foodlabel/dvs.html›.

————. "The Food Label." May 1999. ‹http://www.fda.gov/opacom/ backgrounders/foodlabel.html›.

U.S. Geological Survey. "United States Magnetic Field Charts for 1995." ‹http://geomag.usgs.gov/usimages.html›.

U.S. Treasury. Department of Engraving and Printing. "Your New Currency." *Bureau of Engraving and Printing.* 2002. ‹http://www.bep.treas.gov/ section.cfm/4›.

Index